Peterson's

MASTER THE ASVAB BASICS

PETERSON'S

A nelnet COMPANY

About Peterson's

To succeed on your lifelong educational journey, you will need accurate, dependable, and practical tools and resources. That is why Peterson's is everywhere education happens. Because whenever and however you need education content delivered, you can rely on Peterson's to provide the information, know-how, and guidance to help you reach your goals. Tools to match the right students with the right school. It's here. Personalized resources and expert guidance. It's here. Comprehensive and dependable education content—delivered whenever and however you need it. It's all here.

For more information, contact Peterson's, 2000 Lenox Drive, Lawrenceville, NJ 08648; 800-338-3282; or find us on the World Wide Web at www.petersons.com.

© 2010 Peterson's, a Nelnet company

Previously published as *ASVAB Basics* © 1990, 1994, 1998, 1999 by Ronald M. Kaprov and Ronald Bronk; © 2002, 2005, 2007 by Ronald M. Kaprov and Steffi R. Kaprov.

Stephen Clemente, Managing Director, Publishing and Institutional Research; Bernadette Webster, Director of Publishing; Mark D. Snider, Editor; Ray Golaszewski, Manufacturing Manager; Linda M. Williams, Composition Manager

ISBN-13: 978-0-7689-2829-7
ISBN-10: 0-7689-2829-X

Printed in the United States of America

10 9 8 7 6 5 4 3 2 1   12 11 10

First Edition

By printing this book on recycled paper (40% post-consumer waste) 200 trees were saved.

OTHER RECOMMENDED TITLES

Master the ASVAB

Master the Officer Candidate Tests

Contents

PART IV: OVERVIEW OF THE ASVAB VERBAL

PART V: THREE PRACTICE TESTS

Before You Begin

Peterson's Master the ASVAB Basics has helped thousands of young men and women prepare to take the Armed Services Vocational Aptitude Battery (ASVAB) test. The format is clear and well organized, making the book easy to use. This revised edition contains up-to-date information necessary for success on the current version of the ASVAB. You have made an excellent decision in choosing this book to help you prepare for the ASVAB.

Peterson's Master the ASVAB Basics offers you:

- Intensive practice in math and verbal skills
- Clear, easy-to-follow instructions
- General tips for taking tests
- Special preparation ideas for improving math and verbal skills
- Specific hands-on instruction

HOW THIS BOOK IS ORGANIZED

Part I provides a general introduction to the ASVAB. Chapter 1 gives an overview of the pencil-and-paper test and the computer-based test (CAT-ASVAB). The chapter also includes suggestions for test preparation, strategies to improve your study skills, and tips on how to best use this book. Chapter 2 explains your ASVAB scores in detail.

Part II details enlistment opportunities in the U.S. Military. It contains a chapter on general enlistment qualifications, enlisting in the military, military training, descriptions of the different military branches, pay and benefits information, and a summary of employment benefits.

Part III introduces you to the ASVAB math subtests. The Arithmetic Reasoning and Mathematics Knowledge sections guide you on how to work through concepts that are troublesome to many test takers.

Part IV introduces you to the ASVAB verbal subtests. The materials used in the Paragraph Comprehension section are engaging and varied, with the inclusion of many contemporary topics designed to interest and motivate you to keep improving your language skills. The Word Knowledge section will help you develop a broader vocabulary. We've included the types of words often found on the ASVAB, as well as explanations to help you further expand your vocabulary.

Part V consists of Practice Tests for the four subtests enlistees must take to qualify for the armed services. There are three Practice Tests for each of the Armed Forces Qualification Test (AFQT) qualifying exams. Please be sure to adhere to the stated time limits if you plan to take the pencil-and-paper test. If you plan to take the

CAT-ASVAB, refer to Figure 2 in Chapter 1 for the appropriate number of test items and time allotments, and modify your test taking accordingly.

SPECIAL STUDY FEATURES

Peterson's Master the ASVAB Basics is designed to be as user-friendly as it is complete. To this end, it includes significant features to make your preparation more efficient.

Overview

Each chapter begins with a bulleted overview listing the topics covered in the chapter. This allows you to quickly target the areas in which you are most interested.

Summing It Up

Each chapter ends with a point-by-point summary that reviews the most important items in the chapter. The summaries offer a convenient way to review key points.

YOU'RE WELL ON YOUR WAY TO SUCCESS

You've made the decision to join the armed services and have taken a very important step in that process. *Peterson's Master the ASVAB Basics* will help you increase your score and prepare you for everything you'll need to know on the day of the ASVAB test.

GIVE US YOUR FEEDBACK

Peterson's publishes a full line of resources to guide you through the armed services admission process. Peterson's publications can be found at your local bookstore, library, and high school or college guidance office. You can access us online at www.petersons.com.

We welcome any comments or suggestions you may have about this publication and invite you to complete our online survey at www.petersons.com/booksurvey. Or, you can fill out the survey in the back of this book, tear it out, and mail it to us at:

Publishing Department
Peterson's, a Nelnet Company
2000 Lenox Drive
Lawrenceville, NJ 08648

Your feedback will help us make your educational dreams possible.

PART I

OVERVIEW OF THE ASVAB

An Introduction to the ASVAB Test

OVERVIEW

- **What Is the ASVAB?**
- **How to use this book**
- **How to prepare for the ASVAB**
- **Summing it up**

Congratulations on deciding to take the ASVAB! This is an important first step toward a career in the armed services. The job outlook for military personnel is excellent and should remain this well way into the future. Nearly 200,000 military personnel must be recruited each year to take the place of those who have retired or fulfilled their commitment. Military personnel have the most important job in the world—keeping our country safe. Because of this, our military must be comprised of the best young men and women available.

ASVAB stands for Armed Services Vocational Aptitude Battery. The ASVAB is divided into subtests. How you perform on these subtests will help you and the military determine your skills and talents and the type of job that bests suits you. Your test might indicate that you would be an outstanding aircraft mechanic or air traffic specialist. Because the ASVAB can help you choose a suitable career, some high school students enrolled in a Career Exploration Program take it even though they do not plan to enlist in the military. Taking the ASVAB is not a commitment to enlist.

WHAT IS THE ASVAB?

There are three different versions of the ASVAB: (1) the pencil-and-paper ASVAB, (2) the CAT-ASVAB (computer-based), and (3) the student ASVAB. The student ASVAB is given in high schools and is the same as the pencil-and-paper test, except it does not include the Assembling Objects (AO) subtest. *Note:* The Armed Forces Classification Test (AFCT), which is used when military personnel want to change jobs, also does not contain the AO subtest.

ASVAB testing for applicants is conducted at Military Entrance Processing Stations, known as MEPS. If a student does not live near a MEP station, the ASVAB can be administered at a satellite location called a Military Entrance Test (MET) site. The ASVAB tests given at METs are pencil-and-paper tests, so the pencil-and-paper test is often referred to as the MET-site ASVAB.

chapter 1

The ASVAB subtests are designed to measure general abilities and information in specific areas covered in the general high school program or acquired through an interest or a hobby. Figure 1 presents an overview of the pencil-and-paper ASVAB, the time allowed for the administration of each subtest, the number of items in each subtest, and a description of the abilities or knowledge it measures. Figure 2 presents the CAT-ASVAB, the time allowed for each subtest, the number of items in each subtest, and descriptions of the abilities or knowledge measured.

The pencil-and-paper ASVAB and the CAT-ASVAB are slightly different. The CAT-ASVAB divides the Auto & Shop Information (AS) subtest into two separate subtests, which appear as Auto Information (AI) and Shop Information (SI). So, the CAT-ASVAB contains ten subtests (where as the pencil-and-paper exam contains only nine). The CAT-ASVAB has fewer questions, and consequently, less testing time available, but the two tests contain essentially the same information. For the purposes of this book, the Practice Tests will include the number of items and time allotment conducive to the pencil-and-paper exam. Since the content of the two ASVAB tests is virtually identical, these Practice Tests will also provide excellent preparation for the CAT-ASVAB. By referring to Figure 2, test takers may modify their time allotment and test items appropriately to simulate conditions for the CAT-ASVAB.

FIGURE 1

Pencil-and-Paper ASVAB			
TEST	**TIME**	**ITEMS**	**DESCRIPTION**
General Science (GS)	11 minutes	25	Measures knowledge of physical and biological sciences.
Arithmetic Reasoning (AR)	36 minutes	30	Measures ability to solve arithmetic word problems.
Word Knowledge (WK)	11 minutes	35	Measures ability to select the correct meaning of words presented in context and identify the best synonym for a given word.
Paragraph Comprehension (PC)	13 minutes	15	Measures ability to obtain information from written passages.
Mathematics Knowledge (MK)	24 minutes	25	Measures knowledge of general mathematics principles, including algebra and geometry.
Electronics Information (EI)	9 minutes	20	Measures knowledge of electricity, radio principles, and electronics.

Auto & Shop Information (AS)	11 minutes	25	Measures knowledge of automobiles, tools, and shop terminology and practices.
Mechanical Comprehension (MC)	19 minutes	25	Measures knowledge of mechanical and physical principles and ability to visualize how illustrated objects work.
Assembling Objects (AO)	15 minutes	25	Measures spatial reasoning and speed while performing tasks in a timed context.

FIGURE 2

CAT-ASVAB			
TEST	**TIME**	**ITEMS**	**DESCRIPTION**
General Science (GS)	8 minutes	16	Measures knowledge of physical and biological sciences.
Arithmetic Reasoning (AR)	39 minutes	16	Measures ability to solve arithmetic word problems.
Word Knowledge (WK)	8 minutes	16	Measures ability to select the correct meaning of words presented in context and identify the best synonym for a given word.
Paragraph Comprehension (PC)	22 minutes	11	Measures ability to obtain information from written passages.
Mathematics Knowledge (MK)	20 minutes	16	Measures knowledge of general mathematics principles, including algebra and geometry.
Electronics Information (EI)	8 minutes	16	Measures knowledge of electricity, radio principles, and electronics.
Auto Information (AI)	7 minutes	11	Measures knowledge of automobiles.
Shop Information (SI)	6 minutes	11	Measures knowledge of tools and shop terminology and practices.

| Mechanical Comprehension (MC) | 20 minutes | 16 | Measures knowledge of mechanical and physical principles and ability to visualize how illustrated objects work. |
| Assembling Objects (AO) | 16 minutes | 16 | Measures spatial reasoning and speed while performing tasks in a timed context. |

Your scores on the ASVAB subtests are reported individually. Some subtests are also grouped together and are reported as composite scores. You'll learn more about scoring in Chapter 2, but for now, be aware of an important composite score—the Armed Forces Qualifications Test (AFQT) score, which is also called the Military Entrance Score. The AFQT is used to determine who is allowed to enlist in the military. The AFQT is calculated using these subtests and this formula:

$$\text{AFQT Raw Score} = 2 \times \begin{bmatrix} \text{Word Knowledge} \\ \text{score} + \text{Paragraph} \\ \text{Comprehension} \\ \text{score} \end{bmatrix} + \begin{bmatrix} \text{Arithmetic} \\ \text{Reasoning score} \\ + \text{Mathematics} \\ \text{Knowledge score} \end{bmatrix}$$

The AFQT Raw Score is converted into a percentile score, which is used to determine who is eligible to enlist in the military. You'll learn more about this conversion in Chapter 2.

FIGURE 3

ACADEMIC ABILITY SCORE	VERBAL ABILITY SCORE	MATH ABILITY SCORE
Word Knowledge + Paragraph Comprehension + Arithmetic Reasoning + Mathematics Knowledge	Word Knowledge + Paragraph Comprehension	Arithmetic Reasoning + Mathematics Knowledge
Purpose: Measures potential for further formal education.	*Purpose:* Measures capacity for verbal activities.	*Purpose:* Measures capacity for mathematical activities.

HOW TO USE THIS BOOK

Everything you need to know to get a good score on the ASVAB is in this book, which is easy to use and allows you to work at your own pace. This chapter provides an overview of the structure and content of the ASVAB, and Chapter 2 offers explanations of how the ASVAB is scored.

Chapter 3 details enlisted opportunities in the U.S. Military and will help you plan ahead for a military career before and after you take the ASVAB.

Parts III and IV of *Peterson's Master the ASVAB Basics* are organized into six accessible chapters to help you increase your score:

Chapter 4   General tips and test-taking tips for mathematical problems

Chapter 5   Comprehensive review and exercises for Arithmetic Reasoning problems

Chapter 6   Comprehensive review and exercises for Mathematics Knowledge problems

Chapter 7   General tips and test-taking tips for verbal problems

Chapter 8   Comprehensive review and exercises for Word Knowledge problems

Chapter 9   Comprehensive review and exercises for Paragraph Comprehension problems

Finally, Part V contains three Practice Tests with answer keys and explanations. Each Practice Test includes the four AFQT subtests for a total of twelve subtests in all.

Four Strategies for Success

❶ **Practice with exercises.** Complete the mathematical exercises in Part III and the verbal exercises in Part IV. Check your answers with the answer explanations at the end of each test. The skill tested by each question is included in the answer explanation.

❷ **Practice necessary skills.** Review the math topic reviews, verbal word skills, and comprehension skill for the questions in the exercises that you answered incorrectly.

❸ **Take the Practice Tests.** Practice Tests for each AFQT subtest are included in this book: Arithmetic Reasoning, Mathematics Knowledge, Word Knowledge, and Paragraph Comprehension.

❹ **Review.** Review any items that you had trouble with. Concentrate on the sections in which you made the most errors.

HOW TO PREPARE FOR THE ASVAB

Four-Step Timeline

1. Begin reading this book about two months before the test. Follow the strategies you just learned.

2. One month before the test, focus on the sections containing material that was difficult for you.

3. One week before the test, review the material in this book, and practice doing problems from the math and verbal skills sections.

4. Go to bed early the night before the test. Try to relax and maintain a positive attitude when you wake in the morning.

Study Skills to Increase Retention and Motivation

Follow these steps to make the best use of the time you spend preparing for the test.

- **Find a good place to study.** Find a quiet place in your home to study. Create a work area in this place. Keep your pens, pencils, highlighters, and scrap paper in your work area. Study at least a half an hour a day. Don't forget to schedule time to study.

- **Keep your chin up.** Be optimistic and maintain a good attitude about taking the ASVAB. Imagine yourself doing well. Make positive statements such as, "I know I can do well on the ASVAB."

- **Take care of yourself.** You'll perform better on the test if you feel good and are healthy. Try to get 7 or 8 hours sleep each night. Exercise as often as you can. Exercise will enable you to better concentrate when you study.

- **Review often.** Review the material you have studied. If you can, review with someone else who is taking the ASVAB. If you can't do this, review out loud. This will help you remember what you have learned.

Five Test-Taking Suggestions

Follow these suggestions on the day of the test:

1. Wear comfortable clothing. Layer your clothes, so you can remove a layer if you're too warm.

2. Wear a watch in case there isn't a clock in the room. You need to keep track of testing time.

3. Arrive early. You'll become stressed if you rush. Find the test center ahead of time, so you know how to get there on the day of the test.

4 Listen carefully to oral directions, and read written directions carefully.

5 Answer every question. Begin with those that are easiest for you. Then, go back and answer the more difficult questions. If you can't determine the answer, eliminate answer options that you're sure are incorrect and make a good guess. Check to make sure you're recording each answer in the right place on the answer sheet. Good luck!

SUMMING IT UP

- The Armed Services Vocational Aptitude Battery (ASVAB) is the selection and classification test used by all branches of the U.S. Armed Services.

- There are three different versions of the ASVAB test: (1) the pencil-and-paper AS-VAB test, (2) the CAT-ASVAB (computer-based) test, and (3) the student ASVAB test. The student ASVAB is the same as the pencil-and-paper test, except it does not include the Assembling Objects (AO) subtest. The CAT-ASVAB divides the Auto & Shop Information (AS) subtest into two separate subtests, which appear as Auto Information (AI) and Shop Information (SI).

- An important score derived from ASVAB is the Armed Forces Qualification Test (AFQT) Raw Score, which is used to determine who gets into the armed forces. This score is calculated from the Arithmetic Reasoning, Mathematics Knowledge, Word Knowledge, and Paragraph Comprehension subtests.

- This book provides four strategies for success:

  ❶ Practice with exercises.
  ❷ Practice necessary skills.
  ❸ Take the Practice Tests.
  ❹ Review.

Scoring the ASVAB

OVERVIEW

- ASVAB student results
- Percentile scores
- Summing it up

ASVAB STUDENT RESULTS

After you take the ASVAB, you'll receive a summary report of your scores. This report includes your Career Exploration Scores, standard score bands for each subtest, and your Armed Forces Qualification Test (AFQT) score, which is also called the Military Entrance Score.

As you learned in Chapter 1, you might take the ASVAB as part of a Career Exploration Program in high school. This program is designed to identify students' individual strengths and limitations in a variety of academic and vocational areas. Only the paper-and-pencil version of the ASVAB is available to students in the Career Exploration Program.

The Career Exploration Scores are derived from several sections of the ASVAB. These scores help you identify the areas in which you excel at this point in your academic career. They can also help you determine which subjects you might like to study in the future.

The standard score bands show how well you did on each subtest in relation to other students in your grade. These scores can also help indentify your strengths and the areas in which you need additional instruction.

Lastly, you'll receive an AFQT score or Military Entrance Score. The various branches of the armed forces use this score as a way to predict how you might perform in military training or occupations. For this score, your results are compared to a sample of 6,000 American youths ages 18 to 23. You can read more about this score and what it means for your entrance into the armed forces later in this chapter.

Your ASVAB score can be used for any branch of the military, no matter which version of the test you take. For example, if you take the ASVAB to join the U.S. Army and then decide that you would rather join the U.S. Navy, you don't have to retake the ASVAB. To convert your score from one branch of service to another, you simply need to obtain and sign a 714-A form. Your school counselor or recruiter can give you more information about obtaining this form.

chapter 2

PERCENTILE SCORES

ASVAB scores are reported as percentiles, which determine your standing in a certain field by comparing your scores to a sample of young men and women from across the country.

Your percentile scores don't measure the percent of questions you answered correctly on the test but rather how well you did in comparison to other men and women ages 18 to 23. If you received a percentile of 72 in the Verbal Ability Score, this means that you did as well or better than 72 out of every 100 people who took the test.

Composite Scores

You'll receive three composite scores when you receive your ASVAB results. These scores are combinations of your results on two or more subtests. Composite scores measure your academic, verbal, and math ability.

Academic Ability

Your Academic Ability Score predicts the probability of your future academic success. This composite score combines the results from the Word Knowledge, Paragraph Comprehension, Arithmetic Reasoning, and Mathematics Knowledge subtests.

Verbal Ability

The Verbal Ability Score is used to determine how well you absorb information from written materials. This composite score combines the results from the Word Knowledge and Paragraph Comprehension subtests.

Math Ability

The Math Ability Score predicts how well you'll perform in future math-related courses or occupations. This composite score combines the results from the Arithmetic Reasoning and Mathematics Knowledge subtests.

ASVAB Codes

When you receive your ASVAB scores, you'll also get a primary and secondary ASVAB code. Use these codes with the book *Exploring Careers: The ASVAB Workbook*, which comes free during the Career Exploration Program, to investigate good occupations for someone with your skill set. The book is also available for free at http://www.eric.ed.gov/ERICDocs/data/ericdocs2sql/content_storage_01/0000019b/80/16/91/03.pdf.

Individual Test Scores

Your ASVAB results will also tell you how you performed on each subtest. These scores are not used to determine your ASVAB codes. Students and guidance counselors often use individual test scores to identify areas of academic strength and weakness.

Military Career Scores

The Military Career Score combines your Academic Ability Score with your scores on the Mechanical Comprehension and Electronics Information subtests. When your ASVAB results arrive, you'll also receive the book *Military Careers,* which describes the many occupational paths available in today's military. You can use your Military Career Score with *Military Careers* to estimate your chances of qualifying for enlisted occupations in the military.

The Armed Forces Qualification Test (AFQT)

As you learned earlier, the armed services use your AFQT score to predict how well you would perform during military training or in a military occupation.

The AFQT Raw Score is a composite score that combines the scores from four ASVAB subtests. As you learned in Chapter 1, this is the formula used to obtain this score:

$$\text{AFQT Raw Score} = 2 \times \begin{bmatrix} \text{Word Knowledge} \\ \text{score} + \text{Paragraph} \\ \text{Comprehension} \\ \text{score} \end{bmatrix} + \begin{bmatrix} \text{Arithmetic} \\ \text{Reasoning score} \\ + \text{Mathematics} \\ \text{Knowledge score} \end{bmatrix}$$

Then, the AFQT Raw Score is converted into a percentile score to assess your eligibility for the armed services. The percentile scores are grouped into categories. These categories not only determine which applicants gain admittance to various branches of the armed services, but also whether an individual is eligible for an enlistment bonus. The following are the categories of percentile scores:

AFQT Percentile	AFQT Category
93–99	I
65–92	II
50–64	III-A
31–49	III-B
21–30	IV-A
16–20	IV-B
10–15	IV-C
1–9	V

While the minimum AFQT score requirement varies depending on the branch of the armed services, most branches prefer applicants from Categories I, II, and III-A or III-B. However, depending on the needs of the armed services, a limited number of applicants who fall into Category IV may also enlist. Speak with a recruitment officer to learn more about what your AFQT score means to your future in the armed services.

SUMMING IT UP

- ASVAB results include Career Exploration Scores, standard score bands for each testing area, and a Military Entrance Score.

- The ASVAB can be used in any branch of the military. A 714-A form is needed to convert your score from one branch to another.

- ASVAB scores are reported as percentiles, which indicate your standing in relation to a national sample of students.

- Composite scores are the results of two or more subtests and include the following:
  - Academic Ability Score: Word Knowledge + Paragraph Comprehension +Arithmetic Reasoning + Mathematics Knowledge
  - Verbal Ability Score: Word Knowledge + Paragraph Comprehension
  - Math Ability Score: Arithmetic Reasoning + Mathematics Knowledge

- Score reports include two ASVAB codes, a primary ASVAB code and a secondary ASVAB code, that can be used with *Exploring Careers: The ASVAB Workbook* to identify occupations in which workers have similar aptitude levels.

- The Military Careers Score is a composite of the Academic Ability Score, Mechanical Comprehension subtest score, and the Electronics Information subtest score. It can be used with *Military Careers* to estimate your chances of qualifying for enlisted occupations in the military.

- The AFQT Raw Score is twice the result of the Word Knowledge and Paragraph Comprehension scores plus the result of the Arithmetic Reasoning score and the Mathematics Knowledge score.

- Typically, the military prefers candidates who score in the following categories:
  - Category I (percentile score: 93 and over)
  - Category II (percentile score: 65 to 92)
  - Category III (percentile score: 31 to 64)

PART II

OVERVIEW OF U.S. MILITARY OPPORTUNITIES

CHAPTER 3   Enlisted Opportunities in the U.S. Military

Enlisted Opportunities in the U.S. Military

OVERVIEW

- **General enlistment qualifications**
- **Enlisting in the military**
- **Military training**
- **Servicemembers Opportunity Colleges**
- **Military branches**
- **Pay and benefits**
- **Summing it up**

Most people assume that military service limits a person's career choices to either law enforcement or intelligence. This, of course, is not the case. Those enlisted in the service pursue opportunities in more than 2,000 job specialties in such diverse fields as finance, social work, communications, international relations, and culinary services. This chapter not only discusses the career opportunities available to enlisted servicemembers, but also the process of joining the military, the training servicemembers receive, and the benefits they earn.

GENERAL ENLISTMENT QUALIFICATIONS

You must meet certain eligibility requirements to gain entrance into the military. These requirements assess your citizenship status, physical condition, and educational experience.

- **Age**: Applicants must be between the ages of 18 and 35. Applicants who are 17 may enlist with the permission of a parent or legal guardian.

- **Citizenship status**: You must be a U.S. citizen or a permanent resident alien (with an INS I-151/I-551 Green Card) to enlist in the military. Noncitizens may enlist, but may only serve one term unless they become naturalized U.S. citizens. Certain countries require noncitizens to obtain a waiver before enlisting.

- **Physical condition**: Health and physical fitness standards vary in the military, depending on the branch of service and duty status of the servicemember. Generally, the military requires applicants to be in good health. Certain chronic illnesses or conditions, such as diabetes or epilepsy, prevent some applicants from enlisting. All applicants receive a physical exam to assess their health before basic training. Applicants must meet special weight and height standards to enlist in certain military branches or programs.

- **Education**: Applicants must have a high school diploma or acceptable alternative credentials. While candidates with GEDs may enlist, they aren't always afforded the same opportunities as those with diplomas.

- **Aptitude**: As you already know, all military candidates must take the ASVAB before enlisting. The scores on this test help a recruiter determine the best branch and field of service.

- **Moral character**: Applicants must meet certain moral standards to enter the military. Recruiters examine criminal and school records to determine if a candidate is suited to military life.

- **Marital status and dependents**: Married people can enlist in the military. Each branch has its own policies regarding married individuals and those with dependents. Generally, the military doesn't accept applicants who have two or more dependents under the age of 18. The military grants waivers to individuals on a case-by-case basis.

Service Obligation

Once you enlist in the military, you'll be obligated to serve for a predetermined period in exchange for your pay and benefits. Your service obligation will depend on a number of factors, including your chosen field of service and required training. Many first-time applicants serve a four-year tour of active duty, but some programs offer two-, three-, and six-year plans. Applicants who join the U.S. Reserves and the U.S. National Guard serve part-time. Generally, they serve one weekend every month and two weeks of active duty every year. After spending a period on active duty, recruits move into inactive reserve status. These individuals don't participate in combat unless the military calls them to active duty.

Enlistment Programs

The five services—the U.S. Army, Navy, Air Force, Marine Corps, and Coast Guard—offer different enlistment programs. The military devises various programs to meet its ever-changing recruitment demands. Some enlistment programs offer cash bonuses or other incentives to qualified applicants, which is another reason to aim for a good score on the ASVAB. Candidates with excellent scores usually receive some sort of incentive when they enlist.

Enlistment Contracts

Once you chose an enlistment program, you'll sign an enlistment contract. This includes the chosen enlistment program, the enlistment date, the enlistment term, and other job-training options or incentives. If the military can't meet its part of the agreement (e.g., you don't receive the job training you were guaranteed), you aren't bound by the contract. Before signing your contract, discuss its terms and conditions with your recruiter.

High School Graduates

As you learned earlier, the military requires applicants to have a high school diploma or acceptable alternative credentials. Research shows that high school graduates tend to adjust to military life more quickly and are more likely to complete their initial tours of duty. This is why the military encourages students to stay in school and graduate.

ENLISTING IN THE MILITARY

Learn as much as you can about the military and discuss your decision to enlist with family and friends before speaking to a recruiter. If, after careful consideration, you decide to enlist, you'll follow a four-step process:

Step 1: Talking with a Recruiter

Once you've decided to enlist in the military, make an appointment to speak with a local recruiter. It's the recruiter's job to answer your questions and provide you with information about military service. Your recruiter will also assess your enlistment eligibility. If your recruiter doesn't foresee any problems, then he or she will examine your credentials and schedule your enlistment processing.

Step 2: Qualifying for Enlistment

As you already know, one of the most important steps in the enlistment process is taking the ASVAB. While some students take the exam at their high school, others take it at a local Military Entrance Processing Station (MEPS). Most applicants also receive the medical examinations required to determine if they are fit for service at a MEPS.

Your ASVAB results determine whether you meet the requirements for entry into the military. The Military Career Score determines which field of job training suits your skills. Your ASVAB scores are good for two years. After that time, you need to take the test again to enlist.

Step 3: Meeting with a Military Career Counselor

A military career counselor is a career information specialist who determines which jobs applicants qualify for based on their interviews and ASVAB scores. The military career counselor can answer specific questions about various job-training programs and help you understand the responsibilities of each occupation.

Step 4: Enlisting in the Service

Next, you'll select an enlistment date. Because certain job-training programs aren't immediately available, some applicants choose the Delayed Enlistment Program, which allows them to delay enlistment until the program they desire is available. You have three options if the job-training program you select isn't available when it's time for you to enlist: You can (1) choose another enlistment date and hope that your program will be available in the near future, (2) pick another occupation, or (3) opt not to join the service. As you'll recall, you aren't obligated to serve if the military can't fulfill its part of the enlistment contract.

Those who delay enlistment will return to their local MEPS on a scheduled enlistment date. Applicants who select immediate enlistment receive their travel papers and move to a military base for basic training.

MILITARY TRAINING

The military trains thousands of individuals for a variety of occupations every year. The five services provide four types of training for servicemembers:

1. Recruit training
2. Job training
3. Advanced training
4. Leadership training

Recruit Training

Recruit training, also called basic training or boot camp, is an intense introduction to military life. This program prepares the recruits for the physical, mental, and emotional pressures of military service. The location and duration of training depends on the service and job-training program the recruit has selected. Generally, training lasts between eight and twelve weeks.

At basic training, recruits receive instruction in first aid and combat skills. Recruits split their time each day between classes, exercise routines, and military training sessions. Although this period is strenuous, more than 90 percent of all recruits complete basic training without issue.

Job Training

After basic training, recruits receive job training for their chosen specialties. Job training not only prepares recruits for military assignments, but also provides an excellent foundation for future civilian occupations. Recruits receive hands-on experience both in the classroom and on the job. Refresher and continuing education courses maintain and build on the skills they acquired in their initial job-training programs.

The U.S. Army, Navy, and Marine Corps also offer apprenticeship programs for some occupations through the Department of Defense (DoD).

Advanced Training

As servicemembers advance through the ranks, they receive additional training in their field of choice. Advance training provides servicemembers with new information about their job specialties. This is especially important to recruits who work in technological fields. While some training requires classroom instruction, other courses can be completed through distance education programs.

Leadership Training

The military also provides noncommissioned officers with various leadership-training courses, which prepare them for the challenges they face on a day-to-day basis. Classes focus on developing leadership skills, implementing service regulations, and learning techniques to train new recruits.

SERVICEMEMBERS OPPORTUNITY COLLEGES

The Servicemembers Opportunity Colleges (SOC) is a consortium of more than 1,800 accredited colleges and universities across the United States that helps servicemembers and their families receive college degrees. Receiving a degree through the SOC is beneficial in many ways. An SOC institution offers college credit for military experience and accredited military training programs. You can also transfer credits between various SOC institutions if you need to relocate. For more information on the SOC, go to www.soc.aascu.org.

MILITARY BRANCHES

The five services have similar systems for assigning personnel to jobs. The military designs these systems to satisfy the staffing needs of a particular service while attempting to meet the desires of individual servicemembers and offering them opportunities for career development. The duty-assignment process determines where enlisted personnel work, how often they move, and the opportunities available to them.

All services require members to travel. Enlisted personnel are stationed in each of the fifty states and in twenty countries all over the world. The military routinely reassigns employees after two-, three-, or four-year tours of duty. For many, this is a major attraction of service life; they join for the opportunity to travel, live in foreign countries, and see different parts of the United States.

U.S. Army

The U.S. Army offers its more than 400,000 enlisted servicemembers training in at least 200 occupational specialties. Currently, the army divides jobs into these fields:

administrative support, arts and media, combat, computers and technology, construction and engineering, intelligence and combat support, mechanics, medical and emergency, and transportation and aviation.

Many career opportunities are available within these fields. Servicemembers can train for jobs as communications managers, combat mission support specialists, and artillery and missile crewmembers. The army also employs musicians, religious program specialists, graphic designers, and food service managers. As one of the nation's largest employers, the army also needs finance and accounting managers, lawyers, administrative specialists, doctors, firefighters, and social workers. Almost every job within the U.S. Army has a counterpart in the civilian world, making it easy for servicemembers to find employment once they leave the military.

U.S. Navy

Servicemembers who join the U.S. Navy are responsible for protecting the freedom of the seas. Navy recruits often fulfill a number of technical jobs as sonar technicians, air traffic controllers, radio electrician technicians, and fire control technicians.

The navy also offers recruits the unique opportunity to train as nuclear propulsion specialists who oversee nuclear propulsion technology, a key component in powering the navy's submarines and aircraft carriers. However, because of the sensitive nature of this occupation, the navy selects only a handful of recruits for its Nuclear Propulsion Officer Candidate Program. Recruits in this program are college juniors and seniors pursuing degrees in mathematics, chemistry, physics, or engineering. Recruits with excellent grades will receive specialized training at the Officer Candidate School in Pensacola, Florida, after graduation.

Qualified navy servicemembers can also join the Aviation Officer/Naval Flight Officer Programs, which accepts college seniors who are interested in becoming navy pilots or flight officers.

U.S. Air Force

The U.S. Air Force trains recruits for careers in a number of technical, administrative, and electrical fields. After they enlist, they are automatically enrolled in the Community College of the Air Force (CCAF), the largest community college in the United States. This institution allows recruits to get their applied science associate's degrees in aircraft and missile maintenance, electronics and telecommunications, allied health, logistics and resources, or public and support services. Many recruits seek opportunities that allow them to assist pilots in defending our air and space interests, but others pursue careers in general fields such as medicine, communications, and linguistics.

U.S. Marine Corps

The main objective of the U.S. Marine Corps is to transform recruits into world-class soldiers. After basic training, enlistees pursue opportunities in ground, aviation, and logistics combat missions.

Marines involved in ground combat missions work in the infantry, artillery, intelligence, and combat engineering fields. The aviation combat unit comprises enlisted aircrew members, air traffic controllers, air support and anti-air warfare specialists, aviation operators, and aviation supply and maintenance professionals. The U.S. Marine Corps also employs logistics professionals who oversee the movements of military operations. These marines coordinate troop transportation, maintain vehicles, and oversee communication between various units.

U.S. Coast Guard

The U.S. Coast Guard is responsible for protecting our nation's waterways from various threats. Coast guard enlistees perform search-and-rescue missions, coordinate environmental cleanups, and assist in law enforcement operations.

Enlistees can pursue careers in many fields, including health services, marine sciences, and communication technologies. College graduates in the coast guard may train for careers in law, aviation, engineering, and intelligence. Members of the U.S. Coast Guard Reserve may train to become port security specialists, investigators, and data processing technicians.

PAY AND BENEFITS

The military pays all servicemembers according to the same pay scale, which is based on pay grade and number of years served. Each year, the U.S. Congress grants a cost-of-living increase to those in the military. In addition to basic pay, servicemembers receive a number of valuable benefits, including health care, tuition assistance, and retirement packages.

Enlisted Pay Grades

The military has nine pay grades for enlistees. New enlistees start at pay grade E-1 and gradually work their way up through promotions and years of service. Servicemembers are usually up for promotions every six to twelve months. Supervisors examine the job performance, test scores, and leadership abilities of enlistees who are eligible for promotion.

Basic Pay

The following charts show the monthly base pay for enlisted service members and the base pay for commissioned officers.

ENLISTED SERVICEMEMBERS MONTHLY BASE PAY

Rank	Years Served			
	2 or Less	Over 2	Over 3	Over 4
E-1<4 months	$1,294.50	N/A	N/A	N/A
E-1>4 months	$1,399.50	$1,399.50	$1,399.50	$1,399.50
E-2	$1,568.70	$1,568.70	$1,568.70	$1,568.70
E-3	$1,649.70	$1,753.50	$1,859.70	$1,859.70
E-4	$1,827.60	$1,920.90	$2,025.00	$2,1270.60

COMMISSIONED OFFICERS MONTHLY BASE PAY

Rank	Years Served			
	2 or Less	Over 2	Over 3	Over 4
O-1	$2,655.30	$2,763.60	$3,340.50	$3,340.50
O-2	$3,058.80	$3,483.90	$4,012.50	$4,148.10
O-3	$3,540.30	$4,013.40	$4,332.00	$4,722.90
O-4	$4,026.90	$4,661.40	$4,972.20	$5,041.80

Incentives and Special Pay

Servicemembers may receive incentives and special pay for specific types of duty or specialized skills. Enlistees who volunteer for hazardous duties such as parachute jumping, submarine travel, and flight deck work receive a monthly incentive in addition to their base pay. The military also dispenses bonuses for specialized occupations.

Allowances

During the first year of service, many enlistees live in military housing where they receive necessities such as food and clothing free of change. The military grants servicemembers who live off base quarters subsistence allowances for housing and food.

Employment Benefits

In addition to their monthly pay, servicemembers receive an attractive benefits package for themselves and members of their immediate family. Benefits include medical and dental care, tuition assistance for college, and free job training. The military gives each servicemember thirty days vacation per year. Servicemembers also enjoy access to on-base sports and recreational facilities and discounts on a range of goods and services including airfare and movie tickets.

Retirement Benefits

Servicemembers who joined the military after August 1, 1986, are eligible to choose from two retirement packages after fifteen years of service. Those who choose the first option receive a cash bonus of $30,000 after agreeing to complete a twenty-year active-duty career. After twenty years, the servicemember receives a pension at a rate of 40 percent of the average of the highest thirty-six months of the individual's base pay. Those who choose not to receive the cash bonus up front and complete their twenty years of active-duty service collect a pension at a rate of 50 percent of the average of their highest thirty-six months of base pay.

Servicemembers may also contribute to the Thrift Savings Plan (TSP), which is similar to a 401K investment plan. However, unlike private employers, the government will not match contributions to this plan.

Veterans' Benefits

The U.S. Congress and the Department of Veterans Affairs provides veterans with certain benefits. In most cases, these include guarantees for home loans, hospitalization, survivor benefits, educational benefits, disability benefits, and assistance in finding civilian employment.

SUMMING IT UP

- The military provides job assignment, pay, benefits, and occupational training. In return, enlistees agree to serve for a certain period.

- Enlistment programs vary by service, but all services offer a Delayed Entry Program (also called Delayed Enlistment Program). If the service cannot meet its part of the agreement, then the applicant is not required to serve.

- Enlisting in the military is a four-step process:
  - Step 1: Talking with a recruiter
  - Step 2: Qualifying for enlistment
  - Step 3: Meeting with a military career counselor
  - Step 4: Enlisting in the service

- The military generally provides its personnel with four kinds of training:
  1. Recruit training
  2. Job training
  3. Advanced training
  4. Leadership training

- The Servicemembers Opportunity Colleges (SOC) program enables members and their families to receive college degrees through a group of more than 1,800 colleges, universities, and technical institutes.

- The five military services offer career opportunities in a variety of fields.

- The military pays all personnel according to the same pay scale. Servicemembers receive substantial benefits in addition to their pay and allowances. The military provides many necessities, such as food, clothing, and housing, or pays monthly allowances for them.

- After fifteen years of service, servicemembers may choose a retirement plan that suits their needs.

PART III

OVERVIEW OF THE ASVAB MATH

An Introduction to ASVAB Math

OVERVIEW

- General tips
- Four test-taking tips for the ASVAB math subtests
- Summing it up

GENERAL TIPS

You use math every day without even thinking about it. You might figure out how much time you have until a class ends. When cooking, you might double or halve a recipe. You might determine how long it will take you to travel to a new place.

To improve your math skills, use math whenever you can. When you buy groceries, round the prices up or down and estimate your bill. When you shop at a department store, try to determine how much sales tax you will have to pay. For example, if you're purchasing a $40 jacket and your state requires you to pay a 6 percent sales tax, you will have to pay $42.40 for the jacket. If you travel 12 miles to work each day, figure out how many feet you travel. The more you use math, the better your math skills will become.

FOUR TEST-TAKING TIPS FOR THE ASVAB MATH SUBTESTS

1 **Use scrap paper to organize your thoughts.** If you use more than one page, number each page, so you don't become confused. Neatly line up numbers and rows, so you don't make careless mistakes.

2 **Keep track of your time during the test.** Estimate how much time it will take you to solve each problem using this formula:

Total time for the section/Total number of problems =
The approximate time you should spend on one problem

If you're unsure of the answer to a question, eliminate answer choices that you know are incorrect. Then, make a good guess as to the best answer. Put a question mark in the margin of the test paper if you're unsure of your answer. Return to it when you complete the rest of the problems in that section—if you have time.

3 **Make sure the problem and the solution make sense.** Use common sense when choosing an answer. For example, if you are to add one number to another, the correct answer should be greater than either number.

chapter 4

❹ Estimate your answers. Before you spend a great deal of time doing computations to find the exact answer, you might be able to estimate your answer by rounding numbers. This will help you eliminate incorrect answer choices—possibly even all incorrect answer choices.

These exercises will show you which mathematical skills will be tested on the ASVAB. Solve each problem, and then check your answers against the solutions that follow the exercises.

EXERCISES: ARITHMETIC REASONING

Directions: Now try these exercises. Each problem is followed by four possible answers. Solve each problem. When you have completed these exercises, check your answers against the answer explanations that follow these exercises.

1. Cara, a druggist, wants to know how many antibiotic pills she can make out of 2.5 kilograms of drug X if each pill requires 5 milligrams of drug X.
   1-A   2,500
   1-B   50,000
   1-C   500,000
   1-D   1,500,000

2. Emile and Tenisha have a budget of $2,000 to purchase furniture for their living room. If they buy a sofa and loveseat for $900, 2 rugs for $150 each, a coffee table for $180, and two lamps for $80 each, how much money is left in their furniture budget?
   2-A $460
   2-B $540
   2-C $1,310
   2-D $3,540

3. If roses are bought for $7 a dozen and sold for $20 a dozen, what is the profit on the sale of 3 dozen roses?
   3-A $14.00
   3-B $21.00
   3-C $26.00
   3-D $39.00

4. One-half of the 240 students in Marcy's sophomore class play a sport. Of these, 55% play soccer, 30% play basketball, and 15% play golf. How many of these students play soccer?
   4-A   65
   4-B   66
   4-C   120
   4-D   132

5. Jeremy, Keisha, and Frank played basketball and scored 4, 8, and 12 points, respectively. What was the average number of points scored?
   5-A   6
   5-B   8
   5-C   10
   5-D   22

6. Renee is fixing some broken posts in a fence. If each post is 4.5 feet in length, how many posts can Renee make out of a board that is 18 feet long?
   6-A   18
   6-B   5
   6-C   4
   6-D   2

7. A small bag of jelly beans contains 4 orange, 2 pink, 6 black, and 6 green jelly beans. If the small bag contains the same distribution of jelly beans as is found in an extra-large bag holding 360 jelly beans, how many green jelly beans will be found in the large bag?
   7-A   180
   7-B   120
   7-C   60
   7-D   6

QUESTIONS 8 TO 10 REFER TO THE FOLLOWING GRAPH.

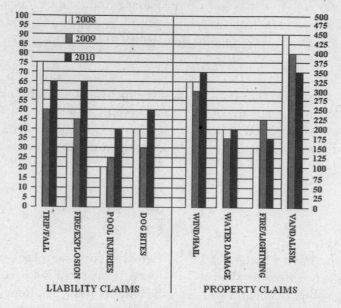

NUMBER OF INSURANCE CLAIMS FOR COMMUNITY X, 2008-2010

8. In 2010, the incidence of which of the following insurance claims was greater than in the two previous years?

8-A   Trip/Fall

8-B   Water Damage

8-C   Pool Injuries

8-D   Fire/Lightening

9. The above graph indicates that the percentage increase in Trip/Fall claims from 2009 to 2010 is

9-A   5%

9-B   15%

9-C   30%

9-D   65%

10. Which of the following cannot be determined because there is not enough information in the graph to do so?

10-A   For the three-year period, what percentage of liability claims involved pool injuries in 2008?

10-B   Which claims followed a pattern of continuing yearly increases for the three-year period?

10-C   For 2010, what was the ratio of wind/hail, water damage, and fire/lightening claims?

10-D   For the three-year period, what percentage of liability claims was made in the first six months of 2008?

ANSWER KEY AND EXPLANATIONS

1. C	3. D	5. B	7. B	9. C
2. A	4. B	6. C	8. C	10. D

1-C   Step 1: Make a sketch.

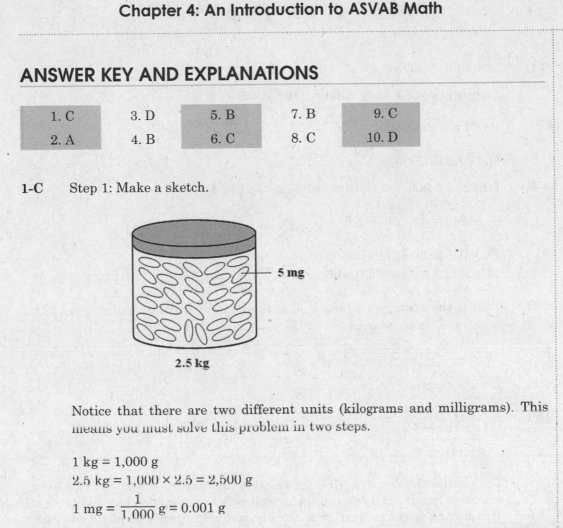

5 mg

2.5 kg

Notice that there are two different units (kilograms and milligrams). This means you must solve this problem in two steps.

1 kg = 1,000 g

2.5 kg = 1,000 × 2.5 = 2,500 g

$1 \text{ mg} = \dfrac{1}{1,000} \text{ g} = 0.001 \text{ g}$

5 mg = 0.001 × 5 = 0.005 g

Step 2: Divide the total amount of drug X by the amount of drug X in each pill:

$$\text{Total/amount per pill} = \frac{2,500}{0.005} = \frac{2,500,000}{5} = 500,000 \text{ pills}$$

2-A   List the items and their costs:

Sofa and loveseat = $900

2 rugs: 2 × $150 = $300

1 coffee table = $180

2 lamps: 2 × $80 = $160

Total = $1,540

Be careful! This is not the answer.

To find out how much money is left, subtract:

$2,000 − $1,540 = $460

3-D   Cost of 3 dozen roses = $7 × 3 = $21.00

Selling price of 3 dozen roses = $20 × 3 = $60.00

Profit = selling price − cost.

$60.00 − $21.00 = $39.00

4-B   Find the number of students who play sports:

$$\frac{1}{2} \text{ of } 240 = \frac{1}{2} \times 240 = 120$$

Find the number who play soccer:
55% of 120 = 0.55 × 120 = 66

5-B   To find the average, find the sum of the number of points and divide by the number of people playing:

$$\text{Average} = \frac{4 + 8 + 12}{3} = \frac{24}{3} = 8$$

6-C   Draw a sketch.

The picture shows that to find the answer, you must divide 4.5 into 18. First, get rid of the decimal point in the divisor by moving it one place to the right. This means you must also move the decimal point in the dividend one place to the right.

$$\frac{18}{4.5} = \frac{180}{45} = 4$$

7-B   Write a fraction that shows the ratio of green jelly beans to all the jelly beans in the small bag:

$$\text{green jelly beans/all jelly beans} = \frac{6}{4 + 2 + 6 + 6} = \frac{6}{18} = \frac{1}{3}$$

"Same distribution" means if $\frac{1}{3}$ of the jelly beans in the small bag are green, then $\frac{1}{3}$ of the jelly beans in the extra-large bag are green:

$$\frac{1}{3} \text{ of } 360 = \frac{1}{3} \times 360 = 120 \text{ jelly beans are green in the extra-large bag.}$$

8-C   The number of pool injuries increased from 20 in 2008 to 25 in 2009 to 40 in 2010.

9-C   The number of Trip/Fall claims went from 50 in 2009 to 65 in 2010. The percent increase is:

$$\frac{15}{50} = 0.3 = 30\%$$

10-D   The graph gives information by year, not by month. It is impossible to determine from the graph the percentage of claims made during the first six months of any year.

EXERCISES: MATHEMATICS KNOWLEDGE

Directions: Now try these exercises. Each problem is followed by four possible answers. Solve each problem. When you have completed these exercises, check your answers against the answer explanations that follow these exercises.

1. If 70 miles is 35% of the total distance between Town A and Town B, how many miles apart are these two towns?
   - **1-A**   0.5 miles
   - **1-B**   24.5 miles
   - **1-C**   140 miles
   - **1-D**   200 miles

2. $4(x + 3) - (3x - 2)$
   - **2-A** $x + 14$
   - **2-B** $x + 5$
   - **2-C** $-12 + 14$
   - **2-D** $7x + 5$

3. Two cars start from the same point at the same time. One car drives north at 40 miles per hour and the other car drives south at 38 miles per hour. How many miles apart are the two cars after 30 minutes?
   - **3-A**   1 mile
   - **3-B**   39 miles
   - **3-C**   58 miles
   - **3-D**   78 miles

4. What is the distance covered in one revolution of a wheel whose diameter is 35 inches?
   (Use $\pi = \frac{22}{7}$)
   - **4-A**   5 in.
   - **4-B**   88 in.
   - **4-C**   110 in.
   - **4-D**   770 in.

5. What is the perimeter of a square with an area of 64 feet?
   - **5-A**   8 ft.
   - **5-B**   16 ft.
   - **5-C**   32 ft.
   - **5-D**   64 ft.

6. What is the area, in square feet, of the triangular plot of land shown below?

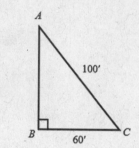

   - **6-A**   2,400 sq. ft.
   - **6-B**   3,000 sq. ft.
   - **6-C**   4,000 sq. ft.
   - **6-D**   4,800 sq. ft.

7. $(2\sqrt{6})^2 =$
   - **7-A**   12
   - **7-B**   24
   - **7-C**   72
   - **7-D**   144

8. What is the next number in the following sequence?

   5.00, 5.06, 5.12, 5.18, 5.24, 5.30, _____
   - **8-A**   5.38
   - **8-B**   5.36
   - **8-C**   5.34
   - **8-D**   5.32

ANSWER KEY AND EXPLANATIONS

1. D	3. B	5. C	7. B	8. B
2. A	4. C	6. A		

1-D Translate the words into an equation and solve.

Let x = total distance between towns. Then 35% of the total distance = $0.35x$.

$0.35x = 70$ (Divide both sides by 0.35.)

$x = \dfrac{70}{0.35}$

$x = 200$ miles

2-A Multiply the first term by 4:
$4(x + 3) = 4x + 12$

Change the signs of the second term:
$-(3x - 2) = -3x + 2$

Follow the rules for addition of signed numbers:
$4x + 12 - 3x + 2 = x + 14$

3-B Make a sketch.

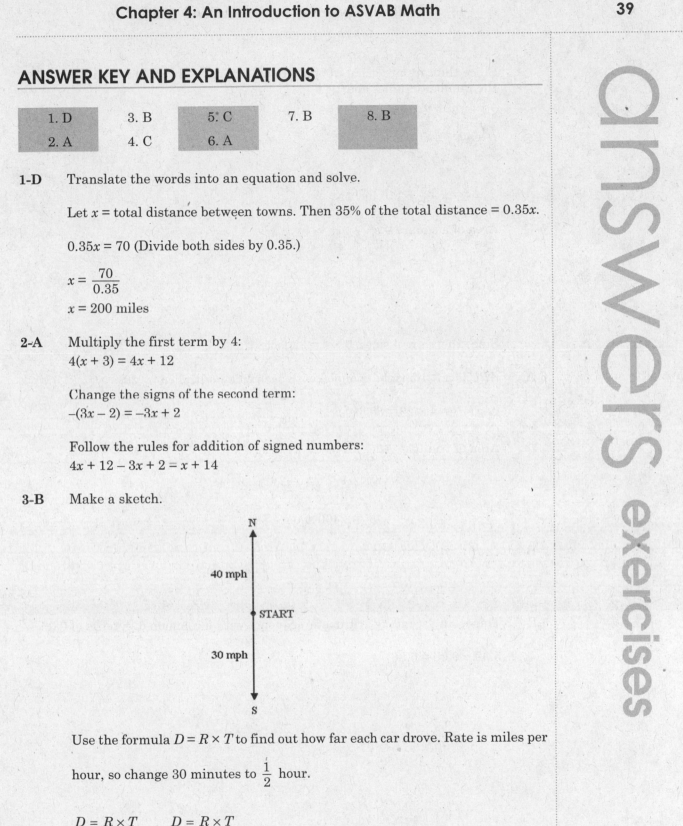

Use the formula $D = R \times T$ to find out how far each car drove. Rate is miles per hour, so change 30 minutes to $\dfrac{1}{2}$ hour.

$$D = R \times T \qquad D = R \times T$$
$$= 40 \times \frac{1}{2} \qquad = 38 \times \frac{1}{2}$$
$$= 20 \text{ miles} \qquad = 19 \text{ miles}$$

Since the cars are going in opposite directions, add the two distances to find the number of miles apart.

20 + 19 = 39 miles

4-C $C = \pi d$

$\quad = \pi \times 35$

$\quad = \dfrac{22}{7} \times \dfrac{35}{1} = 110$ inches

5-C   Area of a square $= s^2$

$\quad\quad 64 = s^2$

$\quad \sqrt{64} = s$

$\quad\quad\ 8 = s$

Since there are 4 sides, $8 \times 4 = 32$ feet.

6-A ABC is a 3-4-5 right triangle, with each side multiplied by 20.

Leg $AB = 4 \times 20 = 80$ feet

Area of triangle $ABC = \dfrac{1}{2}bh$

$\quad\quad\quad\quad\quad\quad\quad = \dfrac{1}{2} \times 60 \times 80$

$\quad\quad\quad\quad\quad\quad\quad = 2{,}400$ square feet

7-B $(2\sqrt{6})^2 = (2)^2 \times (\sqrt{6})^2$

$\quad\quad\quad\quad = 4 \times 6$

$\quad\quad\quad\quad = 24$

8-B   This is an ascending arithmetic sequence with a common difference of 0.06.

$5.30 + 0.06 = 5.36$

SUMMING IT UP

- Each day you perform routine math problems as part of your daily life. Make a point to use math whenever you can to improve your mathematical reasoning and knowledge.

- Use these four test taking tips for the ASVAB math subtests:

  1 Make sure and bring scrap paper so you can organize your thoughts.

  2 Use time wisely when taking the test.

  3 Make sure to use common sense when looking at the problem and solution.

  4 To save time, estimate your answers to eliminate incorrect choices.

- Use the Arithmetic Reasoning and Mathematics Knowledge exercises to gain understanding of what skills will be tested.

- Check the answer keys to make sure you scored well on the exercises.

Arithmetic Reasoning

chapter 5

OVERVIEW

- Decimals and whole numbers
- Making purchases
- Fractions and percents
- Numbers with units
- Parts of a whole
- Ratio and proportion
- Averages
- Graphs
- Summing it up

DECIMALS AND WHOLE NUMBERS

Decimals

Addition and Subtraction of Decimals

You can add and subtract decimals just as you add and subtract whole numbers—but you must keep the decimal points in each number in a vertical line. This determines where the decimal point falls in your answer.

Example: Add 3.14, 0.756, and 5.

SOLUTION:
$$\begin{array}{r} 3.140 \\ 0.756 \\ +\,5.000 \\ \hline 8.896 \end{array}$$

Always insert a place-holding zero in numbers smaller than one to keep your decimal points in line.

Example: Subtract 19.35 from 22.5.

SOLUTION:
$$\begin{array}{r} 22.50 \\ -\,19.35 \\ \hline 3.15 \end{array}$$

Multiplication of Decimals

Multiply decimals just as you would whole numbers. You do not need to line up the decimal points in the numbers. Once you have finished multiplying, add the number of decimal places in the multiplicand to the number of decimal places in the multiplier—this is the number of decimal places needed in the product.

Example: Multiply 4.76 by 0.02.

SOLUTION:
$$\begin{array}{r} 4.76 \\ \times\, 0.02 \\ \hline 0.0952 \end{array}$$

An easy way to multiply a decimal by a power of 10 is to move the decimal point one place to the right for every zero in the power.

Example:
$$0.125 \times 10 = 1.25$$
$$0.125 \times 100 = 12.5$$
$$0.125 \times 1{,}000 = 125$$

Division of Decimals

When only the dividend is a decimal, you can divide as you would with two whole numbers. Once you have the quotient, place the decimal point above the decimal point in the dividend.

Example: Divide 36.40 by 4.

SOLUTION:
$$\begin{array}{r} 9.10 \\ 4\overline{)36.40} \\ -36 \\ \hline 40 \\ -40 \\ \hline \end{array}$$

If both the divisor and the dividend are decimals, remove the decimal point from the divisor, and move the decimal point in the dividend to the right as many places as there were in the divisor. Add a zero to the dividend when there are not enough places.

Example: Divide 2.55 by 0.125.

SOLUTION:
$$0.125\overline{)2.55} = \begin{array}{r} 20.4 \\ 125\overline{)2550} \\ -2500 \\ \hline 50 \end{array}$$

Decimals can be divided by a power of 10 by moving the decimal point one space to the left for every zero in the power. Add zeros in front of the number when there are not enough places.

Example:
$$1.25 \div 10 = 0.125$$
$$1.25 \div 100 = 0.0125$$
$$1.25 \div 1,000 = 0.000125$$

Conversion of Fractions to Decimals

The first step in changing a fraction to a decimal is to divide the numerator by the denominator. Then, work out the division to as many decimal places as required by the problem.

Example: Change $\frac{8}{32}$ to a decimal of two places.

SOLUTION:
$$\frac{8}{32} = 32\overline{)8.00} \quad \begin{array}{r} 0.25 \\ \hline -64 \\ \hline 160 \\ -160 \\ \hline \end{array}$$

Conversion of Decimals to Fractions

You can express a decimal as a fraction by placing the decimal over a denominator of 1. Next, multiply both the top and bottom numbers by the power of 10 indicated by the number of decimal places.

Example: Convert 0.375 to a fraction.

SOLUTION: $\dfrac{0.375}{1} \times \dfrac{1,000}{1,000} = \dfrac{375}{1,000}$

You can then reduce the fraction to lowest terms.

$$\frac{375}{1,000} = \frac{3}{8}$$

Whole Numbers

Rounding Off Numbers

To round a number, locate the rounding digit and look to the right of it. If the number to the right is 0, 1, 2, 3, or 4, the rounding digit will not change. If the number to the right of the rounding digit is 5 or higher, the rounding digit rounds up one number. Omit all digits to the right of the rounding digit.

Example: Round 23.1472 to the nearest thousandths place.

SOLUTION: 23.1472 = 23.147

Example: Round 23.147 to the nearest hundredths place.

SOLUTION: 23.147 = 23.15

Example: Round 23.15 to the nearest tenths place.

SOLUTION: 23.15 = 23.2

Example: Round 23.15 to the nearest units place.

SOLUTION: 23.2 = 23

Example: Round 23 to the nearest tens place.

SOLUTION: 23 = 20

When rounding to the tens place, a zero must remain in the rounding digit's place as a placeholder.

Final Zeros

When multiplying whole numbers, leave off the final zero as you work out the problem. Just remember to transfer the zero to your final answer.

Example:

$$\begin{array}{r} 350 \\ \times\ 250 \\ \hline 175 \\ +\ 700 \\ \hline 87,500 \end{array}$$

Final zeros also play a part in dividing whole numbers. If there is a final zero in the divisor, but no final zero in the dividend, you can move the decimal point in both numbers to the left as many places as there are final zeros in the divisor and omit the final zeros.

Example: $700\overline{)1,455} = 7\overline{)14.55}$

EXERCISES: DECIMALS AND WHOLE NUMBERS

Directions: Now try the exercises below. Each question is followed by four possible answers. Solve each problem. When you have completed the exercises, check your answers against the answer explanations that follow.

1. Add 19.50, 1.642, 112.3, and 17.041.
   - 1-A   15.0483
   - 1-B   150.483
   - 1-C   150.00
   - 1-D   1504.83

2. Subtract 3.2508 from 8.
   - 2-A   4.7492
   - 2-B   4.4792
   - 2-C   3.8451
   - 2-D   3.5482

3. Find the product of 4.14 and 17.5.
   - 3-A   0.7245
   - 3-B   7.245
   - 3-C   72.45
   - 3-D   724.5

4. Divide 12.35 by 1.9, carried out to 1 decimal point.
   - 4-A   65
   - 4-B   6.5
   - 4-C   1.65
   - 4-D   0.165

5. What is $\frac{6}{25}$ in decimal form (to the nearest hundredth)?
   - 5-A   0.24
   - 5-B   0.024
   - 5-C   24
   - 5-D   240

6. Four friends go to dinner. One meal costs $10.52, the second costs $9.75, the third costs $14.85, and the fourth costs $11.22. How much is the total?
   - 6-A $34.46
   - 6-B $36.44
   - 6-C $44.36
   - 6-D $46.34

7. A customer's total purchase at a clothing store costs $50.95. The customer has a gift card with a remaining balance of $16.23. If the customer uses the gift card, how much is the new total?
   - 7-A $27.43
   - 7-B $32.74
   - 7-C $24.37
   - 7-D $34.72

8. 2,300 × 10 =
   - 8-A   230,000
   - 8-B   23,000
   - 8-C   2300
   - 8-D   230

9. Change $\frac{4}{32}$ to a decimal of three places.
   - 9-A   0.322
   - 9-B   0.248
   - 9-C   0.125
   - 9-D   0.008

10. Round 7.2571 to the nearest hundredth.
    - 10-A   .7
    - 10-B   7.3
    - 10-C   7.26
    - 10-D   7.257

ANSWER KEY AND EXPLANATIONS:

1. B	3. C	5. A	7. D	9. C
2. A	4. B	6. D	8. B	10. C

1-B   Line up the decimal points before adding the numbers.

$$
\begin{array}{r}
19.500 \\
1.642 \\
112.300 \\
+\,17.041 \\
\hline
150.483
\end{array}
$$

2-A   Add a decimal point and four zeros to the 8. Then, line up the decimal points and subtract.

$$
\begin{array}{r}
8.0000 \\
-\,3.2508 \\
\hline
4.7492
\end{array}
$$

3-C   You need the same number of decimals in the product as there are in the two multiplers.

$$
\begin{array}{r}
4.14 \\
\times\,17.5 \\
\hline
2070 \\
28980 \\
+\,41400 \\
\hline
72.45
\end{array}
$$

4-B   Move the decimal point in the divisor one place to the right. Move the decimal point in the dividend one place to the right and add one zero to carry the answer to the number of decimal places instructed in the problem.

$$
\begin{array}{r}
6.5 \\
19\overline{)123.5} \\
-114 \\
\hline
95 \\
-95 \\
\hline
\end{array}
$$

5-A Divide the numerator by the denominator.

$$
\begin{array}{r}
0.24 \\
25\overline{)6.00} \\
-\,50 \\
\hline
100 \\
-\,100 \\
\hline
\end{array}
$$

6-D Line up the decimal points before adding the numbers.

$$
\begin{array}{r}
\$10.52 \\
\$9.75 \\
\$14.85 \\
+\,\$11.22 \\
\hline
\$46.34 \\
\end{array}
$$

7-D Line up the decimal points before subtracting the amount of the gift card from the total.

$$
\begin{array}{r}
\$50.95 \\
-\,\$16.23 \\
\hline
\$34.72 \\
\end{array}
$$

8-B Drop the final zeros in each number during computation. Add them to the final product.

$$
\begin{array}{r}
2,3\cancel{00} \\
\times\ 1\cancel{0} \\
\hline
23,\underline{000} \\
\end{array}
$$

9-C Divide the numerator by the denominator and work out the division to three decimal places.

$$
\begin{array}{r}
0.125 \\
32\overline{)4.000} \\
-\,32 \\
\hline
80 \\
-\,64 \\
\hline
160 \\
-\,160 \\
\hline
\end{array}
$$

10-C The rounding digit is rounded up, and all the numbers to the left are dropped.

$7.2\underline{5}71 = 7.26$

MAKING PURCHASES

You often come across decimals in problems involving money. In our monetary system, each cent is equal to one-hundredth of a dollar. In decimal form, a penny is represented as 0.01.

Adding and Subtracting Dollars and Cents

You can add and subtract dollars and cents in the same way that you add and subtract decimals. Line up all the decimal points in the problem before adding or subtracting.

If a number does not have a decimal point, as in $20, add one and place two zeros after it.

Example: Janet is paying her monthly utility bills. She owes $40 for electric, $15.63 for water, and $52.27 for heat. How much will Janet spend on utilities this month?

SOLUTION: First, you need to line up all the decimal points. Total the numbers and place the decimal point in the sum directly under the decimal points in the problem.

$$\begin{array}{r} \$40.00 \\ \$15.63 \\ + \ \$52.27 \\ \hline \$107.90 \end{array}$$

Multiplying Dollars and Cents

When multiplying a monetary amount by a whole number, place the decimal point before the last two digits in the product.

Example: Brandon's monthly car payment is $196.56. How much does Brandon spend on his car in a year?

SOLUTION: There are 12 months in a year.

$$\begin{array}{r} \$196.59 \\ \times \ 12 \\ \hline 39318 \\ + \ 196590 \\ \hline \$2,359.08 \end{array}$$

Multiple Purchases

For problems involving multiple purchases, multiply the cost of each group of items first before adding all numbers together to find the total cost.

Example: A customer purchases the following items:

> 2 frozen dinners @ $2.49 each
> 3 cucumbers @ $0.52 each
> 4 pounds of chicken @ $0.99 per pound

How much change will the customer receive from $20?

SOLUTION: Multiply the cost of each group of items separately.

> Frozen dinners: $2.49 × = $4.98
> Cucumbers: $0.52 × 3 = $1.56
> Chicken: $0.99 × 4 = $3.96

Line up all numbers to find the total cost of the purchases.

```
   $4.98
   $1.56
 + $3.96
 ───────
  $10.50
```

Subtract this amount from $20 to see how much change the customer will receive.

```
   $20.00
 − $10.50
 ───────
    $9.50
```

EXERCISES: MAKING PURCHASES

Directions: Now try the exercises below. Each question is followed by four possible answers. Solve each problem. When you have completed the exercises, check your answers against the answer explanations that follow.

1. Anita and Rick are planning a vacation. They purchase 2 round-trip plane tickets at $425.50 each, a 7-night hotel stay for $119 per night, and round-trip ground transportation for $30 per person. How much did they spend?

   1-A $574.50

   1-B $1,430.50

   1-C $1,560.00

   1-D $1,744.00

2. Jamal is painting his living room. At the home improvement store, he notices that paint is on sale for $12.49 per can. He purchases 3 cans of paint. How much change should he receive from $50?

   2-A $11.27

   2-B $12.53

   2-C $13.31

   2-D $14.75

3. Matt purchased a new refrigerator on a monthly payment plan. He pays $140.44 per month for six months. How much is the total cost of the refrigerator?

   3-A $685.24

   3-B $753.12

   3-C $842.64

   3-D $922.88

4. A group of students is raising money for a local charity. They hope to raise $1,000 by the end of the year. So far, Anna has raised $175, Jason has raised $89, and Elliot has raised $203. How much more do they need?

   4-A $467

   4-B $482

   4-C $533

   4-D $559

5. Andrea has agreed to watch her sister's cat for a week. At the pet store, she purchases cat treats for $1.99, a cat toy for $4.03, and cat food for $6.57. Andrea has a coupon for $5 off her entire purchase. How much will she spend?

   5-A $7.59

   5-B $8.41

   5-C $9.32

   5-D $10.11

6. Jose needs supplies to bake a pumpkin pie. He purchases eggs for $0.89, flour for $1.23, sugar for $1.99, and pumpkin pie filling for $0.69. How much change can he expect from $10?

   6-A $4.30

   6-B $4.80

   6-C $5.20

   6-D $5.50

7. Tonya has $50 to spend on party decorations. If she purchases balloons for $23, candles for $15, and streamers for $17.50, how much more money does she need?

   7-A $2.50

   7-B $3.50

   7-C $4.50

   7-D $5.50

8. Four friends go to dinner at a restaurant. Alice's meal costs $13.20, Steve's meal costs $15.40, Jamie's meal costs $12.75, and Tyrone's meal costs $16.37. Each person ordered a soda, which costs $2.15 per person. How much is the total bill?

   8-A $66.32

   8-B $57.72

   8-C $55.44

   8-D $53.69

9. Bethany needs to purchase 3 textbooks for her class. One book costs $23.15, another costs $15.75, and the last one costs $30.99. How much change will she receive from $100.00?

   9-A $30.11

   9-B $35.75

   9-C $41.52

   9-D $44.52

10. Louis is fixing his bathroom. At the hardware store, he purchases a box of nails for $1.89, a caulking gun for $7.83, and glue for $3.25. He has a coupon for $2.00 off the price of the caulking gun. What is his total?

    10-A $9.75

    10-B $10.97

    10-C $11.88

    10-D $12.97

exercises

ANSWER KEY AND EXPLANATIONS

1. D	3. C	5. A	7. D	9. A
2. B	4. C	6. C	8. A	10. B

1-D   Figure out the cost of each purchase separately before you calculate the total.

$$2 \times \$425.50 = \$851.00$$
$$7 \times \$119 = \$833.00$$
$$\underline{2 \times \$30 = \quad\$60.00}$$
$$\text{Total} = \$1,744.00$$

2-B   Figure out the total cost of the paint first.

$$3 \times \$12.49 = \$37.47$$

Expected change from $50:

$$\$50.00$$
$$\underline{- \$37.47}$$
$$\$12.53$$

3-C   Multiply the number of months by the monthly payment amount to find the total cost.

$$\$140.44$$
$$\underline{\times\ 6}$$
$$\$842.64$$

4-C   Add the amount each group member raised first.

$$\$175.00$$
$$\$89.00$$
$$\underline{+ \$203.00}$$
$$\$467.00$$

Amount needed to reach $1,000 goal:

$$\$1,000.00$$
$$\underline{- \$467.00}$$
$$\$533.00$$

5-A   Add all purchases together first to find the total.

        $1.99
        $4.03
   + $6.57
        $12.59

   Total after using coupon:

        $12.59
   − $5.00
        $7.59

6-C   Figure out the total cost of all the items first.

        $0.89
        $1.23
        $1.99
   + $0.69
        $4.80

   Total change from $10:

        $10.00
   − $4.80
        $5.20

7-D   Figure out the total cost of all the items first.

        $23.00
        $15.00
   + $17.50
        $55.50

   Total $50 = additional money needed:

        $55.50
   − $50.00
        $5.50

8-A   Determine the cost of the meals first.

        $13.20
        $15.40
        $12.75
   + $16.37
        $57.72

Calculate the cost of the drinks.

$4 \times \$2.15 = \$8.60$

Add the cost of the meals and the drinks to find the total amount.

$$\begin{array}{r} \$57.72 \\ + \$8.60 \\ \hline \$66.32 \end{array}$$

9-A   Add the cost of all textbooks.

$$\begin{array}{r} \$23.15 \\ \$15.75 \\ + \$30.99 \\ \hline \$69.89 \end{array}$$

Subtract this amount from $100.00.

$$\begin{array}{r} \$100.00 \\ - \$69.89 \\ \hline \$30.11 \end{array}$$

10-B   Take $2.00 off the price of the caulking gun before adding all the purchases.

$$\begin{array}{r} \$7.83 \\ - \$2.00 \\ \hline \$5.83 \end{array}$$

Add all the purchases to find the total.

$$\begin{array}{r} \$1.89 \\ \$5.83 \\ + \$3.25 \\ \hline \$10.97 \end{array}$$

FRACTIONS AND PERCENTS

Fractions

A fraction is a part of a unit. Each fraction has a numerator and a denominator. In the fraction $\frac{2}{3}$, 2 is the numerator, and 3 is the denominator. In all fractions, the numerator is divided by the denominator. Therefore, in the fraction $\frac{2}{3}$, 2 is being divided by 3.

Think of a fraction as a small part of a larger whole. With fractions, the whole quantity is 1. Any fraction in which the numerator and denominator are the same number is equal to 1.

Example: $\frac{3}{3} = 1$

A *mixed number* is an integer (any of the natural numbers) followed by a proper fraction.

Example: $2\frac{3}{4}$ is a mixed number.

An *improper fraction* is one in which the numerator is greater than or equal to the denominator.

Example: $\frac{4}{3}$ and $\frac{8}{8}$ are improper fractions.

You can change a mixed number to an improper fraction by multiplying the denominator of the fraction by the integer and adding the numerator to the product. Place this sum over the denominator of the fraction.

Example: $3\frac{4}{8}$

$$3 \times 8 = 24$$
$$24 + 4 = 28$$
$$3\frac{4}{8} = \frac{28}{8}$$
$$= \frac{7}{2}$$

Change an improper fraction to a mixed number by dividing the numerator by the denominator. The quotient becomes the integer, and the remainder is placed over the denominator.

Example: Change $\frac{57}{12}$ to a mixed number.

SOLUTION:

$$12\overline{)57}$$
$$\underline{-48}$$
$$9$$

$$\frac{57}{12} = 4\frac{9}{12}$$
$$= 4\frac{3}{4}$$

You should always change an improper fraction to a mixed number as a final answer to a problem. Also, reduce all fractions to the lowest possible terms.

Addition of Fractions

You can only add fractions that have the same denominator. Add the numerators and place them over the common denominator.

Example : $\frac{1}{4} + \frac{2}{4} = \frac{3}{4}$

To add fractions with different denominators, convert the fractions so that they have the same denominator. This can be done by finding the *least common denominator (LCD)*, the smallest number that the various denominators can divide into evenly.

To add fractions with different denominators, first find the LCD. You can do this by listing the multiples of each denominator.

Example: Find the sum of $\frac{1}{6} + \frac{5}{9} + \frac{2}{3}$

Multiples of 3: 3, 6, 9, 12, 15, 18, 21...
Multiples of 6: 6, 12, 18, 24, 30...
Multiples of 9: 9, 18, 27, 36, 45...

In this case, the LCD is 18. You can convert your fractions by multiplying each denominator by a number that will give you an LCD of 18. Multiply the numerator by the same number as the denominator.

SOLUTION: $\frac{1}{6} \times \frac{3}{3} = \frac{3}{18}$

$$\frac{5}{9} \times \frac{2}{2} = \frac{10}{18}$$

$$\frac{2}{3} \times \frac{6}{6} = \frac{12}{18}$$

Add the converted fractions. Remember to convert any improper fraction to a mixed number in your final answer.

$$\frac{3}{18} + \frac{10}{18} + \frac{12}{18} = \frac{25}{18}$$

$$\frac{25}{18} = \quad \begin{array}{r} 1 \\ 18\overline{)25} \\ -18 \\ \hline 7 \end{array}$$

$$= \frac{18}{7}$$

To add mixed numbers with different denominators, find the LCD of the fractions and then add the integers.

Example: Add $2\frac{2}{3}$ and $4\frac{1}{8}$

> Multiples of 3: 3, 6, 9, 12, 15, 18, 21, 24, 27...
> Multiples of 8: 8, 16, 24, 32, 40, 48, 56...
> The LCD is 24.

SOLUTION: $2\frac{2}{3} = 2\frac{16}{24}$

$$4\frac{1}{8} = 4\frac{3}{24}$$

$$2\frac{16}{24} + 4\frac{3}{24} = 6\frac{19}{24}$$

Subtraction of Fractions

Subtraction of fractions involves only two numbers at a time. As with addition, you can only subtract fractions with the same denominator.

To subtract fractions, find the LCD and convert the fractions so that they have the same denominator. Subtract the numerator of the second fraction from the numerator of the first fraction. Place the difference over the LCD and reduce if possible.

Example: Find the difference of $\frac{2}{3}$ and $\frac{1}{7}$.

> LCD is 21.

SOLUTION: $\frac{2}{3} = \frac{14}{21}$

$$\frac{1}{7} = \frac{3}{21}$$

$$\frac{14}{21} - \frac{3}{21} = \frac{11}{21}$$

Subtracting mixed numbers is similar to adding mixed numbers. In some cases, you may need to borrow from an integer so that the fractional part of the first term is larger than the fractional part of the second term. Make sure the denominators of the fractions are the same. Subtract the fractional parts and reduce before subtracting the integers.

Example: Find the difference of $4\frac{1}{5}$ and $3\frac{2}{3}$.

The LCD is 15.

SOLUTION: $4\frac{1}{5} = 4\frac{3}{15}$

$3\frac{2}{3} = 3\frac{10}{15}$

Note that $\frac{3}{15}$ is less than $\frac{10}{15}$. Borrow 1 from 4, change it to $\frac{15}{15}$, and add it to the fraction.

$4\frac{3}{15}$ becomes $3\frac{18}{15}$

$3\frac{18}{15} - 3\frac{10}{15} = \frac{8}{15}$

Multiplication of Fractions

Fractions do not need to have the same denominator to be multiplied. Remember that whole numbers have an understood denominator of 1. You should also note that the word "of" often means "multiply."

Before multiplying, change any mixed numbers to improper fractions. Multiply the numerators and place this product over the product of the denominators. Reduce your answer to the lowest possible terms.

Example: Multiply $\frac{1}{4} \times 8 \times 2\frac{3}{5}$.

SOLUTION: $2\frac{3}{5} = \frac{13}{5}$

$\frac{1}{4} \times \frac{8}{1} \times \frac{13}{5} = \frac{104}{20}$

$\frac{104}{20} = \frac{26}{5} = 5\frac{1}{5}$

You can use *cancellation* to make it easier to multiply fractions. When you use cancellation, you divide a numerator and a denominator in the problem by the same number.

Example: Multiply $\frac{3}{4}$ and $\frac{8}{10}$.

SOLUTION: 4 and 8 are both divisible by 4.

$\frac{3}{\cancel{4}_1} \times \frac{\cancel{8}^2}{10} = \frac{6}{10}$

$= \frac{3}{5}$

To multiply a whole number by a mixed number, first multiply the whole number by the fractional part of the mixed number. Next, multiply the whole number by the integral part of the mixed number. In the final step, add both products together.

Example: $5\frac{7}{9} \times 10$

SOLUTION: $\frac{10}{1} \times \frac{7}{9} = \frac{70}{9} = 7\frac{7}{9}$

$10 \times 5 = 50$

$7\frac{7}{9} + 50 = 57\frac{7}{9}$

Dividing Fractions

Before you divide fractions, change any mixed numbers to improper fractions. Next, invert the second fraction and multiply it by the first fraction. Remember to reduce your answer to the lowest possible terms.

Example: Divide $\frac{2}{3}$ by $\frac{4}{5}$

SOLUTION: $\frac{2}{3} \div \frac{4}{5} = \frac{2}{3} \times \frac{5}{4}$

$\frac{2}{3} \times \frac{5}{4} = \frac{10}{12} = \frac{5}{6}$

A *complex fraction* has a fraction as the numerator, the denominator, or both.

Example: $\dfrac{\frac{2}{3}}{\frac{4}{}}$ is a complex fraction.

You can simplify a complex fraction by dividing the numerator by the denominator.

$\frac{2}{3} \div \frac{4}{1}$

$\frac{{}^1\!2}{3} \times \frac{1}{4_2} = \frac{1}{6}$

Comparing Fractions

When two fractions have the same denominator, the one with the larger *numerator* is the greater fraction.

Example: $\frac{3}{4}$ is greater than $\frac{1}{4}$

When two fractions have the same numerator, the fraction with the larger *denominator* is the smaller fraction.

Example: $\frac{4}{16}$ is smaller than $\frac{4}{8}$

Fraction Problems

Many fraction problems ask, "What fraction of a number is another number?" When examining a problem such as this, take notice of the fraction as well as the words "of" and "is."

When a problem contains a fraction and the word "of," you need to multiply to find the "is" number.

Example: What is $\frac{1}{4}$ of 60?

SOLUTION: Multiply $\frac{1}{4}$ by 60.

$$\frac{1}{\cancel{4}_1} \times \frac{\cancel{60}^{15}}{1} = \frac{15}{1} = 15$$

Another type of fraction problem may look like this:

$\frac{4}{3}$ of what number is 200?

To find the "of" number, divide 200 by $\frac{4}{3}$.

$$200 \div \frac{4}{3}$$

$$\frac{\cancel{200}^{50}}{1} \times \frac{3}{\cancel{4}_1} = \frac{150}{1} = 150$$

You can find the fractional part when the other two numbers are known by dividing the "is" number by the "of" number.

Example: What part of 27 is 9?

SOLUTION: $9 \div 27 = \frac{9}{27} = \frac{1}{3}$

Percents

The percent symbol (%) is used to express parts of a hundred. In some problems, you need to express a fraction or a decimal as a percent, while other problems ask you to express a percent as a fraction or a decimal.

You can change a whole number or a decimal to a percent by multiplying the number by 100 and adding the percent symbol.

Example: Change 10 to a percent.

SOLUTION: $10 \times 100 = 1,000\%$

Example: Change 0.27 to a percent.

SOLUTION: $0.27 \times 100 = 27\%$

In addition, you can change a percent to a decimal by dividing by 100.

Example: Change 5% to a decimal.

SOLUTION: $5 \div 100 = 0.05$

You can change a fraction to a percent by multiplying by 100. Reduce the answer, if possible, and add the percent symbol.

Example: Change $\frac{9}{12}$ to a percent.

SOLUTION: $\frac{9}{12} \times \frac{100}{1} = \frac{900}{12} = \frac{75}{1} = 75\%$

To change a mixed number to a percent, convert the mixed number to an improper fraction. Then, multiply the fraction by 100. Reduce your answer, if possible, before adding the percent symbol.

Example: Change $6\frac{1}{4}$ to a percent.

SOLUTION:
$$6\frac{1}{4} = \frac{25}{4}$$
$$\frac{25}{4} \times \frac{100}{1} = \frac{2,500}{4} = 625\%$$

Solving Percent Problems

When examining a percent problem, look for these quantities:

- The *rate* (R) is followed by the percent symbol (%).
- The *base* (B) follows the word "of."
- The *amount* (P) follows the word "is."

When you know the *rate* (R) and the *base* (B), the *amount* (P) = $R \times B$.

Example: Find 4% of 62.

SOLUTION: Rate = 4%

Base = 62

$P = R \times B$

$P = 4\% \times 62$

$P = 0.04 \times 62 = 2.48$

EXERCISES: FRACTIONS AND PERCENTS

Directions: Now try the exercises below. Each question is followed by four possible answers. Solve each problem. When you have completed the exercises, check your answers against the answer explanations that follow.

1. Frieda has 45 handbags for sale in her store. She sells $\frac{1}{3}$ of the handbags for $35.00 each. How much money did Frieda take in?
   1-A $350.00
   1-B $475.00
   1-C $525.00
   1-D $630.00

2. Ben is baking muffins for a fundraiser. He needs to triple his recipe to have enough muffins. The recipe calls for $2\frac{1}{4}$ cups of flour. How much flour does Ben need to make enough muffins?

   2-A $4\frac{2}{3}$ cups

   2-B $5\frac{4}{5}$ cups

   2-C $6\frac{3}{4}$ cups

   2 D $7\frac{1}{8}$ cups

3. What is $\frac{1}{3}$ of 327?

   3-A   109
   3-B   118
   3-C   121
   3-D   127

4. What part of 512 is 32?

   4-A $\frac{1}{12}$

   4-B $\frac{2}{3}$

   4-C $\frac{3}{4}$

   4-D $\frac{1}{16}$

5. Jim is studying for an exam. He spent $\frac{1}{2}$ of the entire day Saturday studying and $\frac{1}{4}$ of the entire day Sunday studying. How many hours did Jim study?
   5-A   6 hr.
   5-B   12 hr.
   5-C   18 hr.
   5 D   20 hr.

6. Last year, 2,300 freshman students entered Southern University. This year, the population of the freshman class has increased by $\frac{3}{4}$. How many freshmen entered the university this year?
   6-A   3,520
   6-B   3,750
   6-C   3,955
   6-D   4,025

7. Manuel spent $\frac{1}{12}$ of his savings on a vacation that cost $8,500. How much money did he have in his savings?

    7-A $78,250

    7-B $89,535

    7-C $99,775

    7-D $102,000

8. Marianne takes out a loan of $4,800. She pays back $300 in the first month. What part of the loan is still unpaid?

    8-A $\frac{5}{12}$

    8-B $\frac{1}{6}$

    8-C $\frac{15}{16}$

    8-D $\frac{7}{13}$

9. Kendra and Manny are buying their first home. The home costs $130,000. They need to pay 4% of $130,000 as the down payment. How much money do they need?

    9-A $3,900

    9-B $5,200

    9-C $6,100

    9-D $7,800

10. Gomez is shopping for a new car. The car he is interested in costs $9,500. The dealer is willing to take 5% off the price if Gomez purchases the car today. How much will the car cost if Gomez purchases it today?

    10-A $4,750

    10-B $4,975

    10-C $9,025

    10-D $9,155

11. What percent is $\frac{3}{5}$?

    11-A   35%

    11-B   60%

    11-C   75%

    11-D   80%

12. What percent of $\frac{5}{8}$ is $\frac{1}{16}$?

    12-A   1%

    12-B   5%

    12-C   8%

    12-D   10%

ANSWER KEY AND EXPLANATIONS

1. C	4. D	7. D	9. B	11. B
2. C	5. C	8. C	10. C	12. D
3. A	6. D			

1-C First, find the number of handbags Frieda sold.

$$\frac{1}{3} \times \frac{45}{1} = \frac{45}{3} = 15$$

Multiply this number by the price of each handbag.

$$15 \times \$35.00 = \$525.00$$

2-C Since Ben is tripling his recipe, he needs to multiply the mixed number by 3.

$$\frac{1}{4} \times \frac{3}{1} = \frac{3}{4}$$

$$2 \times 3 = 6$$

$$\frac{3}{4} + 6 = 6\frac{3}{4}$$

$$6\frac{3}{4} \text{ cups}$$

3-A The word "of" indicates that you should multiply the fraction by the whole number to find the answer.

$$\frac{1}{3} \times \frac{327}{1} = \frac{327}{3} = 109$$

4-D Divide the "is" number by the "of" number.

$$32 \div 512 = \frac{32}{512} = \frac{1}{16}$$

5-C There are 24 hours in a day.

Saturday: $\frac{1}{2} \times \frac{24}{1} = \frac{12}{1} = 12 \text{ hr}.$

Sunday: $\frac{1}{4} \times \frac{24}{1} = \frac{6}{1} = 6 \text{ hr}.$

$$12 + 6 = 18 \text{ hr}.$$

6-D $\frac{3}{4}$ of 2,300 = increase

$$\frac{3}{4} \times \frac{2,300}{1} = \frac{1,725}{1} = 1,725 \text{ increase}$$

$$1,725 + 2,300 = 4,025$$

7-D $\frac{1}{12}$ of savings is $8,500. Divide the amount spent on the vacation by the fraction to find the amount of Manuel's savings.

$$8,500 \div \frac{1}{12}$$

$$\frac{8,500}{1} \times \frac{12}{1} = \frac{102,000}{1} = \$102,000$$

8-C   Figure out what part of the loan is paid. What part of $4,800 is $300?

$$300 \div 4,800 = \frac{300}{4,800} = \frac{1}{16}$$

Since $\frac{16}{16} = \$4,800$ you need to subtract $\frac{1}{16}$ from $\frac{16}{16}$, then $\frac{16}{16} - \frac{1}{16} = \frac{15}{16}$

9-B   The rate is 4%. The base is $130,000.

rate × base = amount

Convert 4% to a decimal.

$4 \div 100 = 0.04$

Multiply the rate by the base.

$0.04 \times \$130,000 = \$5,200$

10-C   Multiply the rate (5%) by the base ($9,500). Convert 5% to a decimal.

$5 \div 100 = 0.05$

$0.05 \times \$9,500 = \$475$

Subtract this amount from the original cost of the car:

$$\begin{array}{r} \$9,500 \\ -\$475 \\ \hline \$9,025 \end{array}$$

11-B   To change a fraction to a percent, multiply by 100.

$$\frac{3}{5} \times \frac{100}{1} = \frac{300}{5} = 60\%$$

12-D   base $= \frac{5}{8}$

amount $= \frac{1}{16}$

rate = amount ÷ base

$$\text{rate} = \frac{1}{16} \div \frac{5}{8}$$

$$\frac{1}{16_2} \times \frac{8^1}{5} = \frac{1}{10} = 10\%$$

NUMBERS WITH UNITS

Adding and Subtracting Numbers with Units

When adding or subtracting denominate numbers (numbers with units), arrange the numbers in columns by unit and then add or subtract the numbers.

Example: Add 4 yd. 1 ft. 5 in., 3 yd. 2 ft. 7 in., and 5 yd. 6 ft. 9 in.

SOLUTION:

$$
\begin{array}{r}
4\,\text{yd}.\,1\,\text{ft}.\,5\,\text{in}.\\
3\,\text{yd}.\,2\,\text{ft}.\,7\,\text{in}.\\
+5\,\text{yd}.\,6\,\text{ft}.\,9\,\text{in}.\\
\hline
12\,\text{yd}.\,9\,\text{ft}.\,21\,\text{in}.
\end{array}
$$

= 12 yd. 10 ft. 9 in. (because 21 in. = 1 ft. 9 in.)
= 15 yd. 1 ft. 9 in. (because 10 ft. = 3 yd. 1 ft.)

When subtracting denominate numbers, it may be necessary to borrow to increase the number of a certain unit.

Example: Subtract 4 gal. 5 qt. from 9 gal. 3 qt.

SOLUTION. 9 gal. 3 qt. − 8 gal. 7 qt. (*Note:* 1 gallon was borrowed from 9 gallons to make 7 quarts. There are 4 quarts in 1 gallon.)

$$
\begin{array}{r}
8\,\text{gal}.\,7\,\text{qt}.\\
-4\,\text{gal}.\,5\,\text{qt}.\\
\hline
4\,\text{gal}.\,2\,\text{qt}.
\end{array}
$$

Multiplying and Dividing Numbers with Units

If the denominate number has only one unit, multiply the numbers and write the unit after the product.

Example: 12 yd. × 4 = 48 yd.

When the denominate number contains several units, multiply the number of each unit by the given number separately (do not carry). Simplify, if possible.

Example: Multiply 2 yd. 4 ft. 3 in. by 7.

SOLUTION:

$$
\begin{array}{r}
2\,\text{yd}.\,4\,\text{ft}.\,3\,\text{in}.\\
\times\,7\\
\hline
14\,\text{yd}.\,28\,\text{ft}.\,21\,\text{in}.
\end{array}
$$

= 14 yd. 29 ft. 9 in. (because 21 in. = 1 ft. 9 in.)
= 23 yd. 2 ft. 9 in. (because 29 ft. = 9 yd. 2 ft.)

To divide a denominate number by a given number, convert all the units to the smallest unit before dividing.

Example: Divide 5 yd. 4 in. by 2.

$$3 \text{ ft.} = 1 \text{ yd.}$$
$$12 \text{ in.} = 1 \text{ ft.}$$
$$5 \text{ yd.} = 15 \text{ ft.}$$

SOLUTION: $15 \text{ ft.} = 180 \text{ in.}$

$$180 \text{ in.} + 4 \text{ in.} = 184 \text{ in.}$$

$$2\overline{)184} = 92 \text{ in.}$$

$$92 \text{ in.} = 7 \text{ ft. } 6.6 \text{ in.}$$

Converting One Unit to Another

To convert from one unit to another, you need to know how many of the units that it takes to make up one unit of the quantity you already know.

For example, it takes 12 inches to make 1 foot. Knowing this makes it is easy to convert from feet to inches, or vice versa. When converting from one unit to another, multiply to find a smaller unit and divide to find the larger unit.

Example: How many inches are in 5.5 feet?

SOLUTION: Multiply 5.5 by 12.

$$5.5 \times 12 = 66 \text{ in.}$$

Example: How many feet are in 120 inches?

SOLUTION: Since you are converting to the larger unit, divide by 12.

$$12\overline{)120} = 10 \text{ ft.}$$

Metric Measurement

The metric system has three basic units of measurement. The meter (m.) is used for length, the gram (g.) is used for weight, and the liter (l.) is used for volume.

Below are the prefixes and abbreviations used in the metric system:

Prefix	Abbreviation	Meaning
micro	μ	one millionth (0.000001)
milli	m	one thousandth (0.001)
centi	c	one hundredth (0.01)
deci	d	one tenth (0.1)
deka	da or dk	ten times (10)
hector	h	one hundred times (100)
kilo	k	one thousand times (1000)
giga	G	one billion times (1,000,000,000)

When converting from a prefixed metric unit to a basic metric unit, multiply by the number indicated in the prefix.

Example: Convert 45 centimeters to meters.

SOLUTION: 45 cm = 45 × 0.01 = 0.45 m

Example: Convert 23 dekaliters to liters.

SOLUTION: 23 dal. = 23 × 10 = 230

Convert all units to the same unit before adding, subtracting, multiplying, or dividing any metric measurements.

Example: Subtract 25 milliliters from 4 liters.

SOLUTION: 25 ml. = 25 × 0.001 = 0.025

$$
\begin{array}{r}
4.000 \\
-\ 0.025 \\
\hline
3.975
\end{array}
$$

To convert from a metric measure to an English measure, first consult the Table of English-Metric Conversions to find how many units of the desired measure are equal to one unit of the measure given in the problem.

Multiply the given number by the number found in the table.

Example: Find the number of yards in 7 meters.

SOLUTION: 1 m. = 1.1 yd.

7 m. = 7 × 1.1 = 7.7 yd.

Example: Sandra weighs 120 pounds. How many kilograms does she weigh?

SOLUTION: 1 lb. = 454 g.

1,000 g. = 1 kg.

120 lb. = 120 × 454 = 54,480 g.

$$1{,}000 \overline{)54{,}480}^{\,54.48} = 54.48 \, \text{kg}.$$

TABLE OF MEASURES

English Measures
Length
1 foot (ft. or ') = 12 inches (in. or ")
1 yard (yd.) = 36 inches
1 yard = 3 feet
1 mile (mi.) = 5,280 feet
1 mile = 1,760 yards
Weight
1 pound (lb.) = 16 ounces
1 ton (T) = 2,000 pounds
Area
1 square foot (ft.²) = 144 square inches (in.²)
1 square yard (yd.²) = 9 square feet (ft.²)
General Measures
Time
1 minute (min.) = 60 seconds (sec.)
1 hour (hr.) = 60 minutes
1 day = 24 hours
1 week = 7 days
1 year = 52 weeks
1 calendar year = 365 days

Liquid Measures
1 cup (c.) = 8 fluid ounces (fl. oz.)
1 pint (pt.) = 2 cups
1 quart (qt.) = 2 pints
1 gallon (gal.) = 4 quarts
1 barrel (bl.) = $31\frac{1}{2}$ gallons
Dry Measure
1 quart (qt.) = 2 pints (pt.)
1 peck (pk.) = 8 quarts
1 bushel (bu.) = 4 pecks
Volume
1 cubic foot (ft.³ or cu. ft.) = 1,728 cubic inches
1 cubic yard (yd.³ or cu. yd.) = 27 cubic feet
1 gallon = 231 cubic inches
Angles and Arcs
1 minute (') = 60 seconds (")
1 degree (°) = 60 minutes
1 circle = 360 degrees
Counting
1 dozen = 12 units
1 gross = 12 dozen
1 gross = 144 units

TABLE OF ENGLISH-METRIC CONVERSIONS (APPROXIMATE)

English to Metric
1 inch = 2.54 centimeters
1 yard = 0.9 meters
1 mile = 1.6 kilometers
1 ounce = 28 grams
1 pound = 454 grams
1 fluid ounce = 30 milliliters
1 liquid quart = 0.95 liters
1 liter = 1,000 cubic centimeters (cm.³)
1 milliliter = 1 cubic centimeter
1 liter of water weighs 1 kilogram
1 milliliter of water weighs 1 gram

Metric to English
1 centimeter = 0.39 inches
1 meter = 1.1 yards
1 kilometer = 0.6 miles
1 kilogram = 2.2 pounds
1 liter = 1.06 liquid quart

THE METRIC SYSTEM

Length

Unit	Abbreviation	Number of Meters
myriameter	mym.	10,000
kilometer	km.	1,000
hectometer	hm.	100
dekameter	dam.	10
meter	m.	1
decimeter	dm.	0.1
centimeter	cm.	0.01
millimeter	mm.	0.001

Area

Unit	Abbreviation	Number of Square Meters
square kilometer	sq. km. or km.²	1,000,000
hectare	ha.	10,000
are	a.	100
centare	ca.	1
square centimeter	sq. cm. or cm.²	0.0001

Volume

Unit	Abbreviation	Number of Cubic Meters
dekastere	das.	10
stere	s.	1
decistere	ds.	0.10
cubic centimeter	cu. cm. or cm.³ or cc.	0.000001

Capacity

Unit	Abbreviation	Number of Liters
kiloliter	kl.	1,000
hectoliter	hi.	100
dekaliter	dal.	10
liter	l.	1
deciliter	dl.	0.10
centiliter	cl.	0.01
milliliter	ml.	0.001

Mass and Weight

Unit	Abbreviation	Number of Grams
metric ton	MT or t.	1,000,000
quintal	q.	100,000
kilogram	kg.	1,000
hectogram	hg.	100
dekagram	dag.	10
gram	g. or gm.	1
decigram	dg.	0.10
centigram	cg.	0.01
milligram	mg.	0.001

EXERCISES: NUMBERS WITH UNITS

Directions: Now try the exercises below. Each question is followed by four possible answers. Solve each problem. When you have completed the exercises, check your answers against the answer explanations that follow.

1. Ava is traveling in England. The road sign tells her that it is 27 kilometers to London. How many miles must Ava travel to reach London?
   - 1-A   14 miles
   - 1-B   16.2 miles
   - 1-C   17.5 miles
   - 1-D   20 miles

2. Samuel's car weighs 2.5 tons. How many pounds does the car weigh?
   - 2-A   2,500 lb.
   - 2-B   3,000 lb.
   - 2-C   4,500 lb.
   - 2-D   5,000 lb.

3. Kevin is taking a trip to visit some relatives. He spends 4 hours 52 minutes on a plane and 3 hours 14 minutes in a car. How long was Kevin's journey?
   - 3-A   7 hr. and 4 min.
   - 3-B   7 hr. and 50 min.
   - 3-C   8 hr. and 6 min.
   - 3-D   8 hr. and 15 min.

4. Yasmin originally had 3 yards and 1 foot of fabric. She then used 48 inches of fabric to make a pillow. How much fabric is left?
   - 4-A   1 yd. 1 ft.
   - 4-B   2 yd.
   - 4-C   2 yd. 2 ft.
   - 4-D   3 yd.

5. How many centimeters are in 45 inches?
   - 5-A   114.3 cm.
   - 5-B   144 cm.
   - 5-C   154.5 cm.
   - 5-D   167 cm.

6. Yvette has 1 gallon of milk. She uses 8 fluid ounces of milk in a recipe. How many fluid ounces of milk are left?
   - 6-A   32 fl. oz.
   - 6-B   48 fl. oz.
   - 6-C   96 fl. oz.
   - 6-D   120 fl. oz.

7. Susan is 4 feet 9 inches tall. Her brother Jacob is 6 feet 1 inch tall. How much taller is Jacob?
   - 7-A   9 in.
   - 7-B   11 in.
   - 7-C   1 ft. 4 in.
   - 7-D   1 ft. 6 in.

8. Amber is purchasing apples for her restaurant. She buys 2 gross worth of apples. Her chef uses 3 dozen apples to make the night's dessert. How many apples are left?
   - 8-A   144
   - 8-B   252
   - 8-C   288
   - 8-D   300

9. To qualify for the lightweight division, a boxer must weigh between 130–135 pounds. Jeremy weighs 63 kilograms. How many pounds does he need to lose to reach 135 pounds?
   - 9-A   1.5 lb.
   - 9-B   2.87 lb.
   - 9-C   3.6 lb.
   - 9-D   3.94 lb.

10. Kim is purchasing carpet for her living room. She needs 12.2 square yards of carpet. The hardware store sells carpet for $2.98 per square foot. How much will 12.2 square yards cost Kim? (Round to the nearest whole number.)

   10-A $110

   10-B $255

   10-C $292

   10-D $327

11. Jude is paid $1,260 every 2 weeks. He works 40 hours each week. How much does Jude make per hour?

   11-A $15.75

   11-B $14.50

   11-C $13.25

   11-D $12.00

12. Cora can run 7.5 kilometers in one hour. If she sticks with this pace, how many hours would it take her to run 18 miles?

   12-A 3.5 hr.

   12-B 4 hr.

   12-C 5.5 hr.

   12-D 6 hr.

ANSWER KEY AND EXPLANATIONS

1. B	4. B	7. C	9. C	11. A
2. D	5. A	8. B	10. D	12. B
3. C	6. D			

1-B   1 kilometer = 0.6 miles

27 km. = 27 × 0.6 = 16.2 miles

2-D   1 ton = 2,000 pounds

2.5 T = 2.5 × 2,000 = 5,000 lb.

3-C   Add each unit separately first.

$$
\begin{array}{r}
4\,\text{hr}.\ 52\,\text{min}.\\
+3\,\text{hr}.\ 14\,\text{min}.\\
\hline
7\,\text{hr}.\ 66\,\text{min}.
\end{array}
$$

= 8 hr. 6 min. (60 min. = 1 hr.)

4-B   Convert inches to yards and feet.

48 inches = 1 yard and 1 foot

$$
\begin{array}{r}
3\,\text{yd}.\ 1\,\text{ft}.\\
-1\,\text{yd}.\ 1\,\text{ft}.\\
\hline
2\,\text{yd}.\ 0\,\text{ft}.
\end{array}
$$

= 2 yd.

5-A   1 in. = 2.54 cm.

45 in. = 45 × 2.54 = 114.3 cm.

6-D   First, you need to figure how many fluid ounces are in 1 gallon.

8 fl. oz. = 1 cup
16 cups = 1 gal.
8 × 16 = 128 fl. oz.
128 fl. oz. = 1 gal.
Yvette used 8 fl. oz.

$$
\begin{array}{r}
128\\
-\ 8\\
\hline
120\,\text{fl. oz}.
\end{array}
$$

7-C   Subtract to find the difference.

$$\frac{\begin{array}{r}6\,\text{ft. }1\,\text{in.}\\-\ 4\,\text{ft. }9\,\text{in.}\end{array}}{}\quad=\quad\frac{\begin{array}{r}5\,\text{ft. }13\,\text{in.}\\-4\,\text{ft. }9\,\text{in.}\end{array}}{1\,\text{ft. }4\,\text{in.}}$$

Borrow to solve: 12 in. borrowed from 6 ft.

Jacob is 1 foot 4 inches taller.

8-B   Look at the Table of Measures chart to find out how many apples are in a gross.
1 gross = 144 units

Amber bought 2 gross.
2 × 144 = 288 apples

The chef uses 3 dozen apples.

$$\frac{\begin{array}{r}12\\\times\ 3\end{array}}{36}$$

36 apples used.

$$\frac{\begin{array}{r}288\\-36\end{array}}{252}$$

252 apples left.

9-C   First, figure out how many pounds Jeremy weighs.
1 kg. = 2.2 lb.

Jeremy weighs 63 kg.
63 × 2.2 = 138.6 lb.

Subtract the 135 from 138.6 to find the amount of weight Jeremy needs to lose.

$$\frac{\begin{array}{r}138.6\\-135.0\end{array}}{3.6}$$

Jeremy must lose 3.6 pounds.

10-D   Figure out how many square feet are in 12.2 square yards.
$1\,\text{yd.}^2 = 9\,\text{ft.}^2$

$$\frac{\begin{array}{r}12.2\\\times\ 9\end{array}}{109.8\,\text{ft.}^2}$$

Multiply this amount by the cost per square foot.

$$\begin{array}{r} 109.8 \\ \times\ 2.98 \\ \hline 327.204 \end{array}$$

Round to the nearest whole number to get $327.

11-A Find out how many hours Jude works in 2 weeks.

$$\begin{array}{r} 40 \\ \times\ 2 \\ \hline 80\ \text{hr.} \end{array}$$

Divide the amount Jude receives in his paycheck by the number of hours he works in 2 weeks.

$$80\overline{)1,260.00}^{\,15.75}$$

Jude makes $15.75/hr.

12-B Find Cora's speed in miles per hour.
(1 km. = 0.6 mile)

$$\begin{array}{r} 7.5 \\ \times\ 0.6 \\ \hline 4.5 \end{array}$$

7.5 km./hr. = 4.5 miles/hr.

Divide 18 by 4.5 to find out how long it will take Cora to run 18 miles.

$$4.5\overline{)18}^{\,4}$$

It will take Cora 4 hours to run 18 miles.

answers exercises

PARTS OF A WHOLE

Joining Small Units

Multiply to join a number of smaller units to find a larger unit.

Example: Jane walks for 15 minutes each day. How many minutes does she walk in a week?

SOLUTION: 15 (min.) × 7 (days) = 105 (min).

         1 hr. = 60 min.

         Simplify your answer by dividing.

$$60 \overline{)\, 105} \quad \frac{1.75}{}$$

         105 min. = 1 hr. 45 min.

Breaking Down Large Units

Divide to break down one larger unit into smaller units.

Example: Pauline has 5 yards of fabric. She needs 2 feet of fabric to make 1 quilting square. How many quilting squares can she make from 5 yards of fabric?

SOLUTION: 1 yd. = 3 ft.

         5 yd. = 15 ft.

$$2 \overline{)\, 15} \quad \frac{7.5}{}$$

         Since 0.5 is not enough to make 1 quilting square, ignore it. Pauline can make 7 quilting squares out of 5 yards of fabric.

Simplifying Results

When multiplying denominate numbers, multiply each unit separately.

$$\begin{array}{r} 8\,\text{hr.}\,25\,\text{min.} \\ \times\,3 \\ \hline 24\,\text{hr.}\,75\,\text{min.} \end{array}$$

Simplify the results.

24 hr. = 1 day

75 min. = 1 hr. 15 min.

Final answer: 1 day, 1 hr., 15 min.

Convert all units to the smallest unit before dividing denominate numbers.

Example: Divide 3 yards, 7 feet by 2.

SOLUTION: Convert 3 yards, 7 feet to feet.

3 yd. 7 ft. = 3 × 3(ft.) + 7(ft.) = 9 + 7 = 16 ft.

$$2\overline{)16}^{\,8}$$

Simplify: 8 ft. = 2 yd. 2 ft.

EXERCISES: PARTS OF A WHOLE

Directions: Now try the exercises below. Each question is followed by four possible answers. Solve each problem. When you have completed the exercises, check your answers against the answer explanations that follow.

1. Seattle, Washington, receives an average rainfall of 142 inches per year. How many feet of precipitation does Seattle receive each year?
   - 1-A   10 ft. 8 in.
   - 1-B   11 ft. 10 in.
   - 1-C   12 ft. 1 in.
   - 1-D   12 ft. 4 in.

2. Gisele has 4 dozen eggs. She uses 3 eggs to bake a cake. How many eggs does Gisele have left?
   - 2-A   45 eggs
   - 2-B   46 eggs
   - 2-C   47 eggs
   - 2-D   48 eggs

3. Henry spends 75 minutes each day, including weekends, studying for his calculus test. How long does Henry spend studying in a week?
   - 3-A   6 hr. 15 min.
   - 3-B   7 hr. 30 min.
   - 3-C   8 hr. 45 min.
   - 3-D   9 hr. 55 min.

4. Martha has 3 pounds of ground turkey. How many 4-ounce servings of turkey does she have? (1 pound = 16 ounces)
   - 4-A   9 servings
   - 4-B   10 servings
   - 4-C   11 servings
   - 4-D   12 servings

5. A truck is carrying crates of canned goods to a local supermarket. Each crate weighs 150 pounds. If there are 40 crates, how many tons is the truck carrying? (1 T = 2,000 lb.)
   - 5-A   2 T
   - 5-B   3 T
   - 5-C   4 T
   - 5-D   5 T

6. Travis has 112 cups of apple cider. How many 1-gallon jugs can he fill? (4 cups = 1 quart)
   - 6-A   3 jugs
   - 6-B   5 jugs
   - 6-C   7 jugs
   - 6-D   9 jugs

7. A farmer chopped down a 50-foot tree on his property. How many 10-inch logs can he cut from the tree?
   - 7-A   45
   - 7-B   60
   - 7-C   75
   - 7-D   80

8. A road sign tells Darren that there is a work zone in 13,200 feet. How many miles will Darren drive before reaching the work zone? (1 mile = 5,280 ft.)
   - 8-A   0.75 miles
   - 8-B   1 mile
   - 8-C   1.75 miles
   - 8-D   2.5 miles

9. It takes Athena 24 hours to crochet a blanket. She spends 45 minutes crocheting each day. In how many days will she finish the blanket?

   9-A 14 days

   9-B 28 days

   9-C 32 days

   9-D 40 days

10. It is 880 feet from one end of Frederick's property to the other. How many times would he have to walk from one end to the other to cover a distance of 3 miles? (1 mile = 5,280 ft.)

    10-A 18

    10-B 22

    10-C 32

    10-D 41

11. Kelsey used a 5-foot 9-inch pipe to create 3 pieces of equal length. How long was each piece of pipe?

    11-A 15 in.

    11-B 23 in.

    11-C 27 in.

    11-D 31 in.

12. It takes 45 minutes for Hank to commute one way to work each day. How many hours does Hank spend driving to and from work during a 5-day workweek?

    12-A 5.5 hr.

    12-B 6 hr.

    12-C 7.5 hr.

    12-D 8 hr.

exercises

ANSWER KEY AND EXPLANATIONS

1. B	4. D	7. B	9. C	11. B
2. A	5. B	8. D	10. A	12. C
3. C	6. C			

1-B Divide 142 by 12.

$$\begin{array}{r} 11 \\ 12\overline{)142} \\ -12 \\ \hline 22 \\ -12 \\ \hline 10 \end{array}$$

142 in. = 11 ft. 10 in.

2-A Multiply 4 by 12.

$$\begin{array}{r} 12 \\ \times 4 \\ \hline 48 \\ -3 \\ \hline 45 \end{array}$$

Gisele has 45 eggs left.

3-C Multiply 75 by 7.

$$\begin{array}{r} 75 \\ \times 7 \\ \hline 525 \end{array}$$

Simplify:
$$\begin{array}{r} 8 \\ 60\overline{)525} \\ -480 \\ \hline 45 \end{array}$$

525 min. = 8 hr. 45 min.

4-D Multiply 3 by 16.

$$\begin{array}{r} 16 \\ \times 3 \\ \hline 48 \end{array}$$

$$\begin{array}{r} 12 \\ 4\overline{)48} \end{array}$$

Martha has twelve 4-ounce servings.

5-B   Multiply 150 by 40.

$$\begin{array}{r} 150 \\ \times\ 40 \\ \hline 6{,}000 \end{array}$$

$$2{,}000\overline{)6{,}000}^{\;3}$$

The truck is carrying 3 tons of canned goods.

6-C   4 cups = 1 qt.

4 qt. = 1 gal.

$4 \times 4 = 16$

16 cups = 1 gal.

$$16\overline{)112}^{\;7}$$

Travis has enough apple cider to fill seven 1-gallon jugs.

7-B   Multiply 50 by 12.

$50 \times 12 = 600$ in.

$$10\overline{)600}^{\;60}$$

The farmer can cut sixty 10-inch logs.

8-D   Divide 13,200 by 5,280.

$$5{,}280\overline{)13{,}200}^{\;2.5}$$

Darren will reach the work zone in 2.5 miles.

9-C   Multiply 24 by 60 (min).

$24 \times 60 = 1{,}440$

$$45\overline{)1{,}440}^{\;32}$$

Athena will finish the blanket in 32 days.

10-A   Divide 5,280 by 880.

$$880\overline{)5{,}280}^{\;6}$$

Frederick would need to walk from one end to the other 6 times to cover 1 mile.

$6 \times 3 = 18$

Frederick would need to walk from one end to the other 18 times to cover 3 miles.

11-B Multiply 5 feet by 12.

$5 \times 12 = 60$ in.

$60 + 9 = 69$ in.

$$3 \overline{)69} ^{23}$$

Each piece of pipe was 23 inches long.

12-C It takes Hank 45 minutes to commute one way to work each day. He drives 45 minutes to work, and it takes him 45 minutes to get home.

$$\begin{array}{r} 45 \\ \times\ 2 \\ \hline 90 \end{array}$$

Hank spends 90 minutes driving each day.

$$\begin{array}{r} 90 \\ \times\ 5 \\ \hline 450 \end{array}$$

Hank spends 450 minutes driving each week. Divide 450 by 60 to find the number of hours he spends driving.

$$\begin{array}{r} 7 \\ 60 \overline{)450} \\ -420 \\ \hline 30 \end{array}$$

Hank spends 7.5 hours (7 hr. 30 min.) driving each week.

RATIO AND PROPORTION

A *ratio* is the quotient of two numbers. Ratios can be expressed as fractions, using the word "to," or with a colon.

Example: $\frac{1}{4}$, 1 to 4, 1:4

The numbers in the ratio are called the *terms*.

A *proportion* tells you that two ratios are equal.

Example: $a:b = c:d$

In the proportion $a:b = c:d$, the inner terms (b and c) are the *means*, and the outer terms (a and d) are the *extremes*.

Example: In the proportion 3:4 = 6:8, the means are 4 and 6, and the extremes are 3 and 8.

In all proportions, the product of the means is equal to the product of the extremes.

Example: In 3:4 = 6:8, or $\frac{3}{4} \times \frac{6}{8}, 3 \times 8 = 4 \times 6$.

In many problems, you'll have to set up a proportion to find an unknown quantity.

Example: Carrie is at the supermarket. She can purchase 1 jar of tomato sauce for $1.50. How many jars can she buy with $9.00?

SOLUTION: x will represent the unknown number of jars.

$$\frac{1 \text{ jar}}{\text{price per jar}} = \frac{\text{unknown number of jars}}{\text{amount spent}}$$

$$\frac{1}{1.50} = \frac{x}{9.00}$$

$$9.00 = 1.50x$$

$$1.50\overline{)9.00}^{\,6}$$

$$x = 6 \text{ jars}$$

Carrie can purchase 6 jars of sauce with $9.00.

Example: Benjamin can type 134 words in 1 minute. How long will it take him to type 1,072 words?

SOLUTION: Let x equal the amount of time it takes for Benjamin to type 1,072 words.

$$\frac{1}{134} = \frac{x}{1,072}$$
$$134x = 1,072$$

$$134\overline{)1,072}^{8}$$

Benjamin can type 1,072 words in 8 minutes.

EXERCISES: RATIO AND PROPORTION

Directions: Now try the exercises below. Each question is followed by four possible answers. Solve each problem. When you have completed the exercises, check your answers against the answer explanations that follow.

1. If 1 U.S. dollar equals 1.05 Canadian dollars, how many Canadian dollars would you receive for 20 U.S. dollars?

   1-A $18.50

   1-B $19.00

   1-C $20.50

   1-D $21.00

2. Ian drives 568 miles in 8 hours. How many miles did he cover in 30 minutes?

   2-A 30

   2-B 35.5

   2-C 39

   2-D 40.5

3. A company conducted a survey of its employees. The survey found that 7 out of every 10 employees would prefer a retirement plan to a dental plan. If the company has 180 employees, how many would prefer a retirement plan?

   3-A 70

   3-B 94

   3-C 113

   3-D 126

4. Julia needs 3 eggs to bake 12 brownies. How many eggs will she need to bake 60 brownies?

   4-A 5

   4-B 12

   4-C 15

   4-D 21

5. Don creates a natural cleaning solution using 2 quarts of water and 16 ounces of distilled white vinegar. How many ounces of white vinegar does he need to make the same strength solution using 2 gallons of water? (4 quarts = 1 gallon)

   5-A 64 oz.

   5-B 72 oz.

   5-C 84 oz.

   5-D 96 oz.

6. It takes Sandra 45 minutes to read 105 pages of a book. How many pages can she read in 3 hours?

   6-A 385

   6-B 420

   6-C 475

   6-D 530

7. To make sweet tea, Ted uses 3 parts sugar to 5 parts tea. If Ted needs 32 ounces of sweet tea, how many ounces of tea does he use?

   7-A 10

   7-B 15

   7-C 20

   7-D 25

8. On a map, 5 centimeters equals 3 miles. How many miles are covered in 40 centimeters?

   8-A 13

   8-B 17

   8-C 21

   8-D 24

9. On a college campus, every 6 out 10 students is female. If there are 3,150 students, how many are female?

9-A 1,580

9-B 1,660

9-C 1,890

9-D 1,960

10. An astronaut weighs 130 pounds on Earth and 22 pounds on the moon. How many pounds would a 195-pound man weigh on the moon?

10-A 33

10-B 35

10-C 47

10-D 49

ANSWER KEY AND EXPLANATIONS

1. D	3. D	5. A	7. C	9. C
2. B	4. C	6. B	8. D	10. A

1-D Let x represent the number of Canadian dollars you will receive for 20 U.S. dollars.

$$\frac{1}{1.05} = \frac{20}{x}$$
$$1x = 21$$
$$x = 21$$

You will receive 21 Canadian dollars for 20 U.S. dollars.

2-B Let x represent the number of miles Ian covered in 30 minutes. (30 min. = 0.5 hr.)

$$\frac{8}{568} = \frac{0.5}{x}$$
$$284 = 8x$$

$$8\overline{)284} \;\; 35.5$$

$$x = 35.5$$

Ian traveled 35.5 miles every 30 minutes.

3-D Let x represent the number of employees who prefer a retirement plan.

$$\frac{7}{10} = \frac{x}{180}$$
$$1,260 = 10x$$

$$10\overline{)1,260} \;\; 126$$

$$x = 126$$

The survey shows that 126 employees would prefer a retirement plan.

4-C Let x represent the number of eggs needed to make 60 brownies.

$$\frac{3}{12} = \frac{x}{60}$$
$$12x = 180$$

$$12\overline{)180} \;\; 15$$

$$x = 15$$

Julia needs 15 eggs to make 60 brownies.

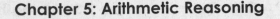

5-A Let x represent the number of ounces of white vinegar Don needs to make the same strength solution using 2 gallons of water.

(2 gal. = 8 qt.)

$$\frac{2}{16} = \frac{8}{x}$$

$$2x = 128$$

$$2\overline{)128} \;\; 64$$

$$x = 64$$

Don needs 64 ounces of white vinegar to make the same strength solution.

6-B Let x represent the number of pages Sandra reads in 3 hours.

(3 hr. = 180 min.)

$$\frac{45}{105} = \frac{180}{x}$$

$$45x = 18,900$$

$$45\overline{)18,900} \;\; 420$$

$$x = 420$$

Sandra can read 420 pages in 3 hours.

7-C Let x represent the ounces of tea needed to make 32 ounces of sweet tea.

3 (parts of sugar) + 5 (parts of tea) = 8 (total number of parts)

$$\frac{5}{8} = \frac{x}{32}$$

$$8x = 160$$

$$8\overline{)160} \;\; 20$$

$$x = 20$$

Ted needs 20 ounces of tea to make sweet tea.

8-D Let x represent the number of miles in 40 centimeters.

$$\frac{5}{3} = \frac{40}{x}$$

$$5x = 120$$

$$5\overline{)120} \;\; 24$$

$$x = 24$$

40 cm. = 24 miles

9-C   Let x represent the total number of female students at the college.

$$\frac{6}{10} = \frac{x}{3,150}$$

$$10x = 18,900$$

$$10\overline{)18,900} \quad \frac{1,890}{}$$

$$x = 1,890$$

There are 1,890 female students on campus.

10-A   Let x represent the 195-pound man's weight on the moon.

$$\frac{22}{130} = \frac{x}{195}$$

$$130x = 4,290$$

$$130\overline{)4,290} \quad \frac{33}{}$$

$$x = 33$$

The 195-pound man weighs 33 pounds on the moon.

AVERAGES

Average or Arithmetic Mean

Problems that ask you to find the "average" or "mean" are looking for the *arithmetic mean*. You find this number by adding the given numbers and dividing the sum by the number of units being averaged.

Example: Find the mean of 1, 15, 22, 45, and 62.

SOLUTION: There are 5 numbers.

$$\frac{1 + 15 + 22 + 45 + 62}{5} = \frac{145}{5} = 29$$

The arithmetic mean is 29.

Median

The *median* is the middle number in a group of numbers arranged in order. When there is no middle number, you can find the median by figuring out the mean of the two middle numbers.

Example: The median of 4, 7, 9, 12, and 17 is 9.

Example: The median of 5, 9, 17, 21, 29, and 30 is the arithmetic mean of 17 and 21.

$$\frac{17 + 21}{2} = \frac{38}{2} = 19$$

Mode

The *mode* is the number that appears most frequently in a group of numbers.

Example: The mode of 7, 8, 5, 19, 7, 45, and 17 is 7.

Weighted Average

To calculate the average of several weighted quantities, set up a table that lists the quantities, their weights, and their values.

Multiply the value of each quantity by its weight. Add the products and add the weights. Divide the sum of the products by the sum of the weights.

Example: Hayden has a homework grade of 85, a quiz grade of 92, and a test grade of 94. Homework counts for 30% of a student's class grade, quizzes count for 10%, and tests count for 60%. What is Hayden's class grade?

SOLUTION:

Type of Grade	Weight	Score
Homework	0.30	85
Quizzes	0.10	92
Tests	0.60	94

$0.30 \times 85 = 25.5$

$0.10 \times 92 = 9.2$

$0.60 \times 94 = 56.4$

$$\begin{array}{r} 25.5 \\ 9.2 \\ +56.4 \\ \hline 91.1 \end{array}$$

Weights:

$$\begin{array}{r} 0.30 \\ 0.10 \\ +0.60 \\ \hline 1.00 \end{array}$$

$$\frac{91.1}{1} = 91.1$$

Hayden's class grade is 91.1.

EXERCISES: AVERAGES

Directions: Now try the exercises below. Each question is followed by four possible answers. Solve each problem. When you have completed the exercises, check your answers against the answer explanations that follow.

1. During the month of July, the weekly average temperatures in Scranton, Pennsylvania, were 82°, 84°, 81°, and 87°. What was the average temperature for the month?

   1-A   82°

   1-B   83.5°

   1-C   84°

   1-D   85.5°

2. What is the median of 55, 91, 72, 5, 36, 81, and 24?

   2-A   24

   2-B   36

   2-C   55

   2-D   92

3. A store had 45 customers on Monday, 30 customers on Tuesday, 45 customers on Wednesday, 60 customers on Thursday, and 57 customers on Friday. What is the mode of these numbers of customers?

   3-A   30 customers

   3-B   45 customers

   3-C   57 customers

   3-D   60 customers

4. Mr. Kaufman tells his students that homework counts for $\frac{1}{4}$ of their class grade, class participation counts for $\frac{1}{4}$ of their grade, and tests count for $\frac{1}{2}$ of their grade. Vera has a homework grade of 89, a class participation grade of 72, and a test grade of 91. What is her class grade?

   4-A   83.25

   4-B   84.50

   4-C   85.00

   4-D   85.75

5. A cooking class has 7 students. The ages of the students are 65, 42, 19, 34, 29, 50, and 41. What is the median age of the students?

   5-A   41

   5-B   42

   5-C   50

   5-D   65

6. The town of Blakeslee has 3 gas stations. The first station sells a gallon of gas for $2.44. The second station sells a gallon of gas for $2.65, and the third station sells a gallon of gas for $2.50. What is the average price of a gallon of gas in Blakeslee?

   6-A $2.45

   6-B $2.49

   6-C $2.53

   6-D $2.57

7. Angela runs 1 mile every morning. For 7 days, she clocked the time it took her to run a mile. Beginning on Monday, her times were 11:15, 10:45, 10:38, 10:51, 10:59, 10:45, and 11:11. What is the mode of these times?

   7-A   10:38

   7-B   10:45

   7-C   11:11

   7-D   11:15

8. Greg's college weights courses by level; 100-level courses have a weight of 1, 200-level courses have a weight of 2, and 300-level courses have a weight of 3. Greg has a 92 in Spanish 101, an 88 in Economics 225, a 98 in Architecture 302, and a 72 in Philosophy 112. What

is Greg's average grade? (Round to the nearest tenth.)

8-A 88.9

8-B 89.2

8-C 90.6

8-D 91.7

9. Tricia is reviewing her cell phone account to see how many minutes she talks per day. She talked for 31 minutes on Monday, 15 minutes on Tuesday, 45 minutes on Wednesday, 22 minutes on Thursday, 29 minutes on Friday, 35 minutes on Saturday, and 52 minutes on Sunday. What is the median of these numbers of minutes?

9-A 15 min.

9-B 22 min.

9-C 29 min.

9-D 31 min.

10. The Johnson family is calculating their grocery expenses for the month. During the first week, the family spent $75.50 on groceries, during the second week they spent $105.50, during the third week they spent $85.75, and during the fourth week they spent $92.25. What was the average amount the Johnson family spent on groceries per week?

10-A $89.75

10-B $91.25

10-C $95.00

10-D $102.50

exercises

ANSWER KEY AND EXPLANATIONS

1. B	3. B	5. A	7. B	9. D
2. C	4. D	6. C	8. C	10. A

1-B   Add all temperatures together. Divide by the number of items being averaged.

$$\frac{82 + 84 + 81 + 87}{4} = \frac{334}{4} = 83.5$$

The average temperature for the month of July was 83.5°.

2-C   First, arrange the numbers in order.

5, 24, 36, 55, 72, 81, 91

Locate the middle number.

The median is 55.

3-B   The mode asks you to find the number that occurs most frequently.

Day of the week	Monday	Tuesday	Wednesday	Thursday	Friday
Number of customers	45	30	45	60	57

45 customers is the mode.

4-D   Convert the fractions to decimals.

$$\frac{1}{4} = 0.24$$

$$\frac{1}{2} = 0.50$$

Type of Grade	Weight	Score
Homework	0.25	89
Class Participation	0.25	72
Tests	0.50	91

$0.25 \times 89 = 22.25$
$0.25 \times 72 = 18$
$0.50 \times 91 = 45.5$

$$
\begin{array}{r}
22.25 \\
18.00 \\
+\ 45.50 \\
\hline
85.75
\end{array}
$$

$$0.25$$
$$0.25$$
$$+\ 0.50$$
$$\overline{1.00}$$

$$\frac{85.75}{1} = 85.75$$

Vera's class grade is 85.75.

5-A Arrange the numbers in order.

19, 29, 34, 41, 42, 50, and 65

The middle number is 41.

The median age of the students is 41.

6-C Add the prices.

$$\$2.44$$
$$\$2.65$$
$$+\ \$2.50$$
$$\overline{\$7.59}$$

Divide by 3.

$$\frac{7.59}{3} = 2.53$$

The average price for a gallon of gas in Blakeslee is $2.53.

7-B The mode is the time that occurs most frequently.

Day of the Week	Monday	Tuesday	Wednesday	Thursday	Friday	Saturday	Sunday
Timed Mile Run	11:15	10:45	10:38	10:51	10:59	10:45	11:11

Since 10:45 occurs twice, the mode is 10:45.

8-C Set up a table listing the class level, grade, and weights.

Class Level	Grade	Weight
101	92	1
225	88	2
302	98	3
112	72	1

Greg has a 92 in Spanish 101, an 88 in Economics 225, a 98 in Architecture 302, and a 72 in Philosophy 112.

answers exercises

Multiply each grade by its respective weight and add the products.

$$92 \times 1 = 92$$
$$88 \times 2 = 176$$
$$98 \times 3 = 294$$
$$72 \times 1 = \underline{+\ 72}$$
$$634$$

Add the weights.

$$1 + 2 + 3 + 1 = 7$$

Divide the sum of the products by the sum of the weights.

$$7\overline{)634}\quad 90.571$$

Rounded to the nearest tenth, Greg's average grade is 90.6.

9-D Arrange the numbers in order.

15, 22, 29, 31, 35, 45, 52

The median is the middle number.

The median is 31 minutes.

10-A Add the given numbers and divide by 4.

$$\frac{75.50 + 105.50 + 85.75 + 92.25}{4} = \frac{359}{4} = \$89.75$$

The Johnson family spent an average of $89.75 on groceries per week.

GRAPHS

People use graphs to demonstrate trends in statistical information. The most common graphs are bar graphs, line graphs, circle graphs, and pictographs.

Bar Graphs

Bar graphs use horizontal or vertical bars to compare various quantities. Each bar can represent one quantity, or it may be divided to represent several quantities.

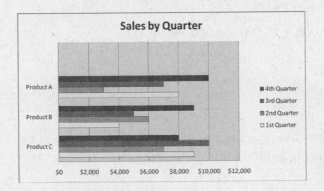

Question: Which product made the most money in the first quarter?

The lightest bar represents the first quarter. The lightest bar for product C is between $8,000 and $10,000. This means that the company sold about $9,000 worth of product C in the first quarter. In the first quarter, this product outperformed product A, which had $8,000 in sales, and product B, which had only $4,000 in sales.

Question: Which product made $10,000 in the fourth quarter?

The darkest bar represents the fourth quarter. This shows that product A made $10,000 in the fourth quarter.

Question: Which product was the most profitable across all four quarters?

Use the bar graph to find out how much each product made during each quarter.

> **Product A**
> 1st Quarter: $8,000
> 2nd Quarter: $3,000
> 3rd Quarter: $7,000
> 4th Quarter: $10,000
>
> 8,000 + 3,000 + 7,000 + 10,000 = $28,000
>
> **Product B**
> 1st Quarter: $4,000

2nd Quarter: $6,000
3rd Quarter: $5,000
4th Quarter: $9,000

4,000 + 6,000 + 5,000 + 9,000 = $24,000

Product C
1st Quarter: $9,000
2nd Quarter: $7,000
3rd Quarter: $10,000
4th Quarter: $8,000

9,000 + 7,000 + 10,000 + 8,000 = $34,000

Product C was the most profitable.

Line Graphs

Line graphs show trends over a period of time. They may have more than one line, with each line representing a different item.

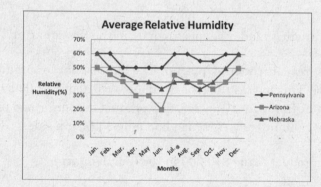

Question: Which state's relative humidity decreased by an average of 5% per month from January to June?

Arizona's relative humidity decreased from 50% in January to 20% in June.

50 − 20 = 30

$$\frac{30 \text{ (decrease in humidity)}}{6 \text{ (number of months)}} = 5\%$$

Question: Which state had a constant relative humidity from March to June?

A straight line indicates a constant rate. Of the three lines, the one representing Pennsylvania stayed straight from March to June.

Circle Graphs

People use *circle graphs* to show the relationship of various parts of a quantity to each other and to the whole quantity. The quantity of each part is often represented by a percentage. The entire circle (360°) represents 100%. Each part of the circle is called a *sector*.

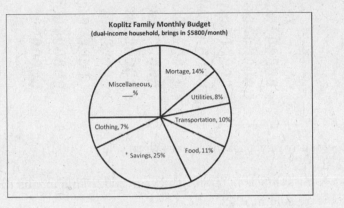

Question: How much of the Koplitz family's budget goes toward miscellaneous expenses?

The graph must total 100%. Find the sum of the other sectors.

14% + 8% + 10% + 11% + 25% + 7% = 75%

100% − 75% = 25%

The Koplitz family spends 25% of the monthly budget on miscellaneous expenses.

Question: How much money does the Koplitz family spend on transportation?

10% × $5,800 = $580

The Koplitz family spends $580 on transportation each month.

Question: How much more money did the Koplitz family spend on their mortgage than they did on utilities?

Mortgage = 14%

Utilities = 8%

14% − 8% = 6%

0.06 × 5,800 = $348

The Koplitz family spends $348 more on the mortgage than they do on utilities.

Pictographs

Pictographs compare quantities using symbols. Each symbol represents a given amount:

New Passenger Cars Sold in the US

each represents 1 million cars

Question: How many new passenger cars were sold in 2002?

The graph has 8 car symbols listed for the year 2002. This means that 8 million new passenger cars were sold in 2002.

Question: How many more new passenger cars were sold in 2001 than in 2004?

There are $8\frac{1}{2}$ symbols for 2001 and $7\frac{1}{2}$ symbols for 2004.

$$8\frac{1}{2} \times 1,000,000 = 8,500,000$$

$$7\frac{1}{2} \times 1,000,000 = 7,500,000$$

$$\begin{array}{r} 8,500,000 \\ -7,500,000 \\ \hline 1,000,000 \end{array}$$

There were 1 million more cars sold in 2001.

EXERCISES: GRAPHS

Directions: Now try the exercises below. Each question is followed by four possible answers. Solve each problem. When you have completed the exercises, check your answers against the answer explanations that follow.

QUESTIONS 1 TO 3 REFER TO THE FOLLOWING GRAPH.

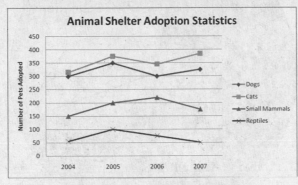

1. Which animal was adopted most often in 2004?

   1-A   dogs

   1-B   cats

   1-C   small mammals

   1-D   reptiles

2. In which year was there an increase in the adoption of all animals?

   2-A   2004

   2-B   2005

   2-C   2006

   2-D   2007

3. In 2007, how many more dogs were adopted than reptiles?

   3-A   100

   3-B   150

   3-C   275

   3-D   300

QUESTIONS 4 TO 7 REFER TO THE FOLLOWING GRAPH.

Intended Academic Majors of First-Year College Students
(3,525 students surveyed)

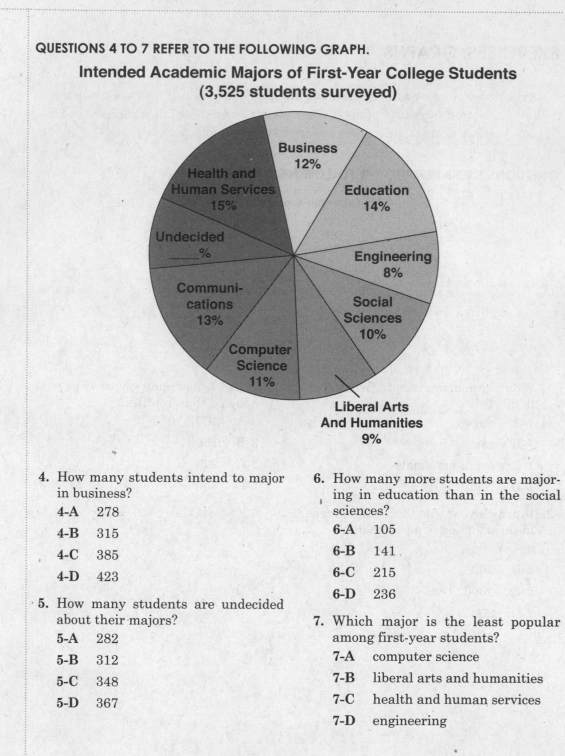

4. How many students intend to major in business?

   4-A   278

   4-B   315

   4-C   385

   4-D   423

5. How many students are undecided about their majors?

   5-A   282

   5-B   312

   5-C   348

   5-D   367

6. How many more students are majoring in education than in the social sciences?

   6-A   105

   6-B   141

   6-C   215

   6-D   236

7. Which major is the least popular among first-year students?

   7-A   computer science

   7-B   liberal arts and humanities

   7-C   health and human services

   7-D   engineering

QUESTIONS 8 TO 11 REFER TO THE FOLLOWING GRAPH.

8. How many pairs of sneakers were sold in January?

   8-A   200

   8-B   250

   8-C   300

   8-D   325

9. If each pair of sneakers costs $30.00, how much money was made in July?

   9-A $3,000

   9-B $4,000

   9-C $5,000

   9-D $6,000

10. How many more pairs of sneakers were sold in September than in August?

    10-A   100

    10-B   150

    10-C   225

    10-D   275

11. What was the total number of pairs of sneakers sold from October to December?

    11-A   1,550

    11-B   1,600

    11-C   1,750

    11-D   1,800

ANSWER KEY AND EXPLANATIONS

1. B	4. D	6. B	8. B	10. B
2. B	5. A	7. D	9. D	11. C
3. C				

1-B   The graph shows that cats were most often adopted in 2004.

2-B   The graph shows that there was an increase in all adoptions in 2005.

3-C   The graph shows that 325 dogs and 50 reptiles were adopted in 2005.

$$325 - 50 = 275$$

In 2005, there were 275 more dogs adopted than reptiles.

4-D   The graph says that 12% of first-year students intend to major in business.

Multiply 12% by the number of students surveyed.

$$0.04 \times 3,525 = 141$$

According to the graph, 423 students intend to major in business.

5-A   There must be a total of 100% in a circle graph.

The sum of the other sectors is 92%.

$$100\% - 92\% = 8\%$$

Remember that the question asks you how many students are undecided.

Multiply 8% by the total number of students surveyed.

$$0.08 \times 3,525 = 282$$

According to the graph, 282 students are undecided about their majors.

6-B   According to the graph, 14% of students intend to major in education and 10% intend to major in the social sciences.

$$14\% - 10\% = 4\%$$

Multiply by the number of students surveyed.

$$0.04 \times 3,525 = 141$$

According to the graph, there are 141 more students intending to major in education than there are students intending to major in the social sciences.

7-D   According to the graph, 11% of students intend to major in computer science, 9% intend to major in the liberal arts and humanities, 15% intend to major in health and human services, and 8% intend to major in engineering.

This makes engineering the least popular major.

8-B The space for January shows $2\frac{1}{2}$ sneaker symbols. This means that there were 250 pairs of sneakers sold in January.

9-D According to the graph, 200 pairs of sneakers were sold in July.

Multiply 200 by $30.00.

$200 \times 30.00 = \$6,000$

10-B According to the graph, 350 pairs of sneakers were sold in August and 500 pairs of sneakers were sold in September.

$500 - 350 = 150$

In September, the store sold 150 more pairs of sneakers than it did in August.

11-C According to the graph, 400 pairs of sneakers were sold in October, 550 pairs were sold in November, and 800 pairs were sold in December.

$400 + 550 + 800 = 1,750$

There were 1,750 pairs of sneakers sold from October to December.

answers exercises

SUMMING IT UP

- Be sure to familiarize yourself with the following topics covered in this chapter: decimals, whole numbers, making purchases with money, fractions, percents, adding and subtracting numbers with units, multiplying and dividing numbers with units, metric measurement, joining small units, breaking down large units, simplifying results, ratio and proportion problems, average or arithmetic mean, median, mode, weighted average, bar graphs, line graphs, circle graphs, and pictographs.

- Use the exercises in this chapter to prepare for taking the Arithmetic Reasoning sections in the three Practice Tests in Part V of this book.

- Check the answer keys to make sure you scored well on the exercises.

Mathematics Knowledge

OVERVIEW

- Solving problems using algebra
- Signed numbers
- Using formulas
- Circles and quadrilaterals
- Triangles
- Powers, roots, and radicals
- Exponents and sequences
- Summing it up

SOLVING PROBLEMS USING ALGEBRA

You can use algebra to solve many problems involving a relationship between a known and an unknown quantity.

Follow these steps when using algebra:

- Carefully read the problem to determine the information you know (the *known quantity*) and the information you don't know (the *unknown quantity*).
- Use a letter, such as *x*, to represent the unknown quantity.
- Write an equation representing the relationship between the quantities.
- Solve the problem.

Example: In 15 years, Rick will be 43 years old. How old is Rick now?

SOLUTION: In this problem, the known quantity is Rick's age in 15 years. The unknown quantity, called the *variable,* is Rick's age now.

An equation has an equal sign, which means that two quantities are equal.

Let x = Rick's age now.

Write an equation: $x + 15 = 43$.

$x + 15 - 15 = 43 - 15$ Subtract 15 from both sides of the equation.
$x = 28$ Rick's age now is 28.

Substitute 28 for x in the equation to check your work: $28 + 15 = 43$.

chapter 6

Transforming Equations

When you rearrange an equation so that the variable is isolated on one side of the equation, you *transform* the equation. When you determine the unknown quantity, you *solve* the equation.

To transform an equation, add or subtract the same quantity from both sides of the equation:

$$y + 3 = 10$$

To transform this equation, subtract 3 from both sides:

$$y + 3 - 3 = 10 - 3$$

The +3 and −3 on the left side of the equation cancel out each other, so that the variable y is on one side of the equation by itself:

$$y = 7$$

You might also have to multiply or divide both sides of an equation by the same quantity.

To solve $2x = 10$, divide both sides by 2:

$$\frac{2x}{2} = \frac{10}{2}$$

$$x = 5$$

To solve $\frac{y}{6} = 18$, multiply both sides by 6:

$$6 \cdot \frac{y}{6} = 18 \cdot 6$$

$$y = 108$$

For some equations, you have to perform more than one operation. Begin by adding or subtracting to isolate the variable on one side of the equation. Then multiply or divide to eliminate a number in front of the variable.

Example: The number 12 is 20 less than 4 times a number. What is this number?

SOLUTION: Let x = the unknown number.

Write the equation: $12 = 4x - 20$

$$
\begin{array}{rcl}
12 & = & 4x - 20 \\
+\,20 & & +\,20 \\
\hline
32 & = & 4x
\end{array}
$$

Adding 20 eliminates −20.

$$32 = 4x$$

$$\frac{32}{4} = \frac{4x}{4} \qquad \text{Dividing by 4 eliminates the 4 in front of the } x.$$

$$8 = x \qquad \text{The solution to the original equation is } x = 8.$$

Substitute 8 for x in the equation to check your work.

$$12 = 4(8) - 20$$
$$12 = 32 - 20$$
$$12 = 12$$

If the variable appears on both sides of the equation, you must add or subtract the number in front of the variable from both sides.

In this equation, eliminate the x-term on the right side of the equation by subtracting $2x$ from both sides:

$$4x + 6 = 2x + 10$$
$$\underline{-2x \qquad -2x}$$
$$2x + 6 = \qquad 10 \qquad \text{Eliminate 6 from the left side by}$$
$$\underline{-6 \qquad -6} \qquad \text{subtracting it from both sides.}$$
$$2x = 4$$
$$\frac{2x}{2} = \frac{4}{2} \qquad \text{Divide by 2 to isolate } x.$$
$$x = 2$$

Substitute 2 for x in the original equation and check your work:

$$4(2) + 6 = 2(2) + 10$$
$$8 + 6 = 4 + 10$$
$$14 = 14$$

Sometimes you have to *simplify* an equation before you can solve it. You might have to remove parentheses or combine like terms:

$$3y - 2(y - 1) = 15$$
$$3y - 2y + 2 = 15 \qquad \text{Remove parentheses.}$$
$$y + 2 = 15 \qquad \text{Combine like terms.}$$
$$y = 15 - 2$$
$$y = 13$$

Substitute 13 for y:

$$3(13) - 2(13 - 1) = 15$$
$$39 - 26 + 2 = 15$$
$$15 = 15$$

Evaluating Algebraic Expressions

You learned earlier in this chapter that an *algebraic equation* has an equal sign. An *algebraic expression,* on the other hand, does not. For example, $4x + 1$ is an expression used to find the perimeter of a geometric figure.

When you plug in values for variables in an algebraic expression, you *evaluate* the expression. When evaluating expressions, perform mathematical calculations by following these six operations:

1. Perform calculations in parentheses first.

2. Calculate all powers and roots.

3. Multiply from left to right.

4. Divide from left to right.

5. Add from left to right.

6. Subtract from left to right.

Example: Evaluate $4x + 1$ when $x = 2$.

SOLUTION: Substitute 2 for x and simplify.

$$4(2) + 1$$
$$9$$

Example: Evaluate $3x^2 - 2y$ if $x = 2$ and $y = 3$

SOLUTION: $3(2)^2 - 2(3)$ Remove the parentheses.

$3 \cdot 2^2 - 2 \cdot 3$	Calculate 2^2.
$3 \cdot 4 - 2 \cdot 3$	Multiply.
$12 - 6$	Subtract.
6	

EXERCISES: SOLVING PROBLEMS USING ALGEBRA

Directions: Now try the exercises below. Each question is followed by four possible answers. Solve each problem. When you have completed the exercises, check your answers against the answer explanations that follow.

FOR ITEMS 1 AND 2, CHOOSE THE CORRECT MATHEMATICAL STATEMENT.

1. Three times a number minus one half equals 20.

   1-A $\quad 3n - \dfrac{1}{2} = 20$

   1-B $\quad 2n + 3 = 20$

   1-C $\quad 3n + \dfrac{1}{2} = 20$

   1-D $\quad 3n - 2 = 20$

2. Twelve added to a number is 98.

   2-A $\quad n + 12 = 89$

   2-B $\quad 98 - 12 = n$

   2-C $\quad 12 + n = 98$

   2-D $\quad n - 12 = 98$

FOR ITEMS 3 TO 6, WRITE THE EQUATION FOR EACH PROBLEM AND THEN SOLVE FOR THE NUMBER.

3. If 5 is subtracted from a given number, the difference is 5.

   3-A $\quad$ 5

   3-B $\quad$ 10

   3-C $\quad$ 15

   3-D $\quad$ 25

4. The product of 9 and a number is 108.

   4-A $\quad$ 8

   4-B $\quad$ 12

   4-C $\quad$ 117

   4-D $\quad$ 972

5. One fourth of a number decreased by 4 is 24.

   5-A $\quad$ 24

   5-B $\quad$ 28

   5-C $\quad$ 96

   5-D $\quad$ 112

6. When 2 is subtracted from 2 times a number, the result is 2.

   6-A $\quad$ 2

   6-B $\quad$ 4

   6-C $\quad$ 6

   6-D $\quad$ 8

7. Solve for b: $0.2b - 4 = 6$

   7-A $\quad$ 5

   7-B $\quad$ 24

   7-C $\quad$ 40

   7-D $\quad$ 50

8. Solve for x: $2x - 2 = 6$

   8-A $\quad$ 2

   8-B $\quad$ 4

   8-C $\quad$ 6

   8-D $\quad$ 8

9. $y = 9x - 6$

   Find y when x is -3.

   9-A $\quad$ -37

   9-B $\quad$ -33

   9-C $\quad$ -27

   9-D $\quad$ -6

10. Solve for b: $b - 2.4 = 8$

   10-A $\quad$ 5.6

   10-B $\quad$ 6.4

   10-C $\quad$ 10.4

   10-D $\quad$ 12.6

ANSWER KEY AND EXPLANATIONS

1. A	3. B	5. D	7. D	9. B
2. C	4. B	6. A	8. B	10. C

1-A   Let n be the number.

$$3n - \frac{1}{2} = 20$$

2-C   Let n be the number.

$$12 + n = 98$$

3-B   Let n be the number.

$$\begin{array}{rl} n - 5 = & 5 \\ \underline{+ 5 \quad + 5} & \quad \text{Add 5 to both sides.} \\ n = & 10 \end{array}$$

4-B   Let n be the number.

$$9n = 108$$
$$\frac{9n}{9} = \frac{108}{9}$$
$$n = 12$$

5-D   Let n be the number.

$$\frac{n}{4} - 4 = 24$$

$$\underline{\quad\quad + 4 \quad + 4} \quad \text{Add 4 to both sides of the equation.}$$

$$\frac{n}{4} = 28$$

$$4\left(\frac{n}{4}\right) = (28)4$$

$$n = 112$$

6-A   Let n be the number.

$$\begin{array}{rl} 2n - 2 = & 2 \\ \underline{+ 2 \quad + 2} & \quad \text{Add 2 to both sides of the equation.} \\ 2n = & 4 \end{array}$$

$$\frac{1}{2}(2n) = \frac{1}{2}(4) \quad \text{Divide both sides of the equation by 2.}$$

$$n = 2$$

7-D $0.2b - 4 = 6$

$\underline{+4+4}$ Add 4 to both sides.

$0.2b = 10$

$\dfrac{0.2b}{0.2} = \dfrac{10}{0.2}$ Divide both sides by 0.2.

$b = 50$

8-B $2x - 2 = 6$

$\underline{+2+2}$ Add 2 to both sides.

$2x = 8$

$\dfrac{2x}{2} = \dfrac{8}{2}$ Divide both sides by 2.

$x = 4$

9-B Substitute the value for x into the equation and perform the indicated operations.

$y = 9(-3) - 6$

$y = -27 - 6$

$y = -33$

10-C Solve for b: $b - 2.4 = 8$

$b - 2.4 = 8$

$\underline{+2.4+2.4}$ Add 2.4 to both sides.

$b = 10.4$

SIGNED NUMBERS

Numbers in algebra are *signed*, which means they have a plus or a minus in front of them. You need to understand the rules to correctly perform operations with signed numbers. Study these rules until you're sure that you know them.

Addition:

To add numbers with the same sign, add the numbers and keep the sign. When adding numbers with different signs, subtract the numbers and use the sign of the larger number.

Add these numbers:

$$
\begin{array}{rrrr}
+9 & -9 & -9 & +9 \\
+3 & -3 & +3 & -3 \\
\hline
+12 & -12 & -6 & +6 \\
\end{array}
$$

Subtraction:

When you subtract signed numbers, change the sign of the number being subtracted. Then, follow the rules for addition.

Subtract these numbers:

$$
\begin{array}{ll}
\begin{array}{r} +9 \\ +3 \\ \hline +6 \end{array} \text{Change to } -3. &
\begin{array}{r} -9 \\ -3 \\ \hline -6 \end{array} \text{Change to } +3. \\
\end{array}
$$

$$
\begin{array}{ll}
\begin{array}{r} -9 \\ +3 \\ \hline -12 \end{array} \text{Change to } -3. &
\begin{array}{r} +9 \\ -3 \\ \hline +12 \end{array} \text{Change to } +3. \\
\end{array}
$$

Multiplication:

Keep this rule in mind when multiplying numbers: If the number of negative signs is odd, the product is negative. If the number of negative signs is even, the product is positive.

Multiply these numbers:

$$(+5)(+6) = +30$$

$$(+5)(-6) = -30$$

$$(-5)(-6) = +30$$

$$(-5)(+6) = -30$$

Division:

If the signs of the numbers in a division problem are the same, the quotient is positive. If the signs are different, the quotient is negative.

Divide these numbers:

$$\frac{+42}{+7} = +6$$

$$\frac{-42}{-7} = +6$$

$$\frac{-42}{+7} = -6$$

$$\frac{+42}{-7} = -6$$

Polynomials

An algebraic expression with one or more terms is called a *polynomial*. The coefficients of the terms in a polynomial are the numbers before the terms. Remember that a term without a number in front of it has a coefficient of 1. Also, a number may appear in a polynomial without a term. This number is still considered a coefficient.

Find the coefficients of the terms in this polynomial:

$$6y^2 + x + 7 - 2x^2$$

The coefficients are +6, +1, +7, and −2.

When you add polynomials, add the coefficients and like terms. Like terms are those with the same term and exponent:

$$+6y^2 + \ x + 7 - 2x^2$$
$$+2y^0 + 3x - 4 + x^2$$
$$\overline{+8y^2 + 4x + 3 - x^2}$$

When you subtract polynomials, subtract the coefficients of like terms. Remember to change the signs of the terms being subtracted:

$$+8x - 3y + 2z$$
$$-6x - \ y + 4z$$
$$\overline{+14x - 2y - 2z}$$

When multiplying a single term by a single term, multiply the coefficients and add the exponents. Note that a single term is called a *monomial*. A term without an exponent is considered to have an exponent of 1.

$$3b^2 \cdot 2b = 6b^3$$

$$x^4 \cdot x^5 = x^9$$

$$2y^3 \cdot 4y^2 = 8y^5$$

$$(-2x^5y^3)(-4x^{10}y^8) = 8x^{15}y^{11}$$

When multiplying a monomial and a polynomial, multiply each term of the polynomial by the monomial.

$$4(3x + 8y) = 12x^3 + 32y$$

$$x^2(2x + 8y) = 12x^3 + 32x^2y$$

$$x^2(2x - 3x^4) = 2x^3 - 3x^6$$

When multiplying two polynomials, multiply each term of the first polynomial by each term of the second polynomial. Then, add like terms.

$$(a + 3)(a + 4) = a^2 + 4a + 3a + 12 = a^2 + 7a + 12$$

$$(x - 2)(y + 3) = xy + 3x - 2y - 6$$

$$(x + 3)(x^2 + 4x - 1) = x^3 + 4x^2 - x + 3x^2 + 12x - 3 = x^3 + 7x^2 + 11x - 3$$

When dividing monomials, divide the coefficient and subtract the exponents.

$$\frac{6x^8}{3x^2} = 2x^6$$

$$\frac{xy^5}{xy^3} = y^2 \text{ (Note that } \frac{x}{x} = 1.)$$

$$\frac{-10a^8b^{10}}{5ab^2} = -2a^7b^8$$

When dividing a polynomial by a monomial, divide each term of the polynomial by the monomial.

$$\frac{16x^2 - 14x}{2} = 8x^2 - 7x$$

$$(20y^3 - 15y^2 + 20y) \div 5y = 4y^2 - 3y + 4$$

Simplifying Expressions by Removing Parentheses

Follow these rules when removing parentheses.

When a positive sign appears before parentheses, eliminate the parentheses.

Example: $2y^2 + (9y + 4) = 2y^2 + 9y + 4$

When there is a negative sign before parentheses, change the sign of each term inside the parentheses, and eliminate the parentheses.

Example: $2 - (3x - y - z) = 2 - 3x + y + z$

When there is a number and/or variable before the parentheses, multiply each term inside the parentheses by the number and/or variable. Then, eliminate the parentheses.

Example: $2y + 4(5x - 2) = 2y + 20x - 8$

Once parentheses have been removed, combine like terms.

Example: $4(x + y) + (3x - 2y) - (2x + 3y)$

$$= 4x + 4y + 3x - 2y - 2x - 3y$$

$$= 5x - y$$

EXERCISES: SIGNED NUMBERS

Directions: Now try the exercises below. Each question is followed by four possible answers. Solve each problem. When you have completed the exercises, check your answers against the answer explanations that follow.

1. When +3 is added to −5, the sum is
    1-A   +8
    1-B   −8
    1-C   −2
    1-D   +2

2. At 9 a.m. the temperature was −5°. If the temperature rose 8 degrees during the next hour, what was the temperature at 10 a.m.?
    2-A   −13°
    2-B   +13°
    2-C   −3°
    2-D   +3°

3. Find the product of (−8), (−6), (−5), and (−3).
    3-A   −21
    3-B   +22
    3-C   +720
    3-D   −720

4. The temperatures reported at hour intervals on a winter evening were +8°, −2°, −3°, +4°, and +3°. Find the average temperature for these hours.
    4-A   −2°
    4-B   +2°
    4-C   −20°
    4-D   +20°

5. Evaluate the expression $6x − 2y + 3z$ if $x = −2$, $y = −3$, and $z = +5$.
    5-A   −8
    5-B   +9
    5-C   +21
    5-D   +28

6. If $5x − 2$ is multiplied by $3x$, the product is
    6-A $15x^2 − 6x$
    6-B $15x^2 − 6$
    6-C $15x^2 − x$
    6-D $8x − 5x$

7. The sum of $2x^2 − 3x + 3$ and $x^2 + x − 2$ is
    7-A $3x^2 − 2x + 1$
    7-B $3x^2 − 4x + 5$
    7-C $x^2 + 2x + 1$
    7-D $2x^2 − 3x − 6$

8. The product of $(2x + 3)$ and $(2x + 3)$ is
    8-A $4x + 6$
    8-B $4x^2 + 6$
    8-C $4x^2 + x + 9$
    8-D $4x^2 + 12x + 9$

9. $3(a + b) − 5(2a + b)$
    9-A $13a + 8b$
    9-B $7a + 2b$
    9-C $−7a − 2b$
    9-D $−30a − 15b$

10. $3(x + 6) − (3x − 2)$
    10-A $3x + 18$
    10-B   16
    10-C $−x + 16$
    10-D   20

ANSWER KEY AND EXPLANATIONS

1. C	3. C	5. B	7. A	9. C
2. D	4. B	6. A	8. D	10. D

1-C To add numbers with different signs, subtract the value of the numbers and use the sign of the number with the greatest value.

$$\frac{\begin{array}{r} -5 \\ +3 \end{array}}{-2}$$

2-D Add +8 to −5.

$$\frac{\begin{array}{r} +8 \\ -5 \end{array}}{+3}$$

Alternatively, use a number line.

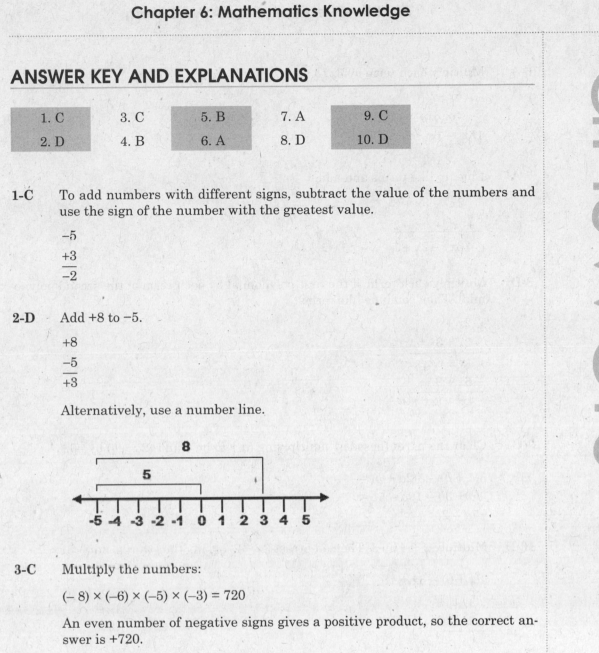

3-C Multiply the numbers:

$(-8) \times (-6) \times (-5) \times (-3) = 720$

An even number of negative signs gives a positive product, so the correct answer is +720.

4-B Add all terms. Then divide by the number of terms.

$$\frac{(+8) + (-2) + (-3) + (+4) + (+3)}{5}$$

$$\frac{+10}{5} = +2$$

5-B Substitute the values for x, y, and z in the original equation and then solve.

$$6x - 2y + 3z = 6(-2) - 2(-3) + 3(5)$$
$$= -12 + 6 + 15$$
$$= 9$$

6-A   Multiply each term by $3x$.

$$\begin{array}{r} 5x - 2 \\ \times\ 3x \\ \hline 15x^2 - 6x \end{array}$$

7-A   Line up like terms and add.

$$\begin{array}{r} 2x^2 - 3x + 3 \\ +\ x^2 +\ x - 2 \\ \hline 3x^2 - 2x + 1 \end{array}$$

8-D   Multiply each term of the first polynomial by each term of the second polynomial. Then combine like terms.

$$\begin{array}{r} 2x + 3 \\ \times\ 2x + 3 \\ \hline 4x^2 + 6x \\ +\ 6x + 9 \\ \hline 4x^2 + 12x + 9 \end{array}$$

9-C   Clear the parentheses by multiplying $(a + b)$ by 3 and $(2a + b)$ by -5.

$$3(a + b) - 5(2a + b) =$$
$$3a + 3b - 10a - 5b =$$
$$-7a - 2b$$

10-D   Multiply $x + 6$ by 3. Then, subtract $3x - 2$, or, in other words, add $-3x + 2$.

$$3(x + 6) = 3x + 18$$

$$\begin{array}{r} 3x + 18 \\ -\ 3x +\ 2 \\ \hline +20 \end{array}$$

USING FORMULAS

Motion Problems

Motion problems are word problems that ask you to determine how far something (or someone) traveled, how fast it moved, and the length of time it took to make the trip. In other words, you'll be asked to determine the distance, rate, or time. In most motion problems, distance is given in miles, rate is given in miles per hour, and time is measured in hours.

Use this formula to solve motion problems:

$$rate \times time = distance$$

Example: A car on a highway traveled 325 miles in 5 hours at the same speed without stopping. How fast was the car traveling?

SOLUTION: Let r = rate

$$rate \times time = distance$$

$$r \cdot 5 = 325$$

$$\frac{5r}{5} = \frac{325}{5}$$

$$r = 65 \text{ miles per hour}$$

Example: Ray and Latoya start at the same time from cities 250 miles apart and travel toward each other. Ray travels at 50 miles per hour, and Latoya travels at 55 miles per hour. In how many hours will they meet?

SOLUTION: Let h = number of hours. Then $50h$ = the distance traveled by Ray, and $55h$ = the distance traveled by Latoya. The total distance is 315 miles.

$$50h + 55h = 315$$

$$\frac{105h}{105} = \frac{315}{105}$$

$$h = 3$$

They will meet in 3 hours.

Percent Problems

To solve percent problems, rewrite the relationship in the problem as an equation.

Example: Twenty-five percent of what number is 32?

SOLUTION: Let n = the unknown number. Twenty-five percent of n is 32.

$$0.25n = 32 \qquad \text{Change the percent to a decimal } (25\% = 0.25).$$

$$25n = 3200 \qquad \text{Multiply both sides by 100 to eliminate the decimal.}$$

$$\frac{25n}{25} = \frac{3200}{25}$$

$$n = 128$$

Example: Ms. Torres receives a salary raise from $35,000 to $42,000. Find the percent of the increase.

SOLUTION: Let p = percent. The increase is $42,000 - 35,000 = 7,000$. What percent of 35,000 is 7,000?

$$35,000p = 7,000$$

$$\frac{35,000p}{35,000} = \frac{7,000}{35,000}$$

$$p = 0.2$$

$$p = 20\%$$

Interest Problems

If a bank loans you money for a car or a house, you will have to pay back the amount plus interest. *Interest* is the price you pay to borrow the money. Interest is also the amount of money you will earn when you invest money.

Use this formula to solve interest problems:

Interest = *principal* (amount you're borrowing) × *rate* (the amount of interest you'll pay expressed as a percent) × *time* (the number of years it will take you to pay back the principal and interest).

This formula is commonly written as:

$$I = prt$$

When this formula is used to calculate the amount of money you will earn when you invest money, the interest is referred to as *simple interest*.

Example: How long must $4,000 be invested at 3% simple interest to earn $360?

SOLUTION: Let t = time

$I = \$360$

$p = \$4,000$

$r = 3\%$ or 0.03

$360 = 4,000(0.03)t$

$\dfrac{360}{120} = \dfrac{120t}{120}$

$3 = t$

The $4,000 must be invested for 3 years.

Profit and Loss Problems

When a dealer pays for an item, he or she adds money to the selling price. This is the dealer's *profit*. Note that the purchase price is 100% of the cost. If the dealer adds 15% to the purchase price, the selling price is 100% + 15%, or 115% of the cost.

Example: An electronic store is selling a leading stereo for $260, which represents a 30% profit over the cost. What was the cost to the store?

SOLUTION: Let c = cost price

$100\% + 30\% = 130\%$

The selling price is 130% of the cost.

130% of $c = \$260$

$1.30c = 260$ Multiply both sides by 100 to eliminate the decimal
    and divide both sides by 130.

$\dfrac{130c}{130} = \dfrac{26,000}{130}$

$c = \$200$

The stereo cost the electronic store $200.

When the sales price of an item is marked down, a *discount* is applied. The *marked price* is 100%. So, if an item is discounted 10%, its selling price is 100% − 10%, or 90%, of its marked price.

Example: A jacket is on sale for $32.00, which is 20% off the regular price. What is the regular price?

SOLUTION: Let r = regular price. The sale price is 100% − 20%, or 80%, of the regular price.

$$80\% \text{ of } r = \$32.00$$

$$0.80r = \$32.00 \qquad \text{Multiply both sides by 100 to eliminate the decimals and divide both sides by 80.}$$

$$\frac{80r}{80} = \frac{3,200}{80}$$

$$r = 40$$

The regular price was $40.

Sometimes an item is sold at a loss, which means it is sold for less than it cost a dealer. When this happens, the amount of the loss is deducted from the cost price. This is the *selling price.* If an item is sold at a 15% loss, it has a selling price of 100% − 15%, or 85%, of the cost price.

Example: Kelly bought a car for $12,000. After a year, she sold it to Mike at a 25% loss. What did Mike pay for the car?

SOLUTION: The car was sold for 100% − 25%, or 75%, of its cost price.

$$75\% \text{ of } \$12,000 = 0.75 \, (12,000)$$

$$= 9,000$$

Mike paid $9,000 for the car.

EXERCISES: USING FORMULAS

Directions: Now try the exercises below. Each question is followed by four possible answers. Solve each problem. When you have completed the exercises, check your answers against the answer explanations that follow.

1. Melanie wishes to buy a jacket that is 30% off the regular price of $62.00. How much money will be deducted from the price of the jacket?

   1-A $1.86

   1-B $18.60

   1-C $32.00

   1-D $43.40

2. In Ken's grade, 160 of the 320 students take the train to school. What percentage of students take the train?

   2-A   25%

   2-B   40%

   2-C   50%

   2-D   60%

3. A dealer buys a used car for $14,000 and wishes to sell it at a 15% profit. What should his selling price be?

   3-A $14,210

   3-B $14,500

   3-C $15,500

   3-D $16,100

4. Deshawn received a bonus of $900, which was 3% of his annual salary. What was his annual salary?

   4-A $27,000

   4-B $30,000

   4-C $30,900

   4-D $90,000

5. A woman traveled a distance of 10 miles at 60 miles per hour and returned over the same route at 40 miles per hour. How long did it take her to make the round trip?

   5-A $\frac{1}{2}$ hr.

   5-B $\frac{1}{4}$ hr.

   5-C $\frac{5}{12}$ hr.

   5-D $\frac{1}{10}$ hr.

6. A store reduced the price of a gallon of milk from $4.00 to $3.00. What was the percent decrease per gallon?

   6-A   100%

   6-B   75%

   6-C   50%

   6-D   25%

7. Jeremy earns $72 for 8 hours of work. At the same rate of pay, how much will he earn for 35 hours of work?

   7-A $2,520

   7-B $648

   7-C $576

   7-D $315

8. Daphne sells appliances, earning an 80% commission on all sales. How much will she need in sales to earn $500 in commission?

   8-A $40.00

   8-B $62.50

   8-C $400.00

   8-D $625.00

9. A driver traveled 200 miles at the rate of 50 mph, and then traveled 100 miles at 55 mph. What was the total amount of time for the entire trip?

9-A   4 hr.

9-B $4\frac{9}{11}$ hr.

9-C   5 hr.

9-D $5\frac{9}{11}$ hr.

10. Two friends start at the same point and walk in opposite directions. If one walks at the rate of 3 miles per hour and the other walks at the rate of 4 miles per hour, in how many hours will they be 21 miles apart?

10-A 2 hr.

10-B 3 hr.

10-C 4 hr.

10-D 5 hr.

ANSWER KEY AND EXPLANATIONS

1. B	3. D	5. C	7. D	9. D
2. C	4. B	6. D	8. D	10. B

1-B Translate the word problem into a mathematical problem. "30% off the price of $62.00" means $0.30 \times 62 = 18.6$. Therefore, the answer is $18.60.

2-C Write a fraction that shows the ratio of students who take the train compared to the number of students altogether:

Train/students in all $= \dfrac{160}{320} = \dfrac{2}{4} = \dfrac{1}{2}$ or 50%

3-D His selling price will be (100% + 15%) of his cost price.

$14,000 \times 0.15 = 2,100$

$14,000 + 2,100 = 16,100$

4-B Let s = Deshawn's salary

3% of s = $900

$0.03s = \$900$

$\dfrac{0.03s}{0.03} = \dfrac{\$900}{0.03}$

$s = \$30,000$

5-C $T = \dfrac{D}{R}$

Time for 10 miles at 60 miles per hour $= \dfrac{10}{60} = \dfrac{1}{6}$ hour

Time for 10 miles at 40 miles per hour $= \dfrac{10}{40} = \dfrac{1}{4}$ hour

Total time $\dfrac{1}{6} + \dfrac{1}{4} = \dfrac{2}{12} + \dfrac{3}{12} = \dfrac{5}{12}$ hour

6-D Original price = $4.00 per gallon
New price = $3.00 per gallon
Decrease = $1.00

Percent of decrease = Amount of decrease ÷ original price

$= \dfrac{1.00}{4.00} = 25\%$

7-D The amount earned is proportional to the number of hours worked.

Let x = unknown pay

$$\frac{x}{35} = \frac{72}{8}$$
$$8x = 35 \times 72$$

$$\frac{8x}{8} = \frac{2,520}{8}$$
$$x = \$315$$

8-D Let s = needed sales

$$0.8s = 500$$
$$\frac{0.8s}{0.8} = \frac{500}{0.8} \quad \text{Divide both sides by 0.8}$$
$$s = \$625.00$$

9-D The first part of the trip took:

200 miles ÷ 50 mph = 4 hours

The second part of the trip took:

100 miles ÷ 55 mph = $1\frac{9}{11}$ hours

4 hours + $1\frac{9}{11}$ hours = $5\frac{9}{11}$ hours

10-B In 1 hour, they are 7 miles apart.

21 ÷ 7 mph = 3 hours

It will take 3 hours to be 21 miles apart.

CIRCLES AND QUADRILATERALS

Circles

A *circle* is a line that forms a closed loop. Every point on the line is equidistant from a point in the middle of the circle called *the center*. A circle has 360°.

The following are some important terms related to circles:

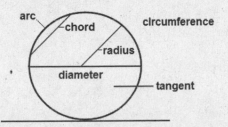

- **Arc**—a part of the circle between the two endpoints of a chord.
- **Chord**—a line segment connecting two points on a circle.
- **Diameter**—a line segment connecting two points on a circle. The diameter must go through the center of the circle.
- **Radius**—a line segment extending from the center of a circle to any point on the line.
- **Semicircle**—an arc connecting a diameter. A semicircle, which is half of a circle, has 180°.
- **Tangent**—a line intersecting a circle at only one point.

Circumference

The *circumference* of a circle is the distance around a circle. (This distance is called *perimeter* when it relates to other geometric shapes.) Use this formula to find the circumference of a circle:

$$C = \pi d \text{ or } C = 2\pi r$$

Pi (π) is approximately equal to $\frac{22}{7}$ or 3.14. When you're asked to make a calculation using pi, the question will indicate whether you should use $\frac{22}{7}$ or 3.14.

Example: Find the circumference of a circle with a diameter of 3 inches. Use 3.14 for pi.

SOLUTION: $C = \pi d$

$$C = 6 \times 3.14 = 18.8 \text{ inches}$$

Example: The circumference of a circle is 11 inches. What is the diameter? Use $\frac{22}{7}$ for pi.

SOLUTION: $D = \dfrac{C}{\pi}$

$$D = 11 \div \frac{22}{7}$$

$$D = 11 \times \frac{7}{22} = \frac{7}{2} = 3\frac{1}{2} \text{ inches}$$

Area

Use this formula to find the area of a circle:

$$A = \pi r^2$$

If the radius of a circle is 4 inches, the area is 16π.

If you're given the area of a circle and asked to find the radius, use this formula:

$$\frac{A}{\pi} = r^2$$

Example: Find the radius of a circle with an area of 225π.

SOLUTION: $\dfrac{225\pi}{\pi} = 225$

$$\sqrt{225} = 15 = \text{radius}$$

Volume

Use this formula to find the volume of a circular cylinder:

$$V = \pi r^2 h$$

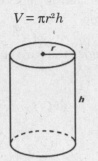

Example: What is the volume of a circular cylinder with a radius of 14 and a height of $\frac{1}{2}$.

SOLUTION: Use $\pi = \frac{22}{7}$

$$\frac{22}{7} \times (14)^2 \times \frac{1}{2} =$$

$$\frac{22}{7} \times 196 \times \frac{1}{2} = 308 \text{ cubic inches}$$

To find the volume of a sphere, use this formula:

$$V = \frac{4}{3} \pi r^3$$

Example: What is the volume of a sphere with a radius of 9 cm. in terms of π?

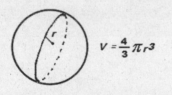

SOLUTION: $\frac{4}{3} \times \pi \times (9)^3 =$

$$\frac{4}{3} \times \pi \times 729 = 972\pi \text{ cubic centimeters}$$

Quadrilaterals

A *quadrilateral* is a four-sided polygon, or closed shape. There are different kinds of quadrilaterals, but all have four sides and four angles whose sum is 360°. Common quadrilaterals include the parallelogram, square, and rectangle.

A *parallelogram* is a quadrilateral with opposite sides and angles that are equal. Opposite sides in a parallelogram are also parallel.

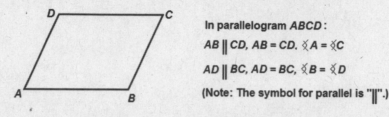

In parallelogram *ABCD*:

$AB \parallel CD$, $AB = CD$, ∡A = ∡C

$AD \parallel BC$, $AD = BC$, ∡B = ∡D

(Note: The symbol for parallel is "$\parallel$".)

The rectangle, square, and rhombus are formed from the parallelogram:

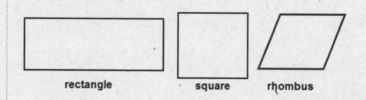

rectangle   square   rhombus

- **Rectangle**—has four right angles and opposite sides that are equal.
- **Square**—has four right angles and four equal sides.
- **Rhombus**—has four equal sides.

A *trapezoid* is a quadrilateral with only one pair of parallel sides.

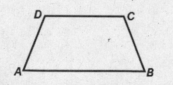

In trapezoid *ABCD*, $AB \parallel DC$.

Perimeter

Perimeter is the distance around a figure. To find the perimeter, add all sides.

Example: The perimeter of the rectangle below is $10 + 5 + 10 + 5 = 30$.

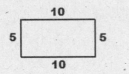

To find the perimeter of a triangle, add all sides.

Example: If the sides of a triangle are 3, 4, and 5, its perimeter is $3 + 4 + 5 = 12$.

If you know the perimeter of a triangle and the length of two sides, you can find the length of the third side by adding the two sides and subtracting this amount from the perimeter.

Example: Two sides of a triangle measure 3 and 4. The perimeter is 12. Find the other side.

SOLUTION: $3 + 4 = 7$

$12 - 7 = 5$

The third side is 5.

When you're asked to find the perimeter, you may have to express some or all sides algebraically.

Example: A rectangle has four sides. The length is two less than three times the width. If the perimeter is 28, find the length and the width.

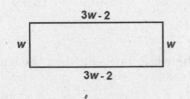

SOLUTION: Let w = width

Then $3w - 2$ = length

The sum of the four sides is 28.

$w + (3w - 2) + w + (3w - 2) = 28$

$$w + 3w - 2 + w + 3w - 2 = 28$$
$$8w - 4 = 28$$
$$8w = 32$$
$$\frac{8w}{8} = \frac{32}{8}$$
$$w = 4$$

$$3w - 2 = 3(4) - 2 = 12 - 2 = 10$$

The width is 4 and the length is 10.

Area

Area is the amount of space inside a flat object such as a rectangle or triangle. Area is expressed in square units, such as square inches, square centimeters, and square miles.

Use this formula to find the area of a square:

$$A = l^2$$

Example: If the length of a side of a square is 7 inches, the area of the square is 7^2 or 49 square inches.

You can find the area of a rectangle by multiplying the length and width:

$$A = l \times w$$

Example: A rectangle has a length of 10 centimeters and a width of 12 centimeters. Therefore, the area is 120 square centimeters.

If you're given the area of a rectangle and either the length or the width, use this formula to find the missing measurement:

$$\frac{A}{l} = w \text{ or } \frac{A}{w} = l$$

If the area of a rectangle is 36 square feet and the width is 3 feet, then the length is 12 feet.

To find the area of a parallelogram, multiply the base times the height, using this formula:

$$A = bh$$

Note that the height of a parallelogram is not a measurement of one side, but the altitude of the parallelogram. The height is represented by a dotted vertical line.

Example:

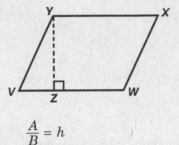

$$\frac{A}{B} = h$$

YZ is the height.

VW is the base.

Example: The base of a parallelogram is 7 inches and the height is 10 inches. What is the area?

SOLUTION: $7 \times 10 = 70$

The area of the parallelogram is 70 square inches.

To find the base or the height of a parallelogram if you're given the area, divide the area by the length or height:

$$\frac{A}{h} = b \text{ or } \frac{A}{b} = h$$

Example: The area of a parallelogram is 24 square centimeters and the base is 4 centimeters. What is the height?

SOLUTION: $\frac{A}{b} = h$ or $\frac{24}{4} = 6$

The height is 6 centimeters.

Volume

A *rectangular solid* is a three-dimensional figure with six faces that meet at right angles. The three dimensions of a rectangular solid are length, width, and height. Look at this rectangular solid. Note the length (l), width (w), and height (h).

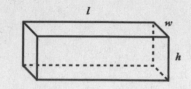

Use this formula to find the volume of a rectangular solid, which is expressed in cubic feet:

$$V = l \times w \times h$$

Example: A rectangular solid has a length of 8 feet, a width of 4 feet, and a height of 6 feet, so its volume is 192 cubic feet. The faces on a cube, which is a rectangular solid, are equal. Note that the length, width, and height on the cube below are labeled as *e,* which stands for edge.

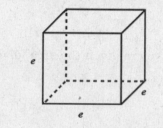

Use this formula to find the volume of a cube:

$$V = e^3$$

Example: What is the volume of a cube with a height of 4 inches?

SOLUTION: $V = (4)^3 = 4 \times 4 \times 4 = 64$ cubic inches

To find the surface area of a cube, multiply the area of any face by 6.

Example: The surface area of a cube with a length of 10 is $10^2 \times 6 = 100 \times 6 = 600$ square inches.

EXERCISES: CIRCLES AND QUADRILATERALS

> **Directions:** Now try the exercises below. Each question is followed by four possible answers. Solve each problem. When you have completed the exercises, check your answers against the answer explanations that follow.

1. If the perimeter of a rectangle is 64 yards and the width is 60 feet, the length is

   1-A　12 yd.

   1-B　24 yd.

   1-C　52 yd.

   1-D　64 yd.

2. How many yards of fencing are needed to enclose a rectangular yard of 112 feet by 84 feet?

   2-A　$65\frac{1}{3}$

   2-B　$130\frac{2}{3}$

   2-C　196

   2-D　392

3. A square is equal in area to a rectangle with a length of 16 and a width of 4. Find the perimeter of the square.

   3-A　20

   3-B　32

   3-C　64

   3-D　128

4. The dimensions of a rectangular living room are 12 feet by 18 feet. How many square yards of carpeting are needed to cover the floor?

   4-A　24 sq. yd.

   4-B　72 sq. yd.

   4-C　216 sq. yd.

   4-D　1,944 sq. yd.

5. A piece of wire is shaped to enclose a square with an area of 144 square inches. It is then reshaped to enclose a rectangle with a length of 14 inches. The area of the rectangle, in square inches, is

   5-A　20 sq. in.

   5-B　24 sq. in.

   5-C　48 sq. in.

   5-D　140 sq. in.

6. The area of a 3-foot sidewalk around a community swimming pool that is 60 feet long and 15 feet wide is

   6-A　126 sq. ft.

   6-B　234 sq. ft.

   6-C　450 sq. ft.

   6-D　486 sq. ft.

7. The figure below is composed of 5 equal squares. If the area of the figure is 125, find its perimeter.

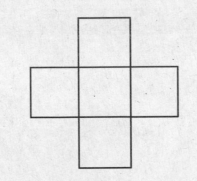

   7-A　120

   7-B　60

   7-C　50

   7-D　25

8. If the area of a square with side x is 10, what is the area of a square with side $4x$?

   8-A   10

   8-B   16

   8-C   160

   8-D   320

9. What will it cost to carpet a room that is 9 feet wide and 12 feet long if carpeting costs $18.90 per square yard?

   9-A $132.30

   9-B $226.80

   9-C $396.90

   9-D $2,041.20

10. The back of a pickup truck that is 6 feet long, 3 feet wide, and 2 feet high is solidly packed with bricks with these dimensions: 6 inches, 3 inches, and 2 inches. The number of bricks in the back of the truck is

   10-A   36

   10-B   132

   10-C   1,728

   10-D   62,208

ANSWER KEY AND EXPLANATIONS

1. A	3. B	5. D	7. B	9. B
2. B	4. A	6. D	8. C	10. C

1-A   Make a sketch.

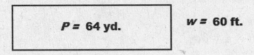

$P =$ **64 yd.** $w =$ **60 ft.**

Perimeter $= 2(l + w)$. Let the length be x yards.

Each width $= 60$ ft., which is 20 yds.

$$2(x + 20) = 64$$
$$2x + 40 = 64$$
$$\underline{-40 = -40}$$
$$2x = 24$$
$$\frac{2x}{2} = \frac{24}{2}$$
$$x = 12$$

2-B   Make a sketch.

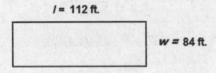

$l =$ **112 ft.**

$w =$ **84 ft.**

Perimeter $= 2(l + w)$
$\qquad\quad = 2(112 + 84)$
$\qquad\quad = 2 \cdot 196$ feet
$\qquad\quad = 392$ feet

$$392 \text{ feet} \times \frac{1 \text{ yard}}{3 \text{ feet}} = 130 \frac{2}{3} \text{ yards}$$

3-B   Make a sketch.

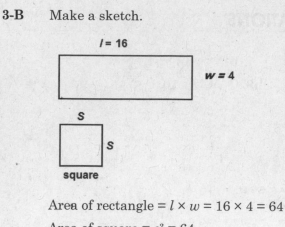

Area of rectangle = $l \times w = 16 \times 4 = 64$

Area of square = $s^2 = 64$

$s = \sqrt{64} = 8$

Perimeter = $4\,(s) = 32$

4-A   Make a sketch.

Find the area in square feet and then convert to square yards by dividing by 9. Remember, there are 9 square feet in one yard.

$(12 \times 18) \div 9 = 216 \div 9 = 24$ square yards

5-D   Make a sketch.

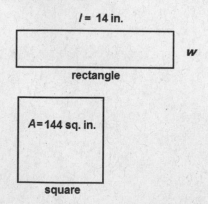

If the area of the square is 144 square inches, each side is $\sqrt{144} = 12$ inches and the perimeter is $4 \times 12 = 48$ inches. The perimeter of the rectangle is then 48 inches. If the two lengths are each 14 inches, their total is 28 inches. $48 - 28 = 20$ inches remain for the two widths. Therefore, each width is equal to $20 \div 2 = 10$ inches.

The area of the rectangle with length 14 inches and width 10 inches is $14 \times 10 = 140$ square inches.

6-D The sidewalk consists of the following:

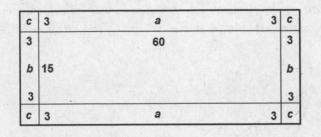

2 rectangles of length 60 feet and width 3 feet:
Area of each is $60 \times 3 = 180$ sq. ft.
Area of both = 360 sq. ft.

2 rectangles of length 15 feet and width 3 feet:
Area of each is $15 \times 3 = 45$ sq. ft.
Area of both = 90 sq. ft.

4 squares, each having a side of 3 feet:
Area of each square is $3^2 = 9$ sq. ft.
Area of 4 squares = 36 sq. ft.
Area of walk = $360 + 90 + 36 = 486$ sq. ft.

You may also solve this problem by finding the area of the pool and the area of the pool plus the sidewalk, and then subtracting to find the area of only the sidewalk.

Area of pool is 900 sq. ft.

Area of pool + sidewalk = $(15 + 3 + 3) \times (60 + 3 + 3) = 21 \times 66 = 1,386$ sq. ft.

Area of only the sidewalk = $1,386 - 900 = 486$ sq. ft.

7-B Area of each square = $\frac{1}{5} \cdot 125 = 25$

Side of each square = 5
Perimeter is made up of 12 sides: $12(5) = 60$

8-C $$x^2 = 10$$
$$(4x)^2 = 16x^2 = 16 \cdot 10 = 160$$

9-B The room is 3 yards by 4 yards or 12 square yards.
$(\$18.90)(12) = \$226.80$

10-C Convert the dimensions of the back of the truck to inches:

6 feet = 72 inches
3 feet = 36 inches
2 feet = 24 inches

Volume of back of truck = $72 \times 36 \times 24$ cubic inches
$\qquad\qquad\qquad\quad = 62,208$ cubic inches

Volume of each brick = $6 \times 3 \times 2 = 36$ cubic inches
$\qquad\qquad 62,208 \div 36 = 1,728$ bricks

TRIANGLES

A *triangle* is a closed figure made of three line segments. All triangles have three angles. Triangles can vary in size and shape. These triangles are shaped differently.

The sum of a triangle's angles is always 180°. If you know the measure of two angles in a triangle, you can find the measure of the third angle by subtracting the first two from 180°.

Example: Two angles of a triangle are 90° and 45°. What is the third angle?

SOLUTION: 90° + 45°= 135°

           180° − 135° = 45°

           The third angle is 45°.

There are different types of triangles:

- An **isosceles triangle** has two equal sides and two equal angles.
- An **equilateral triangle** has three equal sides and three equal angles. Each angle in an equilateral triangle measures 60°.
- A **scalene triangle** has no equal sides.
- An **obtuse triangle** has one angle that is greater than 90°.
- An **acute triangle** has three angles that measure less than 90°.

A *right triangle* has a right angle, which is 90°. The other two angles of a right triangle are *complimentary*, which means their measures add up to 90°. The side opposite the right angle is called the *hypotenuse*, and it is the longest side. The other two sides are called *legs*.

In this right triangle below, the hypotenuse is *BC*. *AB* and *AC* are the legs.

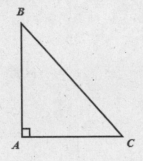

Triangle *ABC* is obtuse; triangle *DEF* is acute in the graphics below.

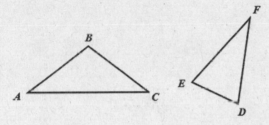

Pythagorean Theorem

The *Pythagorean theorem* states that $a^2 + b^2 = c^2$ or $c^2 = a^2 + b^2$.

The hypotenuse in the triangle below is represented by the letter *C*, and *A* and *B* are the legs of the triangle.

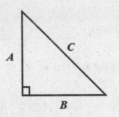

The Pythagorean theorem is sometimes worded differently, depending on the way the triangle is labeled. The points of the following triangle are labeled, but not the sides. For this triangle, the Pythagorean theorem is written this way:

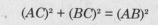
$$(AC)^2 + (BC)^2 = (AB)^2$$

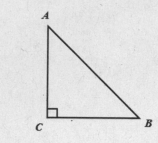

Example: Find the hypotenuse (h) in the triangle below.

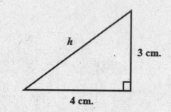

SOLUTION: $a^2 + b^2 = h^3$

$(3)^2 + (4)^2 = h^2$

$25 = h^2$

$\sqrt{25} = h$

$5 = h$

The length of the hypotenuse (h) is 5 centimeters.

Example: One leg of a right triangle is 15 inches. The hypotenuse is 17 inches. How long is the other leg?

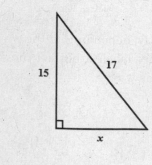

SOLUTION: $a^2 + b^2 = c^2$

$$(15)^2 + b^2 = (17)^2$$
$$225 + b^2 = 289$$
$$-225 \quad = -225$$
$$\overline{\qquad\qquad}$$
$$b^2 = 64$$
$$b = 8$$

The length of the other leg is 8 inches.

A *Pythagorean triple* is a set of three numbers that can be the sides of a right triangle. Memorizing the sets of triples can save you time when you take the test—if you recognize these numbers, you'll be able to find the correct answer without doing math. Also, multiples of these sets also form a Pythagorean triple.

Example: The Pythagorean triple 18-24-30 contains multiples of the set 3-4-5.

The following are some common Pythagorean triples:

3-4-5
6-8-10
5-12-13
8-15-17
7-24-25
10-24-26
12-35-37

Example: If one leg of a right triangle is 30 and the hypotenuse is 34, what is the other leg?

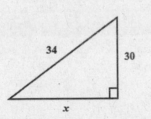

SOLUTION: You can find the answer by applying the Pythagorean theorem, but you'll answer the question much more quickly if you recognize that 30 is 2(15). This should alert you that the triangle is an 8-15-17 triple with each side multiplied by 2. Therefore, the length of the missing leg is 16.

An *isosceles right triangle* has two equal legs. The following applies to this type of triangle:

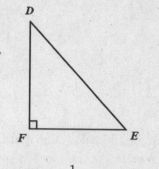

each leg = $\frac{1}{2}$ hypotenuse $\sqrt{2}$

hypotenuse = (leg) $\sqrt{2}$

$DF = EF = \frac{1}{2}(DE)\sqrt{2}$

$DE = (DF)\sqrt{2} = (EF)\sqrt{2}$

Example: In isosceles right triangle *XYZ*:

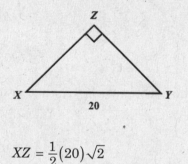

$XZ = \frac{1}{2}(20)\sqrt{2}$

$\quad\quad = 10\sqrt{2}$

$YZ = XZ = 10\sqrt{2}$

Area of a Triangle

To find the area of a triangle, multiply the base and the height and then multiply by $\frac{1}{2}$. The height of a triangle is the perpendicular distance between the highest vertex (point) and the base.

Use this formula to find the area of a triangle: $A = \frac{1}{2}bh$

Example: What is the area of a triangle with a height of 10 inches and a base of 8 inches?

SOLUTION: $\frac{1}{2} \times 10 \times 8 = \frac{1}{2} \times 80 = 40$ square inches

In a right triangle, one leg is the base and the other is the height. So, the area of a right triangle is $A = \frac{1}{2} \times$ leg 1 $\times$ leg 2.

Example: The legs of a right triangle are 12 and 16. Therefore, its area is $\frac{1}{2} \times 12 \times 16$ = 96 square units.

EXERCISES: TRIANGLES

Directions: Now try the exercises below. Each question is followed by four possible answers. Solve each problem. When you have completed the exercises, check your answers against the answer explanations that follow.

1. What is the length, in feet, of h in the triangle shown below.

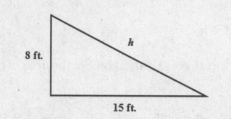

    1-A   15 ft.

    1-B   17 ft.

    1-C   23 ft.

    1-D   289 ft.

2. If the angles of a triangle are in the ratio of 3:4:5, what is the measure of the largest angle?

    2-A   12°

    2-B   15°

    2-C   60°

    2-D   75°

3. What is the area of the figure shown below?

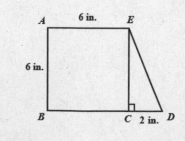

    3-A   14 sq. in.

    3-B   36 sq. in.

    3-C   42 sq. in.

    3-D   72 sq. in.

4. Find the area of a triangle with a base of 12 centimeters and a height of 7.5 centimeters less than the base.

    4-A   4.5 cm.²

    4-B   27 cm.²

    4-C   45 cm.²

    4-D   54 cm.²

5. In isosceles triangle ABC, the measure of angle C is 60° more than the measure of each base angle. Find the number of degrees of each base angle.

    5-A   30°

    5-B   40°

    5-C   100°

    5-D   130°

6. Two small planes leave an airport at the same time, one traveling west at 56 miles per hour and the other traveling north at 105 miles per hour. How many miles apart are the planes after two hours?

    6-A   17 miles

    6-B   119 miles

    6-C   238 miles

    6-D   560 miles

7. Melissa has placed a ladder 9 feet from the base of her house. The ladder rests on the house 12 feet off the ground. How long is the ladder?

    7-A   9 ft.

    7-B   12 ft.

    7-C   15 ft.

    7-D   30 ft.

8. Find the perimeter of right triangle *ABC* if the area of square *AEDC* is 144 and the area of square *BCFG* is 25.

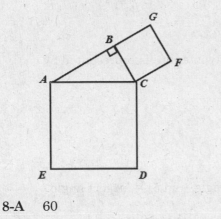

8-A 60

8-B 30

8-C 18

8-D 17

9. A certain triangle has sides that are 15 inches, 20 inches, and 25 inches long, respectively. A rectangle equal in area to that of the triangle has a width of 3 inches. The perimeter of the rectangle, expressed in inches, is

9-A 40 in.

9-B 45 in.

9-C 50 in.

9-D 106 in.

10. The angles of a triangle are in the ratio 1:2:9. This triangle is

10-A right.

10-B acute.

10-C isosceles.

10-D obtuse.

ANSWER KEY AND EXPLANATIONS

1. B	3. C	5. B	7. C	9. D
2. D	4. B	6. C	8. B	10. D

1-B Using the Pythagorean theorem, the hypotenuse is represented by c.

$$a^2 + b^2 = c^2$$
$$(15)^2 + (8)^2 = c^2$$
$$225 + 64 = 289$$
$$\sqrt{289} = 17\,\text{ft}.$$

2-D Let $3x$ = smallest angle, $4x$ = second angle, and $5x$ = largest angle.

The sum of the angles of a triangle is 180°, therefore:
$$3x + 4x + 5x = 180°$$
$$12x = 180°$$
$$x = 15°$$

Largest angle is $5x$ or $5(15) = 75$

3-C Area of $ABCE$ = $6 \times 6 = 36$ in.^{2}

Area of $ECD = \frac{1}{2}bh = \frac{1}{2}(2 \times 6) = \frac{1}{2}(12) = 6\,\text{in.}^2$

Total area = $36 + 6 = 42$ in.^{2}

4-B Base of triangle is 12 cm.

Height of triangle is 12 cm. − 7.5 = 4.5 cm.

Area of triangle = $\frac{1}{2}bh = \frac{1}{2}(12 \times 4.5) = \frac{1}{2}(54) = 27\,\text{cm.}^2$

5-B Let x = base angle   (Base angles of an isosceles triangle are equal.)

Then angle $C = x + 40$

$$x + x + x + 60 = 180$$
$$3x + 60 = 180$$
$$3x = 120$$
$$x = 40$$

6-C   The planes are flying in the shape of a right triangle. Begin by finding the length of the hypotenuse.

$$a^2 + b^2 = c^2$$

$$(56)^2 + (105)^2 = c^2$$

$$3{,}136 + 11{,}025 = 14{,}161$$

$$\sqrt{14{,}161} = 119$$

$$119 \times 2 = 238$$

The planes are 238 miles apart after two hours.

7-C   The ladder forms a right triangle. Use the Pythagorean theorem to find the length of the ladder, and the length of the hypotenuse.

$$a^2 + b^2 = c^2$$

$$(9)^2 + (12)^2 = c^2$$

$$81 + 144 = 225$$

$$\sqrt{225} = 15$$

The ladder is 15 ft. long.

8-B   Area of square $AEDC = s^2 = 144$

$$s = \sqrt{144} = 12$$

Area of square $BFCG = s^2 = 25$

$$s = \sqrt{25} = 5$$

Therefore, right triangle ABC is a 5-12-13 triangle.

Perimeter $5 + 12 + 13 = 30$

9-D   This is a 3-4-5 right triangle. Its area is:

$\dfrac{1}{2} \times 15 \times 20 = 150$ square inches   (area of a triangle is $\dfrac{1}{2}\,bh$)

Therefore, the area of the rectangle is also 150 square inches. If the width of the rectangle is 3 inches, the length is $150 \div 3 = 50$ inches. Then, the perimeter of the rectangle is $2(3 + 50) = 2 \times 53 = 106$ inches.

10-D   Represent the angles as x, $2x$, and $9x$.
They must add up to $180°$.

$$12x = 180$$

$$x = 15$$

The angles are $15°$, $30°$, and $135°$, so the triangle is an obtuse triangle.

POWERS, ROOTS, AND RADICALS

When you multiply two numbers to find a product, the numbers that you multiply are called *factors*. In the example below, 4 and 5 are factors.

Example: $4x \times 5 = 20$

Sometimes, a factor is written repeatedly. Suppose you had to write 3 as a factor 10 times, as in the example below.

Example: $3 \times 3 \times 3 \times 3 \times 3 \times 3 \times 3 \times 3 \times 3 \times 3 = 59{,}049$

Using an exponent makes it easier to write 3 to the tenth power—or even a higher power. The *exponent* indicates the number of times a factor is multiplied.

Example: 3^{10}

When you write a number raised to a power, as in the example above, the number is called the *base* and the power it is raised to is the *exponent*. In this case, 3 is the base and 10 is the exponent.

When you *square* a number, you raise it to the second power. The example below is "five squared."

Example: 5^2

When you *cube* a number, you raise it to the third power. The example below is "five cubed."

Example: 5^3

When the exponent is 4, you say the number has been raised to the "fourth power." The same is true if the exponent is 5, 6, 7, and so on.

A *perfect square* is a square of a whole number.

Example: 36 is a perfect square because $36 = 6^2$.

In the example above, 6 is the square root of 36. The *square root* of a number is written like this:

$$\sqrt{36} = 6$$

Example: $\sqrt{25} = 5$ means that the square root of 25 is 5, or $5 \times 5 = 25$.

Perfect Squares

You can use the table below to learn the most common perfect squares.

Number	Perfect Square	Number	Perfect Square
1	1	10	100
2	4	11	121
3	9	12	144
4	16	13	169
5	25	14	196
6	36	15	225
7	49	20	400
8	64	25	625
9	81	30	900

Finding Square Roots

If you're asked to identify the square root of a large number on the ASVAB, you might be able to choose the correct answer without devoting a great deal of time to answering the question. First, group the numbers into pairs. When there is an odd number of digits before the decimal point, insert a zero at the beginning of a number. When there is an odd number of digits after a decimal point, insert a zero at the end of the number. Now, pair off the numbers. For each pair of numbers, you will have one digit in the square root.

Example: The square root of 9,216 is exactly

    1-A   91

    1-B   96

    1-C   123

    1-D   257

SOLUTION: Pair off the numbers beginning at the decimal point: $\sqrt{9216}$. There are two pairs. This means that the correct answer has two digits, so you can eliminate answer choices C and D. Next, look for a number that when multiplied by itself, ends in 6. This is 6, since $6 \times 6 = 36$. Therefore, the correct answer choice is B: $96 \times 96 = 9,216$.

If you're asked to find the square root of a fraction, find the square root of the numerator and the denominator, as shown in the example below.

Example: $\sqrt{\dfrac{4}{25}} = \dfrac{\sqrt{4}}{\sqrt{25}} = \dfrac{2}{5}$

Cube Roots

Some numbers, such as 27, have three equal factors. Each factor is called a *cube root* of the number. This symbol indicates a cube root: $\sqrt[3]{}$

$\sqrt[3]{27} = 3$ because $3 \times 3 \times 3 = 27$

Radicals

This symbol is called a *radical sign*: $\sqrt{}$. The number underneath a radical sign is called the *radicand*.

Example: $\sqrt{144}$. The number 144 is the radicand and is underneath the radical sign.

Radicals can often be simplified using this formula if the factors chosen contain at least one perfect square: $\sqrt{ab} = \sqrt{a} \cdot \sqrt{b}$

Examples: $\sqrt{40} = \sqrt{10} \cdot \sqrt{4} = 2\sqrt{10}$

$$\sqrt{50} = \sqrt{25} \cdot \sqrt{2} = 5\sqrt{2}$$

$$\sqrt{98} = \sqrt{49} \cdot \sqrt{2} = 7\sqrt{2}$$

$$\sqrt{150} = \sqrt{25} \cdot \sqrt{6} = 5\sqrt{6}$$

When adding and subtracting radicals, add and subtract like terms, just as you would with algebraic expressions.

Like terms: $\sqrt{5}, 2\sqrt{5}$

Example: $\sqrt{5} + 2\sqrt{5} = 3\sqrt{5}$

Note: When a radical doesn't have a coefficient, it is considered to have a coefficient of 1.

Example: $2\sqrt{7} + 2\sqrt{7} - \sqrt{7} = 3\sqrt{7}$

Radicals with unlike terms can be added and subtracted if they can be simplified to be like terms.

Unlike terms: $\sqrt{50}, \sqrt{8}$

Example: $\sqrt{50} - \sqrt{8}$

SOLUTION: $\sqrt{50} = \sqrt{25} \cdot \sqrt{2} = 5\sqrt{2}$

$$\sqrt{8} = \sqrt{4} \cdot \sqrt{2} = 2\sqrt{2}$$

Now, subtract the radicals:

$$5\sqrt{2} - 2\sqrt{2} = 3\sqrt{2}$$

When multiplying radicals, multiply the coefficients first and then the radicands.

Example: $3\sqrt{6} \cdot 2\sqrt{7} = 6\sqrt{42}$

Follow the same procedure when dividing: divide the coefficients first and then the radicands.

Example: $\dfrac{6\sqrt{50}}{3\sqrt{2}} = 2\sqrt{25} = 2 \cdot 5 = 10$

EXERCISES: POWERS, ROOTS, AND RADICALS

Directions: Now try the exercises below. Each question is followed by four possible answers. Solve each problem. When you have completed the exercises, check your answers against the answer explanations that follow.

1. The square of 8 is
   1-A   8
   1-B   16
   1-C   64
   1-D   81

2. The cube of 3 is
   2-A   27
   2-B   729
   2-C   6
   2-D   9

3. The fourth power of 4 is
   3-A   16
   3-B   64
   3-C   256
   3-D   1,024

4. In exponential form, the product $10 \times 10 \times 10 \times 10 \times 10$ may be written
   4-A 10×5
   4-B 5^{10}
   4-C 10^4
   4-D 10^5

5. The value of 2^7 is
   5-A   256
   5-B   128
   5-C   64
   5-D   32

6. Find: $\sqrt{\dfrac{1}{9}}$
   6-A   3
   6-B $\dfrac{1}{3}$
   6-C $\dfrac{1}{18}$
   6-D $\dfrac{1}{81}$

7. The sum of 3^2 and 3^3 is
   7-A   13
   7-B   27
   7-C   36
   7-D   63

8. The square root of 3,969 is exactly
   8-A   60
   8-B   61
   8-C   62
   8-D   63

9. $\sqrt{8} + \sqrt{50} =$
   9-A $7\sqrt{2}$
   9-B $7\sqrt{4}$
   9-C $10\sqrt{2}$
   9-D   58

10. Simplify: $\dfrac{9\sqrt{2}}{\sqrt{3}}$
    10-A $3\sqrt{3}$
    10-B $3\sqrt{6}$
    10-C $27\sqrt{3}$
    10-D $12\sqrt{3}$

ANSWER KEY AND EXPLANATIONS

1. C	3. C	5. B	7. C	9. A
2. A	4. D	6. B	8. D	10. B

1-C $8^2 = 8 \times 8 = 64$

2-A $3^3 = 3 \times 3 \times 3$
$= 9 \times 3$
$= 27$

3-C $4^4 = 4 \times 4 \times 4 \times 4$
$= 16 \times 16$
$= 256$

4-D $10 \times 10 \times 10 \times 10 \times 10 = 10^5$

5-B $2^7 = 2 \times 2 \times 2 \times 2 \times 2 \times 2 \times 2 = 128$

6-B $\sqrt{\dfrac{1}{9}} = \dfrac{\sqrt{1}}{\sqrt{9}} = \dfrac{1}{3}$

7-C $3^2 = 9$

$3^3 = 27$

$9 + 27 = 36$

8-D The correct answer must be a number that when multiplied by itself, will end in 9. This happens only with 63 ($3 \times 3 = 9$).

$63 \times 63 = 3,969$

9-A $\sqrt{8} + \sqrt{50} =$

$\sqrt{4} \cdot \sqrt{2} + \sqrt{25} \cdot \sqrt{2} =$

$2\sqrt{2} + 5\sqrt{2}$

$7\sqrt{2}$

10-B $\dfrac{9\sqrt{2}}{\sqrt{3}} = \dfrac{9\sqrt{2}}{\sqrt{3}} \cdot \dfrac{\sqrt{3}}{\sqrt{3}} = \dfrac{9\sqrt{6}}{3} = 3\sqrt{6}$

answers exercises

EXPONENTS AND SEQUENCES

Exponents

You learned earlier that an exponent raises a number to a power. Exponents follow the ten laws demonstrated by the following examples:

Law I: $x^1 = x$

Example: $5^1 = 5$

Law II: $y^0 = 1$

Example: $5^0 = 1$

Law III: $y^{-1} = \dfrac{1}{y}$

Example: $3^{-1} = \dfrac{1}{3}$

Law IV: $x^a x^b = x^{a+b}$

Example: $y^2 y^3 = y^{2+3} = y^5$

Law V: $\dfrac{x^a}{x^b} = x^{a-b}$

Example: $\dfrac{y^6}{y^3} = y^{6-3} = y^3$

Law VI: $(x^a)^b = x^{ab}$

Example: $(y^2)^3 = y^{2 \times 3} = y^6$

Law VII: $(xy)^a = x^a y^a$

Example: $(xy)^3 = x^3 y^3$

Law VIII: $\left(\dfrac{x}{y}\right)^a = \dfrac{x^a}{y^a}$

Example: $\left(\dfrac{1}{2}\right)^2 = \dfrac{1^2}{2^2} = \dfrac{1}{4}$

Law IX: $x^{-a} = \dfrac{1}{x^a}$

Example: $x^{-3} = \dfrac{1}{x^3}$

Law X: $x^{\frac{a}{b}} = \sqrt[b]{x^a}$

Example: $a^{\frac{2}{3}} = \sqrt[3]{a^2}$

More than one law may apply.

Examples: $(x^2y^2)^3 = x^6y^6$ (Laws VI and VII)

$$\frac{\left(x^{-3}\right)^{-2} \cdot x^2}{x^2} = \frac{x^6 \cdot x^2}{x^2} = \frac{x^8}{x^2} = x^6 \text{ (Laws IV, V, and VI)}$$

To solve equations with a variable and an exponent, express both sides of the equation as powers of the same base. Then, set the exponents equal to each other.

Example: Solve $3^x = 81$

SOLUTION: Write 81 as a power of 3.

$$3^x = 3 \times 3 \times 3 \times 3$$

$$x = 4$$

Example: Solve $216^x = \dfrac{1}{36}$

SOLUTION: $\left(6^3\right)^x = \dfrac{1}{6^2}$

$$6^{3x} = 6^{-2}$$

$$3x = -2$$

$$x = -\frac{2}{3}$$

Sequences

Numbers in a sequence follow a pattern. There are three main types of sequences:

1 **Arithmetic sequence**—Each term in a sequence is being increased or decreased by the same number. The number being added or subtracted is called the *common difference.*

   Example: 3, 6, 9, 12, 15, 18.....

Each term in this sequence is being increased by 3.

2 **Geometric sequence**—Each term in a sequence is being multiplied by the same number. The number each term is being multiplied by is called the *common ratio.*

   Example: 2, 4, 8, 16, 32, 64....

Each term in this sequence is being multiplied by 2.

3 **Miscellaneous sequence**—A sequence that is neither arithmetic nor geometric.

   Example: 10, 9, 11, 10, 12, 11, 13, 12, 14....

This sequence follows the pattern −1, +2

Finding Missing Terms

Follow these three steps to find the missing term in an ascending arithmetic sequence:

1 Subtract a number in the sequence from the number after it to find the common difference.

2 Add the common difference to the number before the missing term.

3 If the missing term is the first number in the sequence, subtract the common difference from the second term.

Example: In this sequence, what number follows 12?

$$2, 4\frac{1}{2}, 7, 9\frac{1}{2}, 12, \underline{\qquad}$$

SOLUTION: $4\frac{1}{2} - 2 = 2\frac{1}{2}, 9\frac{1}{2} - 7 = 2\frac{1}{2}$

The sequence is arithmetic, and the common difference is $2\frac{1}{2}$.

$$12 + 2\frac{1}{2} = 14\frac{1}{2}$$

The missing term is $14\frac{1}{2}$.

Follow these three steps to find the missing term in a descending arithmetic sequence:

1 Subtract a number in the sequence from the number after it to find the common difference.

2 Add the common difference to the number before the missing term.

3 If the missing term is the first number in the sequence, subtract the common difference from the second term.

Example: Find the first term in this sequence:

$$\underline{\qquad}, 48, 40, 32, 24, 16$$

SOLUTION: $16 − 24 = −8, 24 − 32 = −8$

The sequence is arithmetic; the common difference is −8.

$$48 − (−8) = 56$$

The term preceding 48 is 56.

Follow these three steps to find the missing term in a geometric sequence:

1 Divide any term by the one before it to find the common ratio.

2 Multiply the term before the missing term by the common ratio.

3 If the missing term is the first term, divide the second term by the common ratio.

Example: Find the missing term in this sequence:

$$7, 28, 112, 448, \underline{\hspace{1cm}}$$

SOLUTION: $28 \div 7 = 4, 112 \div 28 = 4$

The sequence is geometric, and the common ratio is 4.

$$448 \times 4 = 1,792$$

The missing term is 1,792.

Example: Find the missing term in this sequence:

$$\underline{\hspace{1cm}}, 500, 100, 20, 4$$

SOLUTION: $100 \div 500 = \frac{1}{5}$ (common ratio)

$$500 \div \frac{1}{5} = 500 \times \frac{5}{1} = 2,500$$

The first term is 2,500.

After you've determined that a sequence is neither arithmetic nor geometric, you know that it is miscellaneous. Follow these three steps to find the missing term in a miscellaneous sequence.

1 Experiment to see if the sequence involves a sequence of squares or cubes. A number may be first squared and then cubed.

2 If this isn't the case, then add the first and second term.

3 Then, add the second and third term, and so on.

EXERCISES: EXPONENTS AND SEQUENCES

> **Directions:** Now try the exercises below. Each question is followed by four possible answers. Solve each problem. When you have completed the exercises, check your answers against the answer explanations that follow.

1. $(x^5)^{-2} =$
   - 1-A　x^3
   - 1-B　x^7
   - 1-C　x^{-10}
   - 1-D　x^{10}

2. $\left(\dfrac{-4x^3}{4x}\right)^0 =$
   - 2-A　$-x^4$
   - 2-B　$-x^3$
   - 2-C　0
   - 2-D　1

3. Solve for y: $3^y = \dfrac{1}{9}$
   - 3-A　3
   - 3-B　2
   - 3-C　-3
   - 3-D　-2

4. $4^{2b} \div 16 =$
   - 4-A　$\left(\dfrac{1}{4}\right)^{2b}$
   - 4-B　4^b
   - 4-C　$\left(\dfrac{1}{4}\right)^{b-2}$
   - 4-D　4^{2b-2}

5. Simplify: $\dfrac{\left(x^{-3} \cdot x^4\right)^4}{x^{-7}}$
   - 5-A　x^{11}
   - 5-B　x^{-3}
   - 5-C　x^{-11}
   - 5-D　x^4

FOR ITEMS 6 TO 10, FIND THE MISSING TERM IN EACH OF THE SEQUENCES.

6. ____, 4, 9, 14
   - 6-A　-1
   - 6-B　0
   - 6-C　1
   - 6-D　$\dfrac{1}{2}$

7. 10, 20, 40, ____, 160
   - 7-A　60
   - 7-B　80
   - 7-C　100
   - 7-D　140

8. 62, 58, 54, ____ , 46, 42
   - 8-A　53
   - 8-B　52
   - 8-C　50
   - 8-D　48

9. 2.003, 2.006, 2.009, ____
   - 9-A　2.010
   - 9-B　2.09
   - 9-C　2.012
   - 9-D　2.009

10. 2, 5, 9, 14, ____
    - 10-A　22
    - 10-B　20
    - 10-C　18
    - 10-D　15

ANSWER KEY AND EXPLANATIONS

1. C	3. D	5. A	7. B	9. C
2. D	4. D	6. A	8. C	10. B

1-C $(x^5)^{-2} = x^{(5)(-2)} = x^{-10}$

2-D   Any number raised to the zero power is one.

3-D $3^2 = 9$

$3^{-2} = \dfrac{1}{9}$

4-D $4^{2b} \cdot \dfrac{1}{16} = 4^{2b} \cdot 4^{-2} = 4^{2b-2}$

5-A $\dfrac{\left(x^{-3} \cdot x^4\right)^4}{x^{-7}} = \dfrac{\left(x^1\right)^4}{x^{-7}} = \dfrac{x^4}{x^{-7}} = x^{11}$

6-A   This is an ascending arithmetic sequence in which the common difference is 5. The first term is $4 - 5 = -1$.

7-B   This is a geometric sequence in which the common ratio is 2. The missing term is $40 \times 2 = 80$.

8-C   This is a descending arithmetic sequence in which the common difference is -4. The missing term is $54 - 4 = 50$.

9-C   This is an ascending arithmetic sequence in which the common difference is 0.003. The missing term is $2.009 + 0.003 = 2.012$.

10-B   This sequence is neither arithmetic nor geometric. However, if you look carefully at the numbers, you'll see that they follow this pattern:

$2 + 3 = 5$

$5 + 4 = 9$

$9 + 5 = 14$

$14 + 6 = 20$

answers exercises

SUMMING IT UP

- Be sure to familiarize yourself with the following topics covered in this chapter: solving problems using algebra, transforming equations, and evaluating algebraic expressions; adding, subtracting, multiplying, and dividing signed numbers; working with polynomials and simplifying expressions by removing parentheses; using formulas to solve motion problems, percent problems, interest problems, and profit-and-loss problems; finding the circumference, area, and volume of circles; finding the perimeter, area, and volume of quadrilaterals; using the Pythagorean theorem and finding the area of triangles; understanding powers, roots, and radicals; learning perfect squares and finding square roots and cube roots; and understanding exponents and determining sequences.

- Use the exercises in this chapter to prepare for taking the Mathematics Knowledge sections in the three Practice Tests in Part V of this book.

- Check the answer keys to make sure you scored well on the exercises.

PART IV

OVERVIEW OF THE ASVAB VERBAL

An Introduction to ASVAB Verbal

chapter 7

OVERVIEW

- **General tips**
- **Six test-taking tips for the ASVAB verbal tests**
- **Word knowledge**
- **Paragraph comprehension**
- **Summing it up**

GENERAL TIPS

Verbal comprehension is an important part of everyone's life. Every day, you use your reading and writing skills to communicate with the world around you. The best way to improve your verbal comprehension skills is to read from material that interests you, such as newspapers, magazines, or novels.

It may be helpful to write down any unfamiliar words in a notebook and take a guess at their meaning. Try using alternate words in a sentence to figure out their definitions. Later, look up the meaning of each word in the dictionary. See how many words you were able to interpret on your own.

Word games and crossword puzzles are entertaining ways to improve your vocabulary skills. These games introduce you to words you might not encounter in your everyday reading material. Also, your local library is a great place to find a variety of books and periodicals on different topics that interest you.

The Internet is another wonderful resource for finding reading materials. The Web provides access to news articles, short stories, blogs, and poetry from around the world.

If you dedicate yourself to reading a little each day, you'll improve your chances of success on the ASVAB verbal tests.

SIX TEST-TAKING TIPS FOR THE ASVAB VERBAL TESTS

Keep the following tips in mind when you take the ASVAB Word Knowledge and Paragraph Comprehension subtests:

1 Be mindful of time. Don't spend more time than necessary on any one question. Some questions will take longer than others, so use your time wisely. Read the directions first so you understand what is required.

2 Concentrate on the test. Don't let your surroundings or the other test takers distract you. Keep your thoughts focused on what you're reading. If you take an interest in the topic, it will be easier to concentrate.

3 On the Paragraph Comprehension subtest, make sure you read the question first so you clearly understand what you need to look for as you read.

4 Many of the passages are about common topics. Base your answers only on what you read, and avoid thinking about what you may already know about the topic.

5 Eliminate obviously incorrect choices first. On both the Paragraph Comprehension and Word Knowledge subtests, you'll see answer choices that are either unrelated to the question or obviously incorrect. Eliminate these choices first to narrow down the correct answer. You can also ignore any answer choice that is only partly right. Be sure to select an answer that addresses all parts of the question.

6 It is OK to guess. Your test score is based on the number of questions you answer correctly, so it is perfectly acceptable to guess on some questions. Ignoring obviously incorrect answer choices will increase your odds of guessing correctly.

The following exercises will assess your verbal skills. You'll work on the Word Knowledge exercises first, followed by the Paragraph Comprehension questions. Read the directions carefully before beginning.

WORD KNOWLEDGE

Study the two sample questions below before trying the exercises.

Sample 1.   <u>Malevolent</u> most nearly means

     1-A fixed.

     1-B hateful.

     1-C tired.

     1-D woeful.

1-B   The root of *malevolent* is *mal*, which is Latin for *bad* or *evil*. Choices A and C are unrelated. Choice D, *woeful*, means unhappy or sad. *Hateful* is the best choice.

Sample 2.   The difficult question <u>bewildered</u> the students.

     2-A puzzled

     2-B angered

     2-C excited

     2-D moved

2-A   *Bewildered* is a synonym for *puzzled* and is therefore the correct answer. *Bewilder* means to perplex or confuse, especially by complexity or by a multitude of objects or considerations. A difficult question could easily *puzzle* or *bewilder* students. Choices B, C, and D are unrelated and incorrect.

EXERCISES: WORD KNOWLEDGE

Directions: Now try the exercises below. Each question has an underlined word. Select the answer choice that is closest in meaning to the underlined word. Check your answers against the answer key and explanations that follow.

1. The agile dancer leaps across the stage.
   1-A playful
   1-B harried
   1-C talented
   1-D graceful

2. Prevalent most nearly means
   2-A widespread.
   2-B improved.
   2-C adjacent.
   2-D dynamic.

3. A frugal shopper tries to find the best price.
   3-A casual
   3-B vigorous
   3-C economical
   3-D temperamental

4. Indigenous most nearly means
   4-A found.
   4-B native.
   4-C popular.
   4-D damaging.

5. The detective could not locate the elusive criminal.
   5-A funny
   5-B anxious
   5-C slippery
   5-D dangerous

6. Corrupt most nearly means
   6-A intelligent.
   6-B separate.
   6-C flexible.
   6-D crooked.

7. The museum has an authentic sword from the Middle Ages.
   7-A sturdy
   7-B detailed
   7-C genuine
   7-D valuable

8. Lavish most nearly means
   8-A excessive.
   8-B resourceful.
   8-C indescribable.
   8-D unmistakable.

9. The mother's voice pacified the crying infant.
   9-A reached
   9-B soothed
   9-C elevated
   9-D delighted

10. Futile most nearly means
    10-A careless.
    10-B pointless.
    10-C tempered.
    10-D enraged.

ANSWER KEY AND EXPLANATIONS

1. D	3. C	5. C	7. C	9. B
2. A	4. B	6. D	8. A	10. B

1-D *Agile* means to move with quick, easy grace. Therefore, an *agile* dancer is a *graceful* dancer.

2-A The word *prevalent* refers to something that is *widespread* or common. For example, snowmobiles are *prevalent* in Alaska, meaning they are common in the cold-weather state.

3-C *Frugal* means to be careful in the management of money or *economical*. Therefore, a *frugal* shopper would try to find the best price to ensure that the most *economical* decision was made.

4-B *Indigenous* refers to anything that originated in or is *native* to a particular region. For example, lemurs are *indigenous* or *native* to Madagascar, meaning that they originated there.

5-C *Elusive* means difficult to pin down or *slippery*. Therefore, an *elusive* criminal is one who easily *slips* away from a crime scene.

6-D *Corrupt* means morally degraded or *crooked*. For example, a judge who accepts bribes is corrupt or crooked.

7-C *Authentic* means real or *genuine*. In the sentence, this means that the sword is literally from the Middle Ages.

8-A *Lavish* means to go beyond a normal degree or *excessive*. For example, a *lavish* meal is one that is *excessive* in amount or quality.

9-B The best synonym for *pacified* is *soothed*. A mother's voice has the ability to calm, quiet, and *soothe* her crying baby.

10-B The word *futile* means *pointless*. For example, it would be *futile* or *pointless* to try to lasso the moon; it simply can't be done.

answers exercises

PARAGRAPH COMPREHENSION

Study the two sample questions below before trying the exercises.

Sample 1.   Harry Houdini was a stage magician and an escape artist who rose to fame during the early twentieth century. After struggling to break into show business for several years, Houdini caught a big break when a theater manager saw his handcuff act. Soon, Harry's amazing illusions and death-defying stunts made him an international star. Though Harry made a living by performing stage tricks, he was also a vocal opponent of psychics and mediums. He even lobbied Congress to pass a bill that would make it illegal for anyone to profit from telling fortunes.

Which of the following can be inferred according to the passage?

1-A Houdini's stunts were not dangerous.

1-B Houdini did not believe in psychics.

1-C Houdini had few admirers.

1-D Houdini disliked his job.

1-B   When you infer, you draw a conclusion based on what you have read. The passage tells you that Houdini was an opponent of psychics and that he lobbied Congress to pass a bill that would make it illegal for anyone to profit from telling fortunes. From this, you can infer that Houdini did not believe in psychics. Choice A is incorrect because the passage describes Houdini's stunts as "death-defying," and choice C is incorrect because the passage says that the magician was an international star. Based on the information in the paragraph, you can't assume that Houdini disliked his job. Therefore, choice D is also incorrect.

Sample 2.   Letting your dog out several times a day and waiting patiently by the door for him to finish his business can make you feel more like a door attendant than a pet owner. You can end the constant opening and closing of the door by installing a dog door. First, determine the size of the door you need. Measure your dog's height and width to ensure that you purchase the right-sized door. You will also need a jigsaw and an electric drill to complete this project. You may want to remove the door from its hinges and take it outside before you start sawing to avoid a housekeeping headache later. Trace the outline for the door using the template provided by the manufacturer. Use the jigsaw to cut the door's opening. Line up the frames of the dog door on both sides of the door and screw the frame into place using the electric drill. Secure the flap and replace the door on its hinges. Now your dog has the freedom to go outside whenever he pleases.

The author probably suggests taking the door outside before sawing because

2-A the saw is too big to use indoors.

2-B sawing creates a mess.

2-C the saw will scare your pets.

2-D sawing is dangerous.

2-B The sixth sentence tells you that choice B is correct—the reason you might want to take the door outside is because sawing is messy. Choice A is incorrect because the author never mentions the size of the jigsaw. Choice C is incorrect because it is unrelated to the question. Though sawing is dangerous, the author doesn't say that sawing outside is any safer than sawing indoors. Therefore, choice D is also incorrect. Choice B is the correct answer.

EXERCISES: PARAGRAPH COMPREHENSION

Directions: Now try the exercises below. Choose the best answer for each question. As you finish each exercise, check your answers against the answer key and explanations that follow.

QUESTIONS 1 AND 2 ARE BASED ON THE FOLLOWING PASSAGE.

St. Martin is a tropical island about 180 miles east of Puerto Rico. Though Columbus claimed the 34-square-mile island for Spain in 1493, the territory is now divided between France and the Netherland Antilles. During the mid-seventeenth century, the Spanish, French, and Dutch fought for control of the tiny island, which was valued both for its location and for its large salt deposits. After the Spanish left the island, control shifted between the French and the Dutch for several decades. In 1648, the two sides agreed to divide the island, giving the French control of the northern portion and the Dutch control of the southern portion. The two sides have cohabited peacefully since then.

1. Which of the following makes a good title for this passage?
   - **1-A** "Plan a Trip to St. Martin"
   - **1-B** "Columbus's Discoveries"
   - **1-C** "Islands of the Caribbean"
   - **1-D** "The History of St. Martin"

2. As used in the last sentence, the word *cohabited* probably means
   - **2-A** argued often.
   - **2-B** lived together.
   - **2-C** moved around.
   - **2-D** established contact.

3. Job interviews can be nerve wracking, but preparing beforehand will quell your fears and increase your chances of landing the job. First, decide how you can best market yourself to a particular employer. Have a clear job goal in mind when you go into the interview. Do not assume that a potential employer will know which job best suits you. During the conversation, mention previous work experiences that highlight your skills. Always bring a résumé and a list of references to the interview. Be prepared to toot your own horn and talk about your accomplishments. Remember, you want to market yourself as the best candidate for the job. After the interview, follow up with a letter thanking the employer for the opportunity.

Which of the following statements is TRUE according to the passage?
   - **3-A** Potential employers should know which job best suits your skills.
   - **3-B** It is impolite to talk about your accomplishments at an interview.
   - **3-C** You need to sell yourself as the best potential employee.
   - **3-D** It is unnecessary to bring a résumé to an interview.

4. In baseball, an umpire's ruling can change the fate of any game. Therefore, it is important that all Major League umpires have the proper training and experience to officiate America's national pastime. Potential umpires must attend a five-week training course during baseball's off-season. Here, students not only learn the rules of baseball, but also receive a crash course in the philosophy of umpiring. After graduation, many umpires spend seven to ten years working in the minor leagues before getting called up to the

"big show." Major League Baseball also requires that umpires have excellent vision, a high school diploma or GED, and good communication skills.

The phrase "big show" probably refers to

4-A the major leagues.

4-B the minor leagues.

4-C an important game.

4-D umpire training school.

5. Uluru is a large rock formation in central Australia. Formed 500 million years ago, Uluru is one of the oldest rock formations on Earth. Geologists believe that the formation is the only visible remnant of an ancient mountain range that slowly eroded over a period of millions of years. Several aboriginal tribes consider Uluru sacred because the rock plays a major role in their creation stories. For this reason, they ask that tourists refrain from climbing the rock. Climbing the rock is also very dangerous to tourists and to the plants and animals that call Uluru home. Visitors can still appreciate Uluru's beauty by walking around its base.

Which of the following statements would the author agree with?

5-A Visitors should scale Uluru to enjoy the view.

5-B Geologists do not know when Uluru formed.

5-C Glaciers probably created Uluru.

5-D Tourists should not climb Uluru.

QUESTIONS 6 AND 7 ARE BASED ON THE FOLLOWING PASSAGE.

Though some people do not consider cheerleading a sport, researchers now agree that the popular activity is the most dangerous girls' sport in the United States. Over the years, cheerleading has transformed into an extremely technical and physically demanding sport. Most injuries occur while athletes perform aerial stunts or complicated flips. The National Center for Catastrophic Sports Injury Research found that 65 percent of all serious injuries in high school female athletes during the last twenty-five years were the result of cheerleading accidents. In recent years, dozens of cheerleaders at the high school and college levels have suffered head, spinal, and internal injuries, sometimes leading to paralysis and death. Officials with the American Association of Cheerleading Coaches and Administrators are attempting to prevent serious injuries by implementing new national safety standards.

6. The author's primary message is that

6-A cheerleaders are popular.

6-B cheerleading is dangerous.

6-C cheerleading is not difficult.

6-D cheerleaders are not athletes.

7. The author of this passage would probably agree that

7-A parents should not encourage girls to join cheerleading.

7-B officials must do more to ensure cheerleaders' safety.

7-C cheerleading is not as dangerous as other sports.

7-D cheerleaders should perform more aerial stunts.

8. Feng shui is an ancient Chinese philosophy of aesthetics that seeks to increase positive energy through the arrangement of various objects. The Chinese believe that the world is made of ch'i, the life force inherent in all things. Feng shui teaches practitioners how to balance ch'i in any given space to improve happiness, health, and prosperity. Though the practice has many complicated rules, most of its design principles are rooted in common

exercises

sense. To create a peaceful and positive space, feng shui experts recommend keeping rooms clean and free of clutter, letting in as much natural light as possible and arranging furniture to create a natural flow.

Which of the following can be inferred according to the passage?

8-A   Balance is more important than flow in feng shui.

8-B   You can increase ch'i by installing more lights.

8-C   Many interior designers use feng shui.

8-D   Few people practice feng shui today.

QUESTIONS 9 AND 10 ARE BASED ON THE FOLLOWING PASSAGE.

During the late nineteenth century, young boys from poor families distributed most of the newspapers in New York City. Known as newsboys, these children stood on street corners shouting the day's headlines in an effort to drum up business. Newsboys were not employees of newspaper publishers. Instead, they purchased stacks of 100 papers at wholesale prices and attempted to sell them for a profit by the end of the day. At the time, the two leading papers were William Randolph Hearst's *New York Journal* and Joseph Pulitzer's *New York World*. When newspaper sales dropped off following the end of the Spanish-American War, the two publishers increased the cost of a wholesale stack. The newsboys organized a strike against Hearst and Pulitzer in an effort to get the publishers to lower prices. For several days in July 1899, hundreds of children crowded the streets of New York City, disrupting traffic and stalling news distribution. In the end, the publishers reached an agreement with the newsboys by offering to buy back unsold newspapers.

9. Which of the following statements would the author agree with?

9-A   The newsboys did not get what they wanted.

9-B   Children should not work for newspaper publishers.

9-C   Newsboys were not important to news distribution.

9-D   People did not want to read about the war.

10. Which of the following statements is TRUE according to the passage?

10-A   Newsboys worked for newspaper publishers.

10-B   The price increase did not affect newsboys.

10-C   The war helped Hearst and Pulitzer sell papers.

10-D   The strike did not affect life in New York City.

ANSWER KEY AND EXPLANATIONS

1. D	3. C	5. D	7. B	9. A
2. B	4. A	6. B	8. C	10. C

1-D Choice D, "The History of St. Martin," is the best title because the main idea of the passage is to explain the island's history. Choice A is incorrect because it is unrelated to the passage. Choice C is too general. Choice B reflects only a small detail mentioned in the passage, not the main point.

2-B The only correct answer is choice B, *lived together. Cohabit* means to live together or in company. Choice A is incorrect because the sentence tells you that the French and the Dutch were peaceful. Choice C is incorrect because the French and the Dutch were already settled. Choice D is also wrong because the two sides were already in contact with each other.

3-C In the eighth sentence, the author says that you need to market yourself as the best candidate for the job.

4-A The phrase "big show" refers to the major leagues. Choice B is incorrect because the author says that umpires spend seven to ten years in the minor leagues before moving to the "big show." Choice C is incorrect because it is too general. Choice D is incorrect because umpires must attend school before going to the "big show."

5-D Choice D is correct because the author says that climbing the rock is not only dangerous, but also disrespectful to the traditions of the aboriginal people. Choice A is incorrect because the author says that visitors can appreciate the rock's beauty by walking around its base. Choice B is incorrect because the author says that geologists believe that the rock formed 500 million years ago. Choice C is also incorrect because the passage states that the rock is a remnant of an ancient mountain range.

6-B The main idea is that cheerleading is a dangerous sport that leads to dozens of injuries every year. Therefore, choice B is correct. Choice A is incorrect because there is nothing in the passage to support this claim. Choice C is incorrect because the author calls cheerleading stunts "complicated," and choice D is incorrect because the author refers to cheerleaders as athletes.

7-B The author would agree with choice B—officials must do more to ensure cheerleaders' safety. Choice A is incorrect because nothing in the passage supports this statement. Choice C is incorrect because the author says that cheerleading is the most dangerous girls' sport. Choice D is also incorrect because the author states that aerial stunts lead to injuries.

8-C Since feng shui deals with the placement of objects, you can assume that interior designers use the practice. There is no evidence for choices A, B, and D.

9-A Although the publishers agreed to buy back unsold newspapers, the newsboys' goal was to get them to lower the price of a wholesale stack. Choice A is correct because the newsboys did not achieve this goal. Choice B is incorrect because it is unrelated to the passage. Choice C is incorrect because the passage says that the newsboys' strike disrupted news distribution. Choice D is also incorrect because the passage tells you that newspaper sales dropped off after the war ended. This tells you that people were interested in reading about the war.

10-C Choice C is correct because the passage tells you that sales of newspapers dropped off once the war ended. Choice A is incorrect because the passage tells you that newspaper publishers did not employ newsboys. Choice B is incorrect because the newsboys could not afford the price increase. Choice D is also incorrect because the passage says that the strike disrupted traffic and news distribution.

SUMMING IT UP

- Read a little every day to improve your verbal skills. Select reading material that interests you and take the time to look up the definitions of unfamiliar words.

- Keep an eye on the time when taking the ASVAB verbal tests.

- Try not to let your environment or other test takers distract you.

- On the Paragraph Comprehension subtest, read the question first so you know what to look for as you read.

- Base your answers only on what you read.

- Eliminate obviously incorrect answer choices first.

- Guess when you don't know the answer. Your score is based on the number of questions you answer correctly.

Word Knowledge

OVERVIEW

- Familiar words
- Context clues
- Word parts
- Summing it up

FAMILIAR WORDS

The ability to recognize and define familiar words is vital to your success on the ASVAB Word Knowledge subtest. You use most of the words on the test in your everyday communications. You might see these words in newspapers, magazines, or work memos. The best way to prepare for the Word Knowledge subtest is to read a little every day. If you encounter a word you don't recognize, look it up in the dictionary. Try to memorize the meaning of the word, so you'll recognize it later.

Make a list of unfamiliar words and study it a few nights every week. This will help you improve your vocabulary. You might also enjoy playing word games, such as crossword puzzles, to learn new words.

Completing Familiar Words exercises 1 through 3 will sharpen your vocabulary skills by asking you to find synonyms for a variety of words. A *synonym* is a word that has the same or nearly the same meaning as the test word. When taking the Word Knowledge subtest, look for the word or phrase that has the same meaning as the underlined word.

chapter 8

EXERCISES: FAMILIAR WORDS 1

Directions: Now try the exercises below. Each question has an underlined word. Select the answer that is closest in meaning to the underlined word. Check your answers against the answer key and explanations that follow.

1. Jeer most nearly means
   1-A   trail.
   1-B   waste.
   1-C   taunt.
   1-D   scare.

2. Divulge most nearly means
   2-A   examine.
   2-B   shape.
   2-C   classify.
   2-D   reveal.

3. Gruff most nearly means
   3-A   content.
   3-B   rough.
   3-C   loyal.
   3-D   filthy.

4. Sly most nearly means
   4-A   jolly.
   4-B   clever.
   4-C   eager.
   4-D   greedy.

5. Relevant most nearly means
   5-A   pertinent.
   5-B   liberated.
   5-C   adjusted.
   5-D   indulgent.

6. Tedious most nearly means
   6-A   solemn.
   6-B   anonymous.
   6-C   tiresome.
   6-D   aggressive.

7. Zeal most nearly means
   7-A   passion.
   7-B   harmony.
   7-C   patience.
   7-D   aptitude.

8. Hazard most nearly means
   8-A   intention.
   8-B   freedom.
   8-C   courtesy.
   8-D   danger.

9. Objective most nearly means
   9-A   blame.
   9-B   goal.
   9-C   honor.
   9-D   whole.

10. Valor most nearly means
   10-A   concern.
   10-B   stress.
   10-C   courage.
   10-D   sorrow.

11. Query most nearly means
   11-A   statement.
   11-B   intrigue
   11-C   question.
   11-D   problem.

12. Negligence most nearly means
   12-A   devotion.
   12-B   carelessness.
   12-C   function.
   12-D   sluggishness.

13. <u>Uncouth</u> most nearly means
    13-A crude.
    13-B original.
    13-C lively.
    13-D harmful.

14. <u>Eternal</u> most nearly means
    14-A hopeless.
    14-B imperfect.
    14-C humorous.
    14-D everlasting.

15. <u>Callous</u> most nearly means
    15-A unfeeling.
    15-B disgusting.
    15-C impaired.
    15-D afflicted.

16. <u>Exotic</u> most nearly means
    16-A timeless.
    16-B delicate.
    16-C foreign.
    16-D gorgeous.

17. <u>Haggard</u> most nearly means
    17-A arrogant.
    17-B exhausted.
    17-C indulgent.
    17-D reluctant.

18. <u>Wither</u> most nearly means
    18-A attract.
    18-B shrivel.
    18-C provoke.
    18-D launch.

19. <u>Advocate</u> most nearly means
    19-A labor.
    19-B suspend.
    19-C educate.
    19-D support.

20. <u>Irate</u> most nearly means
    20-A plain.
    20-B pitiful.
    20-C angry.
    20-D clumsy.

exercises

ANSWER KEY AND EXPLANATIONS

1. C	5. A	9. B	13. A	17. B
2. D	6. C	10. C	14. D	18. B
3. B	7. A	11. C	15. A	19. D
4. B	8. D	12. B	16. C	20. C

1-C   *Jeer* means to mock or *taunt*. For example, an audience might *jeer* or *taunt* a comedian for being unfunny. Therefore, choice C is correct. Choices A, B, and D are unrelated to the word.

2-D   *Divulge* means to make known or *reveal*. You might *divulge* or *reveal* a secret to one of your close friends. Choice A, *examine*, means to study, so this isn't correct. As a verb, *shape* means to form. Therefore, choice B is incorrect. *Classify* means to categorize, so choice C is also incorrect.

3-B   *Gruff* means coarse or *rough*. A *gruff* voice would sound *rough*. *Content* means happy and *loyal* means faithful, so choices A and C are incorrect. *Filthy* means dirty, so choice D is also incorrect.

4-B   *Sly* means *clever* or slightly mischievous. For example, you may be familiar with the idiom *sly as a fox*, which is used to describe someone who is cunning or smart. Therefore, choice B is the correct answer.

5-A   *Relevant* means *pertinent*. A commonly related word is *relative*, meaning having relation or connection to something. During a criminal trial, lawyers can only introduce information or material that is *relevant* or *pertinent* to the case.

6-C   *Tedious* means *tiresome*. For example, a student might find lectures *tedious*. Choice A is incorrect because *solemn* means serious. *Anonymous* means unidentified, so choice B is incorrect. Choice D is also incorrect because *aggressive* means violent or hostile.

7-A   *Zeal* means *passion*. It is related to the word *zealous*, which means characterized by zeal. You have probably heard people described as *overzealous*, meaning that they are exceedingly passionate about a person, a cause, or an ideal.

8-D   As a noun, *hazard* means *danger*. *Intention* means purpose, so choice A is incorrect. Choice B is incorrect because *freedom* means liberty. *Courtesy* means civility, so choice C is also incorrect.

9-B   As a noun, *objective* means *goal*. For example, state exams often test students on various learning *objectives*, or *goals*, to see what they have learned.

10-C   *Valor* means *courage*. Choice A is incorrect because *concern* means worry. *Stress* means pressure or strain, so choice B is incorrect. Choice D is incorrect because *sorrow* means sadness.

11-C   *Query* means *question* or inquiry. For example, a business e-mail might ask you to respond to a *query* quickly.

12-B *Negligence* means *carelessness*, or the failure to exercise the caution that a responsible person usually takes. For example, victims of physician *negligence* will often sue for damages because their doctors didn't exercise proper caution.

13-A *Uncouth* is an adjective used to describe a *crude* or rude person or action. For example, an *uncouth* joke might offend some people.

14-D *Eternal* means *everlasting*. For example, many explorers searched for the legendary Fountain of Youth in hopes of learning the secret to *eternal* life.

15-A *Callous* means *unfeeling* or showing no sympathy. Someone who is *callous* might regard the death of a friend's pet as no big deal and show little compassion.

16-C *Exotic* means *foreign* or unusual. At a nursery, you might find some plants from *foreign* countries marked as *exotic*. Choice A is incorrect because *timeless* means enduring. *Delicate* means fragile, so choice B is incorrect. Choice D is also incorrect because *gorgeous* means attractive.

17-B *Haggard* means to have a worn or *exhausted* appearance. Someone who was lost in the woods for days would appear *haggard*.

18-B *Wither* means to *shrivel*. Choice A is incorrect because *attract* means to draw attention. *Provoke* means to irritate, so choice C is incorrect. Choice D is also incorrect because *launch* means to toss.

19-D As a verb, *advocate* means to *support*. For example, an environmentalist would *advocate* or *support* legislation to reduce carbon emissions.

20-C *Irate* means *angry*. For example, after raising rates, an electric company received dozens of *irate* phone calls from its customers.

answers exercises

EXERCISES: FAMILIAR WORDS 2

Directions: Now try the exercises below. Each question has an underlined word. Select the answer that is closest in meaning to the underlined word. Check your answers against the answer key and explanations that follow.

1. Forgo most nearly means
   - 1-A   to take the blame.
   - 1-B   to praise loudly.
   - 1-C   to do without.
   - 1-D   to carry on.

2. Rescind most nearly means
   - 2-A   elect.
   - 2-B   cancel.
   - 2-C   improve.
   - 2-D   prescribe.

3. Ludicrous most nearly means
   - 3-A   distraught.
   - 3-B   frustrated.
   - 3-C   oblivious.
   - 3-D   ridiculous.

4. Imply most nearly means
   - 4-A   to insert.
   - 4-B   to suggest.
   - 4-C   to predict.
   - 4-D   to invest.

5. Enigma most nearly means
   - 5-A   mystery.
   - 5-B   uproar.
   - 5-C   response.
   - 5-D   myth.

6. Titanic most nearly means
   - 6-A   essential.
   - 6-B   diligent.
   - 6-C   colossal.
   - 6-D   inherent.

7. Wary most nearly means
   - 7-A   pensive.
   - 7-B   drastic.
   - 7-C   illicit.
   - 7-D   cautious.

8. Gullible most nearly means
   - 8-A   inane.
   - 8-B   naïve.
   - 8-C   overt.
   - 8-D   tidy.

9. Provocative most nearly means
   - 9-A   hideous.
   - 9-B   exciting.
   - 9-C   stubborn.
   - 9-D   complex.

10. Dormant most nearly means
    - 10-A   undecided.
    - 10-B   modest.
    - 10-C   inactive.
    - 10-D   difficult.

11. Constrict most nearly means
    - 11-A   to squeeze.
    - 11-B   to delay.
    - 11-C   to pacify.
    - 11-D   to remove.

12. Blemish most nearly means
    - 12-A   conflict.
    - 12-B   residue.
    - 12-C   snare.
    - 12-D   flaw.

13. <u>Jeopardy</u> most nearly means
    13-A central point.
    13-B in focus.
    13-C to find.
    13-D at risk.

14. <u>Mimic</u> most nearly means
    14-A ignore.
    14-B imitate.
    14-C pursue.
    14-D present.

15. <u>Staunch</u> most nearly means
    15-A firm.
    15-B evil.
    15-C serious.
    15-D smooth.

16. <u>Obscure</u> most nearly means
    16-A lowly.
    16-B broad.
    16-C unclear.
    16-D outspoken.

17. <u>Nonchalant</u> most nearly means
    17-A indifferent.
    17-B shrewd.
    17-C flimsy.
    17-D various.

18. <u>Rectify</u> most nearly means
    18-A gauge.
    18-B prevent.
    18-C supply.
    18-D correct.

19. <u>Vigor</u> most nearly means
    19-A guile.
    19-B vitality.
    19-C boldness.
    19-D beauty.

20. <u>Thrive</u> most nearly means
    20-A to thrill.
    20-B to alter.
    20-C to prosper.
    20-D to surprise.

exercises

ANSWER KEY AND EXPLANATIONS

1. C	5. A	9. B	13. D	17. A
2. B	6. C	10. C	14. B	18. D
3. D	7. D	11. A	15. A	19. B
4. B	8. B	12. D	16. C	20. C

1-C *Forgo* means *to do without*. For example, a dieter might *forgo* dessert in an effort to lose weight or a confident student might *forgo* studying the night before a test.

2-B *Rescind* means to *cancel* or take back. For example, "I had to *rescind* my offer to assist at the animal shelter after learning I was allergic to cats." Choices A, C, and D aren't synonyms for *rescind*.

3-D *Ludicrous* means *ridiculous*. A ludicrous idea is one that is so implausible that it is laughable. For example, "The teenager's parents quickly rejected his *ludicrous* request to take a road trip with some friends." *Distraught* and *frustrated* mean upset, so choices A and B are incorrect. *Oblivious* means unaware, so choice C is also incorrect.

4-B *Imply* means *to suggest*. For example, "His answer *implied* that he knew more than he was saying."

5-A *Enigma* means *mystery*. A person who is an *enigma* is *mysterious* or difficult to read. Choices B, C, and D aren't synonyms for *enigma*.

6-C *Titanic* means *colossal* or very large. The *RMS Titanic* was the largest passenger steamship in the world before its tragic destruction in 1912. Remembering this fact can help you recognize the meaning of *titanic* when you see it again in your reading.

7-D *Wary* means *cautious*. For example, "The mailman was *wary* of the barking dog." Choice A is incorrect because *pensive* means thoughtful. *Drastic* means radical, so choice B is incorrect. Choice C is also incorrect because *illicit* means illegal.

8-B *Gullible* means *naïve* or easy to fool. For example, criminals often prey on *gullible* tourists who are unfamiliar with a city. Criminals target these people because they are easy to trick.

9-B *Provocative* means *exciting* or provoking. For example, "The magazine received dozens of letters after running a *provocative* article on the mayor." Choices A, C, and D aren't synonyms for *provocative*.

10-C *Dormant* means asleep or *inactive*. For example, a volcano may remain *dormant* for years before violently erupting. *Dormant* comes from the past participle of the French word *dormir*, which means to sleep.

11-A *Constrict* means *to squeeze*. A boa constrictor is a snake that kills its prey by squeezing it to death. During the nineteenth century, many women used corsets to *constrict* or squeeze in the waistline. Use these examples to help you remember the meaning of *constrict*.

12-D A *blemish* is a *flaw* or defect. The word *blemish* is often used to refer to acne because the condition *flaws* a person's complexion. *Conflict*, *residue*, and *snare* aren't synonyms for blemish.

13-D *Jeopardy* means *at risk*. For example, "People who use illegal drugs put their lives in great jeopardy." Choices A, B, and C aren't synonyms for *jeopardy*.

14-B *Mimic* means *imitate*. For example, "Charles could *mimic* his father perfectly." Choice A is incorrect because *ignore* means to overlook. *Pursue* means follow, so choice C is incorrect. Choice D is also incorrect because *present* means to introduce.

15-A *Staunch* means *firm*. For example, "The politician is a *staunch* opponent of capital punishment." This means the politician is firmly against the death penalty.

16-C *Obscure* means *unclear*. For example, "The fog *obscured* the driver's vision." *Lowly*, *broad*, and *outspoken* aren't synonyms for *obscure*.

17-A *Nonchalant* means *indifferent*. Someone who is *nonchalant* is unconcerned. For example, "The actress had a *nonchalant* attitude toward her award nomination."

18-D *Rectify* means *correct*. For example, "The restaurant manager attempted to *rectify* the waiter's mistake by offering the customer a gift certificate." Choice A is incorrect because *gauge* means to measure. *Prevent* means to stop, so choice B is incorrect. Choice C is incorrect because *supply* means to provide.

19-B *Vigor* means *vitality*. Someone who is filled with *vigor* is enthusiastic and animated. *Vigor* is related to the word *vigorous*, which means forceful or spirited.

20-C *Thrive* means *to prosper*. For example, when a business *thrives*, it *prospers*, or succeeds in making a good profit.

answers exercises

EXERCISES: FAMILIAR WORDS 3

Directions: Now try the exercises below. Each question has an underlined word. Select the answer that is closest in meaning to the underlined word. Check your answers against the answer key and explanations that follow.

1. Bestow most nearly means
   1-A give.
   1-B scold.
   1-C reveal.
   1-D withhold.

2. Disperse most nearly means
   2-A claim.
   2-B keep.
   2-C scatter.
   2-D exclude.

3. Procure most nearly means
   3-A arouse.
   3-B obtain.
   3-C damage.
   3-D confess.

4. Sustain most nearly means
   4-A refuse.
   4-B support.
   4-C consider.
   4-D increase.

5. Lucid most nearly means
   5-A amusing.
   5-B bulky.
   5-C rude.
   5-D clear.

6. Unique most nearly means
   6-A essential.
   6-B tiresome.
   6-C unusual.
   6-D guarded.

7. Genial most nearly means
   7-A friendly.
   7-B useful.
   7-C bold.
   7-D silly.

8. Wily most nearly means
   8-A noisy.
   8-B lonely.
   8-C selfish.
   8-D crafty.

9. Hinder most nearly means
   9-A to give up.
   9-B to hold back.
   9-C to win over.
   9-D to make up.

10. Audacity most nearly means
    10-A boldness.
    10-B blessing.
    10-C agreement.
    10-D abundance.

11. Incongruous most nearly means
    11-A insincere.
    11-B reasonable.
    11-C inappropriate.
    11-D disorganized.

12. Overt most nearly means
    12-A serious.
    12-B random.
    12-C obvious.
    12-D avoidable.

13. <u>Yield</u> most nearly means
    - **13-A** to take over.
    - **13-B** to move up.
    - **13-C** to take back.
    - **13-D** to give in.

14. <u>Judicious</u> most nearly means
    - **14-A** exact.
    - **14-B** sensible.
    - **14-C** imaginative.
    - **14-D** judgmental.

15. <u>Narrate</u> most nearly means
    - **15-A** tell.
    - **15-B** ruin.
    - **15-C** correct.
    - **15-D** calculate.

16. <u>Meticulous</u> most nearly means
    - **16-A** effective.
    - **16-B** profitable.
    - **16-C** extreme.
    - **16-D** painstaking.

17. <u>Demure</u> most nearly means
    - **17-A** nimble.
    - **17-B** sharp.
    - **17-C** modest.
    - **17-D** small.

18. <u>Quell</u> most nearly means
    - **18-A** disturb.
    - **18-B** subdue.
    - **18-C** tempt.
    - **18-D** persuade.

19. <u>Chastise</u> most nearly means
    - **19-A** to forbid.
    - **19-B** to follow.
    - **19-C** to punish.
    - **19-D** to prevent.

20. <u>Strife</u> most nearly means
    - **20-A** struggle.
    - **20-B** complaint.
    - **20-C** opinion.
    - **20-D** summary.

exercises

ANSWER KEY AND EXPLANATIONS

1. A	5. D	9. B	13. D	17. C
2. C	6. C	10. A	14. B	18. B
3. B	7. A	11. C	15. A	19. C
4. B	8. D	12. C	16. D	20. A

1-A   *Bestow* means *give*. For example, "Each year, the academy *bestows* its highest honor on one deserving actress." Choice B is incorrect because *scold* means admonish. *Reveal* means show, so choice C is incorrect. Choice D is also incorrect because *withhold* is the opposite of *bestow*.

2-C   *Disperse* means *scatter* or move apart wildly. For example, "The police used tear gas to *disperse* the violent crowd." Choices A, B, and D aren't synonyms for *disperse*.

3-B   *Procure* means *obtain* or take possession of. For example, "The teacher *procured* new textbooks for the students."

4-B   *Sustain* means *support*. For example, "The atmosphere could not *sustain* life." Choice A is incorrect because *refuse* means decline. *Consider* means judge, so choice C is incorrect. Choice D is also incorrect because *increase* means boost.

5-D   *Lucid* means *clear* or not subject to misinterpretation. For example, "Please make the instructions as *lucid* as possible."

6-C   *Unique* means *unusual*. *Unique* comes from the Latin word *unicus*, meaning one. The word *unique* is often used to describe something singular or exceptional. For example, "The bride wanted a *unique* dress that everyone would remember."

7-A   *Genial* means *friendly*. Someone who is *genial* is kind, warm, and welcoming. For example, "The host welcomed her guest with a *genial* smile." Choices B, C, and D aren't synonyms for *genial*.

8-D   *Wily* means *crafty* or full of wiles. *Wile* is Scandinavian in origin and related to the Old Norse word *vēl*, meaning deceit or artifice. One way to remember the meaning of the word is to think of Wile E. Coyote from *Looney Tunes*. The character always thought of *crafty* ideas to trap the Road Runner.

9-B   *Hinder* means *to hold back* or impede. For example, "Snow *hindered* the search party's efforts." This means the snow held back the rescue party.

10-A   *Audacity* means *boldness*. It is related to the word *audacious*. This word comes from the Latin word *audēre*, which means to dare. For example, "I could not believe she had the *audacity* to show up to the party uninvited."

11-C   *Incongruous* means *inappropriate*. It is the opposite of the word *congruous*, which means appropriate. Choice A is incorrect because *insincere* means dishonest. *Reasonable* means the opposite of incongruous, so choice B isn't the correct answer. Although something *incongruous* may also be *disorganized*, the two words aren't synonyms.

12-C *Overt* means *obvious* or open. The word comes from the past participle of the French word *ovrir*, which means to open. Choices A, B, and D aren't synonyms for *overt*.

13-D As a verb, *yield* means *to give in*. For example, "The husband *yielded* control of the TV remote to his wife." You can remember the meaning of *yield* by thinking of the signs on highway entrance ramps. These signs ask you to *yield* or give the right-of-way to other drivers.

14-B *Judicious* means *sensible* or proceeding from good sense. The word is related to *judgment*, which means the forming of opinion through careful consideration. *Exact* and *imaginative* aren't synonyms for judicious. *Judgmental* seems like it would be related to *judicious*, but the word actually means critical.

15-A *Narrate* means *tell*. The word is related to the words *narrator* and *narrative*. A *narrator* is a character that tells a story in a novel or movie. A *narrative* is a fictional account of a series of events, usually told in the first person.

16-D *Meticulous* means *painstaking*. For example, "Our neighbor takes *meticulous* care of his lawn." Choice A is incorrect because *effective* means successful. *Profitable* means gainful, so choice B is incorrect. Choice C is also incorrect because *extreme* means excessive.

17-C *Demure* means *modest* or reserved. For example, "Joan wore a *demure* outfit to the job interview." Choices A, B, and D aren't synonyms for *demure*.

18-B *Quell* means *subdue*. The word comes from the Old English term *cwellan*, which means to kill. For example, "Taking a deep breath helped *quell* her fears."

19-C *Chastise* means *to punish*. For example, "The mother *chastised* her teenage daughter for staying out too late."

20-A *Strife* means *struggle*. The word comes from the Old German term *strītan*, which means to quarrel. For example, "The starlet's life was filled with *strife*."

CONTEXT CLUES

Some of the words on the ASVAB Word Knowledge subtest will be presented in sentences. Use the meaning of the sentence and the surrounding words as context clues. A sentence's context clues can help you determine the meaning of an unfamiliar word.

Sample 1.   Several hotels were built near the stadium to accommodate the expected <u>influx</u> of tourists during the Summer Olympics.

   1-A access

   1-B origin

   1-C arrival

   1-D noise

1-C   The question is asking you to determine the meaning of the word *influx*. The word *accommodate* is the most important context clue. *Accommodate* means house, lodge, or provide accommodation. The sentence tells you that several hotels needed to be built to accommodate or house the expected influx of tourists. This means that there weren't enough hotels to handle all the tourists. The phrase *Summer Olympics* is another context clue. Host cities welcome thousands of tourists from around the world during the Olympics. These context clues suggest that *influx* means *arrival*. Therefore, the answer must be choice C. You can eliminate the other choices because you can't substitute *access*, *origin*, or *noise* for *influx* in the sentence.

Remember to use common sense when examining context clues. You only have a short time to answer each question, so don't waste precious seconds. Find the word that is a synonym for the underlined word and move to the next question.

Complete Context Clues exercises 1 through 3 to get accustomed to using context clues. After you complete each exercise, review the answer key and explanations for examples of how context clues can help you succeed on the ASVAB Word Knowledge subtest.

EXERCISES: CONTEXT CLUES 1

Directions: Now try the exercises below. Each question has an underlined word. Select the answer that is closest in meaning to the underlined word. Check your answers against the answer key and explanations that follow.

1. The <u>feud</u> between the two gangs only grew more violent over the years.
   - 1-A bond
   - 1-B resolve
   - 1-C quarrel
   - 1-D contact

2. The <u>suspense</u> of waiting for her test results was driving the college hopeful crazy.
   - 2-A resource
   - 2-B purpose
   - 2-C status
   - 2-D anxiety

3. The author's friend wrote the <u>preface</u> to the novel, which sets up the story perfectly.
   - 3-A introduction
   - 3-B biography
   - 3-C premise
   - 3-D index

4. The driver <u>averted</u> disaster by swerving to miss the deer.
   - 4-A incited
   - 4-B shunted
   - 4-C verified
   - 4-D prevented

5. The private beach was <u>secluded</u> from the rest of the resort.
   - 5-A cited
   - 5-B hidden
   - 5-C retracted
   - 5-D transformed

6. After the secretary <u>tallied</u> the votes by hand, the teacher announced the new class president.
   - 6-A adhered
   - 6-B gathered
   - 6-C calculated
   - 6-D transitioned

7. The court charged the defendant with several counts of grand <u>larceny</u> for taking more than $1 million from a company fund.
   - 7-A assault
   - 7-B murder
   - 7-C theft
   - 7-D forgery

8. The husband filled the house with flowers, hoping his romantic <u>gesture</u> would raise his wife's spirits.
   - 8-A indication of direction
   - 8-B display of affection
   - 8-C appropriate joke
   - 8-D hand movement

9. A <u>clamor</u> arose from the excited audience when the band walked onstage.
   - 9-A light
   - 9-B song
   - 9-C calm
   - 9-D roar

10. The singer's <u>debut</u> album helped her secure a nomination for best new artist.

10-A first

10-B long

10-C complex

10-D successful

11. The tourist bought a snow globe as a <u>memento</u> of his wonderful vacation.

11-A benefit

11-B reminder

11-C judgment

11-D suggestion

12. The new hair color drastically <u>altered</u> the actress's appearance.

12-A fixed

12-B developed

12-C changed

12-D magnified

13. Our dog groomers use a light-reflecting shampoo to bring out the <u>sheen</u> in your dog's coat.

13-A luster

13-B texture

13-C spots

13-D fur

14. Getting home for the holidays is my highest <u>priority</u>.

14-A new idea

14-B big interest

14-C difficult task

14-D main concern

15. The volcano <u>erupted</u> a week ago, but ash is still spewing from the top.

15-A expired

15-B moved

15-C exploded

15-D resumed

16. The government offers a tax <u>incentive</u> of up to $4,000 for homeowners who purchase energy efficient appliances.

16-A arrangement

16-B motivation

16-C decision

16-D source

17. The mousse left a filmy <u>residue</u> in my hair.

17-A color

17-B deposit

17-C smell

17-D pattern

18. The novel describes a young girl's amazing <u>odyssey</u> across Europe.

18-A journey

18-B dance

18-C education

18-D fantasy

19. The director <u>collaborated</u> with an artist to design the cast's wardrobe.

19-A taught by

19-B contacted

19-C researched

19-D joined forces

20. The members of the winning team <u>flaunted</u> their championship rings in their opponents' faces.

20-A removed

20-B polished

20-C exhibited

20-D grabbed

ANSWER KEY AND EXPLANATIONS

1. C	5. B	9. D	13. A	17. B
2. D	6. C	10. A	14. D	18. A
3. A	7. C	11. B	15. C	19. D
4. D	8. B	12. C	16. B	20. C

1-C The context clues *gangs* and *violent* help you understand the meaning of *feud*. These clues tell you that the two gangs are involved in a *feud* or *quarrel*. If you substitute any of the other choices, the sentence wouldn't make sense. Choice C is the correct answer.

2-D Here the context clue is *waiting*. The college hopeful is restless because she must wait to receive her test results. The best substitution for *suspense* is *anxiety*. The *anxiety* of waiting for these results is upsetting the college hopeful. Choices A, B, and C aren't synonyms for suspense.

3-A The context clue is *set up*. This lets you know that the *preface* comes before the story. Therefore, *preface* means *introduction*. You can eliminate the other choices because you can't substitute *biography*, *premise*, or *index* for *preface*.

4-D The context clues in this sentence are *disaster* and *swerving to miss*. This tells you that the driver avoided or *prevented* disaster by swerving away from the deer. *Averted* means *prevented*. Choices A, B, and C aren't synonyms for *averted*.

5-B The words that give you the correct answer are *private* and *from the rest of*. These words tell you that the beach is far from the rest of

the resort, which means that it is *hidden* from the main part of the resort.

6-C The phrase *by hand* helps you determine the meaning of *tallied*. In a class election, the secretary would have to count the number of votes for each candidate. Therefore, *tallied* means *calculated*. *Adhered* means stuck to, so choice A is incorrect. While the secretary may have also *gathered* the votes, this isn't a synonym for *tallied*. Choice D is incorrect because *transitioned* means changed. Choice C is the correct answer.

7-C The most important word in the sentence is *taking*. The sentence tells you that the defendant was charged with *taking* $1 million from a company fund. Therefore, *larceny* means *theft*. Although the other choices are common crimes, they don't fit the context of the sentence.

8-B Look at the phrase *filled the house with flowers*. This phrase suggests that *gesture* means *display of affection*. This word has several meanings that can include hand movement and indication of direction, but these definitions don't fit the context of this sentence.

9-D The context clue is *excited*. Generally, excited audiences make a lot of noise. This tells you that *clamor* means *roar*. You couldn't replace *clamor* with any of the other choices and retain the logic of the sentence.

10-A   The most important phrase in the sentence is *new artist*. This phrase signals that this was the singer's *first* album. Therefore, *debut* means *first*. There is no way to know if the singer's album was *long* or *complex*, so choices B and C are incorrect. The album may have been *successful*, but this isn't a synonym for *debut*.

11-B   The sentence tells you that the tourist had a wonderful vacation. This tells you that the tourist wants to remember his vacation. Therefore, *memento* means *reminder*. *Memento* comes from the Latin word *meminisse*, which means to remember. The other choices don't fit the context of the sentence.

12-C   The context clues are *new* and *drastically*. These words tell you that the hair color *changed* the actress's appearance. *Fixed, developed*, and *magnified* don't fit the context of the sentence.

13-A   The most important phrase in the sentence is *light-reflecting*. This tells you that the shampoo makes the dog's coat look shiny. From this, you can tell that *sheen* means *luster*. Light-reflecting shampoo wouldn't bring out the *texture* or *spots* in a dog's coat, so choices B and C are incorrect. Choice D is incorrect because a dog's coat is made of *fur*.

14-D   The context clue is *highest*. This tells you that getting home for the holidays is the speaker's *main concern*. You can't substitute *new idea, big interest*, or *difficult task* for *priority* and still retain the original meaning of the sentence.

15-C   The most important word in this sentence is *spewing*. This tells you that *erupted* means *exploded*. The other choices don't fit the context of the sentence.

16-B   Look at the word *for*. This word tells you that the homeowners must do something to receive a tax *incentive*. Because the government wants homeowners to purchase energy efficient appliances, they offer an *incentive*, which is a type of *motivation*, to get homeowners to comply. In this case, the *incentive* is money off the homeowner's taxes.

17-B   The context clue in this sentence is the word *left*. This tells you that a *residue* is something that is left behind or *deposited*. Although mousse could leave a *smell* or a *color* in someone's hair, these aren't synonyms for *residue*. *Pattern* is also incorrect.

18-A   The most important phrase in this sentence is *across Europe*. This should help you realize that *odyssey* means *journey*. You can remember the meaning of *odyssey* by thinking of the Greek hero Odysseus, who spent many years trying to find his way home.

19-D   The word *with* helps you figure out that *collaborated* means *joined forces*. The other choices don't fit the context of the sentence.

20-C   The most important phrase in this sentence is *in their opponents' faces*. This helps you realize that *flaunted* means *exhibited*. *Removed, polished*, and *grabbed* don't fit the context of the sentence.

EXERCISES: CONTEXT CLUES 2

Directions: Now try the exercises below. Each question has an underlined word. Select the answer that is closest in meaning to the underlined word. Check your answers against the answer key and explanations that follow.

1. Looking through her high school yearbook made the former cheerleader feel <u>nostalgic</u>.
   - 1-A   tired
   - 1-B   healthy
   - 1-C   reflective
   - 1-D   interesting

2. Scientists worry that greenhouse gases will <u>deplete</u> the ozone layer, leaving us unprotected from harmful UV rays.
   - 2-A   release
   - 2-B   handle
   - 2-C   detail
   - 2-D   exhaust

3. The unhappy employees filed a <u>grievance</u> against their boss.
   - 3-A   check
   - 3-B   practice
   - 3-C   complaint
   - 3-D   condition

4. The heavy rain caused the already swollen river to <u>exceed</u> its banks.
   - 4-A   shift
   - 4-B   surpass
   - 4-C   narrow
   - 4-D   bisect

5. She faces the <u>dilemma</u> of displeasing her parents or losing a wonderful opportunity.
   - 5-A   problem
   - 5-B   expectation
   - 5-C   assignment
   - 5-D   verdict

6. The police believe the robber <u>lurked</u> outside the house for hours, waiting for the family to leave.
   - 6-A   rested
   - 6-B   foraged
   - 6-C   posted
   - 6-D   prowled

7. His mother dislikes poker because <u>wagering</u> even the smallest amount of money makes her nervous.
   - 7-A   taking
   - 7-B   holding
   - 7-C   betting
   - 7-D   spending

8. The product <u>flaw</u> forced the company to pay thousands of dollars in damages to an injured customer.
   - 8-A   defect
   - 8-B   display
   - 8-C   state
   - 8-D   contract

9. The young boy <u>chronicled</u> his summer adventures in a journal.
   - 9-A   imagined
   - 9-B   recorded
   - 9-C   inflated
   - 9-D   examined

10. The boy believed that it was his <u>destiny</u> to play Major League baseball.
    - 10-A wish
    - 10-B fate
    - 10-C job
    - 10-D dare

11. The argument over where to hold the party caused <u>friction</u> between the family members.

11-A   secrets

11-B   prestige

11-C   hostility

11-D   reprisal

12. The artist mixed some white paint with the teal paint to create a new <u>hue</u>.

12-A   image

12-B   account

12-C   shadow

12-D   shade

13. Many people believe that the Internet was the greatest <u>innovation</u> of the twentieth century.

13-A   advancement

13-B   phenomenon

13-C   catastrophe

13-D   predecessor

14. The foundation addresses the <u>plight</u> of endangered sea turtles.

14-A   locations

14-B   offspring

14-C   troubles

14-D   magnitude

15. She only watched the <u>segment</u> of the show that discussed relieving stress.

15-A   episode

15-B   outline

15-C   time

15-D   part

16. The <u>tension</u> between the warring siblings was evident from the moment they entered the room.

16-A   humor

16-B   strain

16-C   buzz

16-D   hate

17. The groom <u>vowed</u> to care for his bride for the rest of his life.

17-A   hoped

17-B   planned

17-C   complied

17-D   promised

18. The defendant hoped the jury would <u>absolve</u> him from any wrongdoing.

18-A   free

18-B   claim

18-C   grant

18-D   lessen

19. Because of customer complaints, the restaurant owners decided to <u>ban</u> smoking in their facility.

19-A   relieve

19-B   present

19-C   prohibit

19-D   research

20. A family emergency forced the student to <u>defer</u> enrollment in college until the following semester.

20-A   plan for

20-B   put off

20-C   speed up

20-D   take back

ANSWER KEY AND EXPLANATIONS

1. C	5. A	9. B	13. A	17. D
2. D	6. D	10. B	14. C	18. A
3. C	7. C	11. C	15. D	19. C
4. B	8. A	12. D	16. B	20. B

1-C Because the former cheerleader is looking through her high school yearbook, she is probably feeling *reflective*. Therefore, *nostalgic* means *reflective*. *Nostalgia* is related to the Greek word *neisthai*, which means to return. The former cheerleader is using the yearbook as a way to return to her past life.

2-D The context clue in this sentence is *leaving us*. This tells you that scientists fear greenhouse gases will *exhaust* the ozone layer and leave us unprotected. The other choices don't fit the context of the sentence.

3-C The phrase *unhappy employees* tells you that *grievance* means *complaint*. Their boss is making them miserable, so the employees have decided to lodge a *complaint*. *Record, practice,* and *condition* can't be substituted for the word *grievance*.

4-B The context clue is *swollen*. This tells you that the river was already full and that the heavy rain caused the river to exceed or *surpass* its banks. Heavy rain could cause the river to *shift*, but this isn't a synonym for *exceed*. *Narrow* and *bisect* are also incorrect.

5-A The words *displeasing* and *losing* can help you figure out the meaning of *dilemma*. The person in the sentence doesn't want to displease her parents or lose a wonderful opportunity, but she must make

a decision. This tells you that *dilemma* means *problem*.

6-D The robber hung around the house for hours, waiting for the family to leave the house. This means he was carefully watching to see when everyone was gone. This tells you that *lurked* means *prowled*.

7-C The context of the sentence tells you that *wagering* means *betting*. The woman doesn't like poker because risking even the smallest amount of money makes her nervous. *Holding, taking,* and *spending* aren't synonyms for *wagering*.

8-A This sentence implies that something was wrong with the company's product that caused injury to a customer. Because of this, the company had to pay thousands of dollars in damages. From this, you can tell that *flaw* means *defect*.

9-B People often write or *record* important events in a journal. *Recorded* is a synonym for *chronicled*. Though the boy could also use the journal to *imagine* or *examine* his adventures, these words aren't synonyms for *chronicle*. *Inflated* is also incorrect.

10-B The context clue in this sentence is *believed*. The boy believes that he will play Major League baseball because it is his *fate*. The other choices aren't synonyms for *destiny*.

answers exercises

11-C The sentence tells you that the family members were having an argument. From this, you can tell that *friction* means *hostility*. *Secrets*, *prestige*, and *reprisal* aren't synonyms for *friction*.

12-D The context clues are *mixed* and *new*. When you add white to another color, it creates a new *hue* or *shade* of the original color. Though *image* and *shadow* are things that an artist might consider, these aren't synonyms for *hue*. *Account* is also incorrect.

13-A The Internet was an invention in the late twentieth century that changed the world. This tells you that *innovation* means *advancement*. *Phenomenon* means occurrence, which isn't a synonym for *innovation*. *Catastrophe* means disaster, so this choice is also incorrect. *Predecessor* means forerunner, which isn't related to the word *innovation*.

14-C The context clue is *endangered*, which means in danger of becoming extinct. This helps you realize that the word *plight* means *troubles*. The other words aren't synonyms for *plight*.

15-D The word *only* tells you that the person didn't watch all of the show. This tells you that *segment* means *part*. *Episode*, *outline*, and *time* are words that are related to watching a show, but they aren't synonyms for *segment*.

16-B The word *warring* tells you that the two siblings aren't getting along. *Strain* is a synonym for *tension*. The other choices don't fit the context of the sentence.

17-D The word *vowed* means *promised*. During wedding ceremonies, brides and grooms *vow* to love and care for each other for the rest of their lives. The other words aren't synonyms for *vowed*.

18-A The most important phrase in this sentence is *from any wrongdoing*. The defendant wants to be *absolved* or *freed* from any wrongdoing. *Claim*, *grant*, and *lessen* aren't synonyms for *absolve*.

19-C The context clue in this sentence is *complaint*. This tells you that the customers weren't happy about smoking in the restaurant. The restaurant owners decided to deal with this problem by *banning* or *prohibiting* smoking in their facility.

20-B The beginning of the sentence tells you that there was a family emergency. Later, you learn that the student is *deferring* enrollment until the following semester. This tells you that *defer* means *put off*. The other choices aren't synonyms for *defer*.

EXERCISES: CONTEXT CLUES 3

Directions: Now try the exercises below. Each question has an underlined word. Select the answer that is closest in meaning to the underlined word. Check your answers against the answer key and explanations that follow.

1. After several hours of soccer practice, the teenager was <u>famished</u>.
   - 1-A   angry
   - 1-B   upset
   - 1-C   hungry
   - 1-D   lonely

2. The barking dog <u>irked</u> the neighbors as they tried to sleep.
   - 2-A   scared
   - 2-B   pulled
   - 2-C   thrilled
   - 2-D   annoyed

3. The doctor <u>prescribed</u> a cough medicine for his patient.
   - 3-A   created
   - 3-B   ordered
   - 3-C   needed
   - 3-D   wasted

4. The raft will not float because it <u>retains</u> water.
   - 4-A   takes
   - 4-B   holds
   - 4-C   moves
   - 4-D   places

5. After learning of his criminal past, the neighbors <u>shunned</u> the new tenant.
   - 5-A   avoided
   - 5-B   attached
   - 5-C   despised
   - 5-D   concerned

6. Determined not to <u>succumb</u> to her fears, the young girl bravely climbed the stairs to the attic.
   - 6-A   take over
   - 6-B   face up
   - 6-C   give in
   - 6-D   put on

7. Opinions about the town's new noise ordinance <u>vary</u> from approval to outrage.
   - 7-A   refer
   - 7-B   sense
   - 7-C   rate
   - 7-D   differ

8. The humidity <u>warped</u> the wooden door, making it difficult to close.
   - 8-A   soaked
   - 8-B   deformed
   - 8-C   shattered
   - 8-D   stripped

9. The teacher <u>detained</u> the entire class after school to discuss the students' poor behavior.
   - 9-A   held
   - 9-B   left
   - 9-C   blamed
   - 9-D   scolded

10. The second doctor <u>concurred</u> with the first doctor's diagnosis.
    - 10-A   stated
    - 10-B   remained
    - 10-C   agreed
    - 10-D   identified

11. Instead of tearing down the old house, the couple decided to <u>renovate</u> it.
    - 11-A   sell
    - 11-B   move
    - 11-C   restore
    - 11-D   decorate

12. The parents <u>indulged</u> their children's wishes by taking them to the amusement park.

    12-A ignored

    12-B returned

    12-C salvaged

    12-D gratified

13. The coach <u>exploited</u> the other team's weakness by putting in a left-handed pitcher.

    13-A withdraw from

    13-B capitalized on

    13-C to recognize

    13-D spread apart

14. The police arrested the suspect after the evidence <u>negated</u> his claim that he was in the city on the night of the crime.

    14-A invalidated

    14-B retrieved

    14-C suppressed

    14-D violated

15. It took several months for the young man to <u>profess</u> his love for his girlfriend.

    15-A forgive

    15-B retract

    15-C admit

    15-D implore

16. The concerned parents wanted their daughter to <u>sever</u> all ties to the rebellious boy.

    16-A accept

    16-B cut

    16-C expel

    16-D wait

17. Silver <u>tarnishes</u> over time, so it is important to polish flatware every few months to help keep its shine.

    17-A weakens

    17-B yellows

    17-C snares

    17-D dulls

18. The mother told the whining child not to <u>utter</u> another word if he wanted any dessert.

    18-A write

    18-B speak

    18-C laugh

    18-D sing

19. After an expert <u>vouched</u> for the authenticity of the arrowhead, the hiker donated it to a local museum.

    19-A estimated

    19-B presumed

    19-C guaranteed

    19-D renounced

20. The scent of lilacs in the chilly room made her <u>yearn</u> for the warm summer months.

    20-A long

    20-B break

    20-C obtain

    20-D adjust

ANSWER KEY AND EXPLANATIONS

1. C	5. A	9. A	13. B	17. D
2. D	6. C	10. C	14. A	18. B
3. B	7. D	11. C	15. C	19. C
4. B	8. B	12. D	16. B	20. A

1-C The context clue in this sentence is *soccer practice*. This tells you that the teenager spent several hours exercising. This probably means that the teenager worked up an appetite. From this, you can guess that *famished* means *hungry*.

2-D You know that the sound of a barking dog can make it very difficult to fall asleep. This helps you recognize that *irk* means *annoy*. Though a barking dog could *scare* the neighbors, this isn't a synonym for *irk*. *Pulled* and *thrilled* are also incorrect.

3-B Doctors often give patients *prescriptions*, or *orders*, for medication. This tells you that *prescribed* means *ordered*. Choices A, C, and D aren't synonyms for *prescribed*.

4-B The most important context clue is *will not float*. This tells you that *retains* means *hold*. The raft won't float because it *holds* water. The other choices aren't synonyms for *retains*.

5-A The most important part of this sentence is *his criminal past*. This tells you that the neighbors were probably upset about the new tenant. Their fears led them to *shun* or *avoid* the tenant. Though some of the neighbors might also *despise* the tenant, this isn't a synonym for *shun*. *Attached* and *concerned* are also incorrect.

6-C The context clue in this sentence is *bravely*. This tells you that the young girl didn't *succumb* or *give in* to her fear of the attic. The other choices aren't synonyms for *succumb*.

7-D The context clues in this sentence are *approval* and *outrage*. This tells you that some citizens were happy with the noise ordinance, while others were not. From this, you can recognize that *vary* means *differ*. The other choices don't fit the context of the sentence.

8-B From the context of the sentence, you can tell that something has happened to the shape of the door that prevents it from working properly. This helps you recognize that *warped* means *deformed*. Although humidity could potentially *soak* a door, this isn't a synonym for *warp*. *Shattered* and *stripped* are also incorrect.

9-A The context of the sentence tells you that the students did something wrong. The teacher *detained* the students to discuss the problem. From this, you can tell that *detained* means *held*. Though the teacher may have *scolded* the students, this isn't a synonym for *detained*. *Left* and *blamed* are also incorrect because they don't fit the context of the sentence.

10-C From the context of the sentence, you can tell that *concurred* means *agreed*. None of the other answer choices fit the context of the sentence.

11-C   The sentence tells you that the couple didn't want to tear down the old house—they wanted to *renovate* it. This tells you that *renovate* means *restore*. The words *sell*, *move*, and *decorate* are related to home improvement, but they aren't synonyms for *renovate*.

12-D   The context clue in this sentence is *wishes*. This tells you that the parents are doing something that the children enjoy. From this, you can tell that *indulged* means *gratified*. The other choices don't fit the context of the sentence.

13-B   From the context of the sentence, you can tell that *exploited* means *capitalized on*. The coach wanted to use the other team's weakness to help his team win. The other choices aren't synonyms for *exploited*.

14-A   The sentence tells you that the suspect was arrested once the evidence came in. This tells you that the suspect's claim that he was in the city was false. From this, you can tell that *negated* means *invalidated*.

15-C   The context clue in the sentence is *several months*. This tells you that it took a while for the young man to *admit* his love. *Forgive*, *retract*, and *implore* don't fit the context of the sentence.

16-B   From the context of the sentence, you can tell that the parents don't want their daughter to see the rebellious boy. This tells you that *sever* means *cut*. The parents want the daughter to *cut* ties to the boy.

17-D   The sentence tells you that you need to polish silver to prevent it from *tarnishing*. From this, you can recognize that *tarnish* means *dulls*. The other choices don't fit the context of the sentence.

18-B   The context clue in this sentence is *word*. This tells you that *utter* means *speak*. While you can *write* and *sing* words, these aren't synonyms for *utter*. *Laugh* is also incorrect.

19-C   The context clue in this sentence is *authenticity*. The hiker had to have someone *vouch for*, or *guarantee*, the validity of the arrowhead before he could donate it to the museum. The other choices don't fit the context of the sentence.

20-A   From the context of the sentence, you can tell that the subject is somewhere cold. When she catches the scent of lilacs, it makes her *yearn*, or *long*, for the warm summer months. *Break*, *obtain*, and *adjust* aren't synonyms for *yearn*.

WORD PARTS

Another way to determine the meaning of unfamiliar words on the ASVAB Word Knowledge subtest is to use your knowledge of word parts, including prefixes, suffixes, and roots.

PREFIXES

Prefix	Meaning	Example
anti-	against	*antisocial*—against socializing
auto-	self	*automatic*—self-acting
bene-	good, well	*beneficial*—conducive to social well-being
bi-	two	*bicycle*—a vehicle with two wheels
circum-	around	*circumvent*—to manage to get around
com-, co-, col-	with, together	*collaborate*—work together
contra-, contro-, counter-	against	*counterintuitive*—against what one would expect
demi-	half	*demigod*—half god, half human
di-	twice, double	*dioxide*—containing two atoms of oxygen
equi-	equal	*equidistant*—equally distant
extra-	outside, beyond	*extraordinary*—beyond what is normal or regular
fore-	in front of, previous	*foremost*—first in a series
homo-	same, alike	*homogenized*—to make the same
hyper-	too much, over	*hyperactive*—overly active
hypo-	too little, under	*hypoallergenic*—having little likelihood to cause an allergic response
in-, ig-, il-, im-, ir-	not	*ineffective*—not effective *ignore*—not notice *illegal*—not legal *impolite*—not polite *irresponsible*—not responsible
intra-	within, inside	*intramural*—occurring within the limits of a community
mal-	bad, wrong, poor	*maladjusted*—poorly adjusted
mis-	badly, wrongly	*misfit*—someone or something that fits badly

mono-	single, one	*monotheism*—belief in one god
omni-	all	*omnidirectional*—moving in all directions
poly-	many	*polytheism*—belief in many gods
post-	after	*postseason*—after the normal season
pre-	before, earlier than	*prepare*—to make in advance
pro-	in favor of, forward	*promote*—to advance in rank
re-	again, back	*reverse*—to turn back
semi-	half	*semiautomatic*—partially automatic
tele-	far, distant	*telephone*—to speak with from afar
trans-	across	*transatlantic*—across the Atlantic
un-	not	*uncertain*—not certain

SUFFIXES

Suffix	Meaning	Example
-able, -ble	able, capable	*amicable*—capable of being friendly
-age	total, sum of	*acreage*—sum of acres
-al	like, of, suitable for	*comical*—of or relating to comedy
-ance	state of, act of	*assurance*—the act of assuring
-dom	the state of, belonging to	*wisdom*—the state of being wise
-er, -or	that which, one who	*teacher*—one who teaches
-hood	condition or state of	*childhood*—condition of being a child
-ish	a bit like	*girlish*—like a girl
-ism	practice of, belief	*terrorism*—practice of terrorizing
-logy	study of	*biology*—the study of life
-ness	act or quality of	*kindness*—quality of being kind
-ous	having, full of	*anxious*—full of anxiety
-ward	direction of	*eastward*—in an eastern direction
-y	like, full of, somewhat	*smiley*—full of smiles

ROOTS

Root	Meaning	Example
aqua	water	*aquarium*—a tank filled with water
auto	self	*autobiography*—the biography of a person written by himself or herself
biblio	book	*bibliophile*—a lover of books
bio	life, living things	*biography*—an account of a person's life
cede, ceed	move, go with	*secede*—to move on from an organization
chron	time	*chronology*—a time table
clude	close or shut	*exclude*—to shut out
cogn	know about	*cognizant*—to be aware of
flect, flex	turn or bend	*reflect*—to turn in or away
fract	brake	*fracture*—a break or crack
hydr	water	*hydraulic*—operated by water
ject	throw, toss	*eject*—to throw out by force
junct	join	*conjunction*—a word that joins two other words
logue	speech, speaking	*dialogue*—speech between two people
mand	command, order	*demand*—the act of commanding or ordering
manus, mani	hand	*manufacture*—made by hand
ped	foot	*biped*—two-footed animal
port	bring, carry	*import*—to bring from a foreign source
rupt	break	*erupt*—to break free from restraint
scend	climb	*ascend*—climb up
sect	cut apart	*bisect*—cut into two parts
serve	save, keep	*reserve*—to save for later
term	end, finish off	*terminate*—to come to an end in time

EXERCISES: WORD PARTS 1

Directions: Now try the exercises below. Each question has an underlined word. Select the answer that is closest in meaning to the underlined word. Check your answers against the answer key and explanations that follow.

1. The wealthy doctor was the museum's major benefactor.
   - 1-A culprit
   - 1-B director
   - 1-C sponsor
   - 1-D reporter

2. Immobile most nearly means
   - 2-A figured.
   - 2-B expansion.
   - 2-C capable.
   - 2-D motionless.

3. To a teenager, a driver's license represents freedom.
   - 3-A against capture
   - 3-B having many sides
   - 3-C the state of being liberated
   - 3-D in favor of few restrictions

4. The doctors worried that the child suffered from malnutrition.
   - 4-A poor diet
   - 4-B many foods
   - 4-C little strength
   - 4-D bad cooking

5. Portable most nearly means
   - 5-A within a port.
   - 5-B move against.
   - 5-C bring from a foreign land.
   - 5-D capable of being carried.

6. Transfer most nearly means
   - 6-A gauge.
   - 6-B convey.
   - 6-C state.
   - 6-D alert.

7. Courageous most nearly means
   - 7-A after fighting.
   - 7-B full of courage.
   - 7-C like a soldier.
   - 7-D always in action.

8. The sailor pulled the ship safely into port.
   - 8-A moving forward
   - 8-B to be on the water
   - 8-C one who sails
   - 8-D take across

9. Postscript most nearly means
   - 9-A appendix.
   - 9-B letter.
   - 9-C journal.
   - 9-D timeline.

10. The teacher asked the students to put the novel's events in chronological order.
   - 10-A alphabet
   - 10-B location
   - 10-C pattern
   - 10-D sequential

11. The scientist was at the forefront of a major innovation.
   - 11-A line
   - 11-B side
   - 11-C front
   - 11-D moment

12. Biweekly most nearly means
   - 12-A every month.
   - 12-B every two weeks.
   - 12-C divided in two.
   - 12-D too little time.

13. <u>Mythology</u> most nearly means
    13-A mysterious.
    13-B belief in myths.
    13-C the study of myths.
    13-D quality of a mystery.

14. The teenager was told to stop acting so <u>childish</u>.
    14-A like a child
    14-B two children
    14-C condition of being a child
    14-D one who works with children

15. The professor gave a lecture in a dull, <u>monotone</u> voice.
    15-A low pitch
    15-B one tone
    15-C two voices
    15-D little volume

16. <u>Eagerness</u> most nearly means
    16-A full of love.
    16-B one who excites.
    16-C the act of exciting.
    16-D the quality of being eager.

17. <u>Manipulate</u> most nearly means
    17-A command.
    17-B hand over.
    17-C operate with the hands.
    17-D capable of being carried.

18. The couple realized they had been <u>misinformed</u> about the party's location.
    18-A deceived
    18-B adjusted
    18-C believed
    18-D relieved

19. <u>Monologue</u> most nearly means
    19-A little to say.
    19-B many words.
    19-C loud conversation.
    19-D speech by one person.

20. <u>Hydrate</u> most nearly means
    20-A filled with moisture.
    20-B to take up water.
    20-C outside of land.
    20-D overly anxious.

exercises

ANSWER KEY AND EXPLANATIONS

1. C	5. D	9. A	13. C	17. C
2. D	6. B	10. D	14. A	18. A
3. C	7. B	11. C	15. B	19. D
4. A	8. C	12. B	16. D	20. B

1-C The prefix *bene-* tells you that a *benefactor* is someone who does good. While a *director* or *reporter* might do good, a *sponsor* donates money to help a worthy cause or organization.

2-D The prefix *im-* means *not* and *mobile* means *movable*. From this, you can tell that *immobile* means not moveable or *motionless*.

3-C The suffix *-dom* means *the state of being* and *free* means *liberty*. Therefore, *freedom* means *the state of being liberated*. The other choices don't fit the context of the sentence.

4-A *Mal-* means *bad* and *nutrition* means *diet*. *Malnutrition* means *poor diet*. The other choices are related to food and diet, but they don't represent the meaning of *malnutrition*.

5-D The suffix *-able* means *capable* and the prefix *port-* means *carry*. This tells you that *portable* means *capable of being carried*.

6-B *Trans-* means *across*. *Transfer* means to move across from one person, place, or thing. The word *convey* has the same meaning as *transfer*. The other choices don't fit the context of the sentence.

7-B The suffix *-ous* means *full of*. Therefore, *courageous* means *full of courage*. The other choices don't retain the logic of the sentence.

8-C The suffix *-or* means *one who*. This tells you that *sailor* means *one who sails*.

9-A The prefix *post-* means *after* and *script* means *writing*. The term literally means *to write after*. An *appendix* is supplementary material that is attached to the end of a piece of writing. *Appendix* is an appropriate synonym for *postscript*.

10-D The root *chrono-* means *time*. This tells you that the teacher wants students to put the events of the novel in order by time. The word *sequential* means following in order by time. *Chronological* and *sequential* are synonyms.

11-C The prefix *fore-* means *in front*. *Forefront* means *at the front*. The scientist was at the *front* of a major innovation.

12-B *Bi-* means *two*. Therefore, *biweekly* means *every two weeks*. Employers often pay employees on a *biweekly* basis. Magazines and newspapers are sometimes distributed on a *biweekly* schedule.

13-C The suffix *-ology* means *the study of*. From this, you can tell that *mythology* means *the study of myths*. The other choices aren't definitions of *mythology*.

14-A The suffix *-ish* means *a bit like*. *Childish* means *like a child* or marked by immaturity. Toys and games are often considered *childish* activities.

15-B The prefix *mono-* means *single* or *one*. *Monotone* refers to an unvaried tone or voice. A *monotone* speech is most likely very boring.

16-D The suffix *-ness* means *the quality of*. *Eagerness* means *the quality of being eager*. For example, people are usually filled with *eagerness* right before major events or celebrations.

17-C The root *mani* means *hand*. *Manipulate* means to *operate with the hands*. Potters *manipulate* clay with their hands, and puppeteers *manipulate* marionettes with strings attached to their hands.

18-A The prefix *mis-* means *badly* or *wrongly*. *Misinformed* means badly informed. *Deceived* has the same meaning as *misinformed*.

19-D The root *logue* refers to speech or speaking. The prefix *mono-* means *single* or *one*. Therefore, *monologue* means *speech by one person*.

20-B The root *hydra* means *water*. The verb *hydrate* means *to take up water*. A moisturizer helps *hydrate* the skin, providing dry skin with water.

EXERCISES: WORD PARTS 2

Directions: Now try the exercises below. Each question has an underlined word. Select the answer that is closest in meaning to the underlined word. Check your answers against the answer key and explanations that follow.

1. The student was <u>inconsolable</u> after failing to make the cheerleading squad.
   - 1-A   bothersome
   - 1-B   confounded
   - 1-C   devastated
   - 1-D   exhausted

2. <u>Unconscious</u> most nearly means
   - 2-A   not happy.
   - 2-B   overly tired.
   - 2-C   with energy.
   - 2-D   not awake.

3. The driver waited while the <u>pedestrian</u> crossed the road.
   - 3-A   walker
   - 3-B   biker
   - 3-C   citizen
   - 3-D   flyer

4. A ruthless <u>autocrat</u> ruled the country.
   - 4-A   senator
   - 4-B   principal
   - 4-C   dictator
   - 4-D   president

5. <u>Disrupt</u> most nearly means
   - 5-A   not included.
   - 5-B   to break apart.
   - 5-C   to take hold of.
   - 5-D   not breakable.

6. <u>Preclude</u> most nearly means
   - 6-A   thrown over.
   - 6-B   to follow across.
   - 6-C   to shut out in advance.
   - 6-D   having to do with doors.

7. During the drought, the mayor urged citizens to <u>conserve</u> water.
   - 7-A   save
   - 7-B   boil
   - 7-C   filter
   - 7-D   drink

8. The Web site includes a <u>bibliography</u> of the author's work.
   - 8-A   study of writers
   - 8-B   sum of reading
   - 8-C   state of work
   - 8-D   list of books

9. <u>Flexible</u> most nearly means
   - 9-A   finished.
   - 9-B   stretchy.
   - 9-C   static.
   - 9-D   clever.

10. <u>Contradict</u> most nearly means
   - 10-A   assist.
   - 10-B   converse.
   - 10-C   disagree.
   - 10-D   estimate.

11. The car dealer told us that the vehicle gets excellent gas <u>mileage</u>.
   - 11-A   quality of gas
   - 11-B   follow-up service
   - 11-C   total miles traveled
   - 11-D   few mechanical problems

12. After surviving the night on a freezing mountain, it was no wonder that the hiker had <u>hypothermia</u>.
   - 12-A   too much water
   - 12-B   bad circulation
   - 12-C   poor memory
   - 12-D   too little body heat

13. Equality most nearly means
    13-A the state of being equal.
    13-B in favor of differences.
    13-C work with others.
    13-D move against.

14. The school board rejected the students' proposal.
    14-A mocked
    14-B discarded
    14-C recorded
    14-D included

15. Theatrical most nearly means
    15-A full of drama.
    15-B study of acting.
    15-C after the show.
    15-D like the theater.

16. Community most nearly means
    16-A university.
    16-B organization.
    16-C neighborhood.
    16-D government.

17. Many students were involved in the antiwar protest.
    17-A with friends
    17-B against war
    17-C previous battle
    17-D equal aggression

18. The woman used a pedometer to clock her steps.
    18-A total feet
    18-B step counter
    18-C self-propelled
    18-D short distance

19. Extravaganza most nearly means
    19-A lavish show.
    19-B poor quality.
    19-C new production.
    19-D significant book.

20. Forecast most nearly means
    20-A preservation.
    20-B commotion.
    20-C prediction.
    20-D notification.

exercises

ANSWER KEY AND EXPLANATIONS

1. C	5. B	9. B	13. A	17. B
2. D	6. C	10. C	14. B	18. B
3. A	7. A	11. C	15. D	19. A
4. C	8. D	12. D	16. C	20. C

1-C The prefix *in-* means *not* and the suffix *-able* means *capable of*. Therefore, *inconsolable* literally means not capable of being consoled. An acceptable synonym for this would be *devastated*.

2-D The prefix *un-* means *not*. The word *conscious* means *awake*. Using these word parts, you can tell that *unconscious* means *not awake*. The other choices don't fit the definition of the word.

3-A The root *ped* relates to the feet. *Pedestrians* are people who use their feet to get around. An acceptable synonym for *pedestrian* would be *walker*. The other choices aren't examples of people who necessarily use their feet to get around.

4-C *Auto* means *self*. An *autocrat* rules with unlimited authority by him- or herself. The term is derived from the Greek word *autokratōrm*, which means *self-rule*. A *dictator* is someone who rules by him- or herself without any outside influence. This is the only acceptable synonym for autocrat. The other choices represent leaders who must answer to other people in one way or another.

5-B The root *rupt* means *break*. The word *disrupt* means *to break apart*.

6-C The prefix *pre-* means *before* or *earlier than* and the root *clude* means *close* or *shut*. Therefore, *preclude* means *to shut out in* advance. The other choices don't fit the meaning of *preclude*.

7-A The root *serve* means *keep* or *save*. A drought is a period of excessive dryness brought about by a lack of precipitation. During such a period, citizens are encouraged to *save* or *conserve* water. While the other choices are actions that are related to water, they aren't synonyms for *conserve*.

8-D The root *biblio* means *book*. In this case, a *bibliography* is a *list of books* that the author wrote. Sometimes authors include bibliographies of works to which they refer in their own writing.

9-B The root in *flexible* is *flex*, which means to *turn* or *bend*. *Flexible* means bendable or *stretchy*. The other choices aren't acceptable synonyms for *flexible*.

10-C The prefix *contra-* means *against* and *dict* comes from the Latin word *dicere*, which means *to speak*. *Contradict* literally means to speak against. An appropriate synonym for *contradict* is *disagree*. The other words don't have the same meaning as *contradict*.

11-C The suffix *-age* means *total* or *sum of*. *Mileage* refers to the *total miles traveled*. Gas *mileage* is the ratio of the total miles traveled to the number of gallons of gasoline burned.

12-D The prefix *hypo-* means *too little or under*. *Hypothermia* means *too little body heat*. It makes sense that someone who has survived a night on a cold mountain would suffer from too little body heat. The other choices don't fit the context of the sentence.

13-A The prefix *equi-* means *equal*. *Equality* means *the state of being equal*. You might have heard this word used in discussions of the American civil rights movement. During this time, African Americans fought for *equality*. They wanted to have the same rights as all other citizens.

14-B The root *ject* means *to toss* or *throw*. *Rejected* means tossed out or thrown out. The word that is most nearly the same is *discarded*. The other words aren't synonyms for *rejected*.

15-D The suffix *-al* means *like, of,* or *suitable for*. *Theatrical* means *like the theater*. Sometimes, people will make *theatrical* gestures. These gestures are often big because stage actors must use big gestures for the audience to see them.

16-C *Com* means *with* or *together*. *Community* refers to a group of people living *together* in a particular area. The word *neighborhood* is closest in meaning to *community*. The other choices aren't synonyms for *community*.

17-B *Anti-* means *against*. From this, you can tell that *antiwar* means *against war*. As long as there has been war, there have been *antiwar* protests. You have probably seen the prefix *anti-* used to modify many other words. Some examples would be *antifeminist*, *anticlimactic*, and *antibiotic*.

18-B The root *ped* relates to the feet. A *pedometer* is a device used to measure the number of steps taken in a given period. A *pedometer* is a *step counter*.

19-A The prefix *extra-* means *outside* or *beyond* what is normal. An *extravaganza* is a *lavish show*. This word usually refers to a production of the musical or theatrical variety.

20-C The prefix *fore-* means *in front of*. *Forecast* means *to tell ahead of time*. *Predication* is closest in meaning to *forecast*. The other choices don't fit the meaning of *forecast*.

SUMMING IT UP

- Read a little every day to build your verbal skills. Think of ways to remember unfamiliar words. Try to relate these words to other areas of your life, so they become a part of your regular vocabulary.

- Use context clues in sentences to determine the meanings of unfamiliar words.

- Look for familiar word parts. Knowing the meanings of prefixes, suffixes, or roots can help you figure out the definition of a word.

Paragraph
Comprehension

chapter 9

OVERVIEW

- **Finding main ideas**
- **Looking for details**
- **Making inferences**
- **Finding word meanings**
- **Summing it up**

FINDING MAIN IDEAS

On the Paragraph Comprehension subtest of the ASVAB, you'll be asked to read short passages, most of which are a paragraph long. Then, you'll be asked one or more questions about each passage. To answer these questions, you must be able to read and comprehend the passages quickly and correctly. It helps to read the question or questions below the passage *first*—before you read the passage—so you know what to look for as you read. Many of these questions will ask you to find the main idea of a passage.

Questions about the main idea will often begin like this:

This paragraph is mainly about _____.

The main idea above is that _____.

The main point expressed in this passage is that _____.

The best title to this passage is _____.

The author's most important message is that _____.

When a question underneath a passage asks about the main idea, ask yourself questions such as these as you read:

- What is this mostly about?

- What is the author saying?

- What is the main message the author is trying to get across?

Sometimes, the main idea is stated in a topic sentence at the beginning of a paragraph. Other times, the topic sentence is at the end of a paragraph or even in the middle.

The following three sample passages illustrate the kinds of main idea questions you may find on the ASVAB.

Sample 1.   Pluto was discovered in 1930 and was classified as the ninth and smallest planet in the solar system. In 2006, the International Astronomical Union reclassified it as a dwarf planet, dropping the number of planets in the solar system to eight. Mercury, the closest planet to the sun, is now considered the smallest planet. Pluto is the second-largest dwarf planet on the Kuiper belt, a region beyond the planets. It is made up of rock and ice and is one-fifth the size of Earth's moon. Pluto has three moons orbiting it.

This passage is mainly about the

1-A solar system.

1-B Kuiper belt.

1-C planet Pluto.

1-D planet Mercury.

1-C   The passage tells us about Pluto, which was once classified as the ninth planet in the solar system, but is now considered a dwarf planet. Therefore, only choice C is correct. Choices A, B, and D provide details from the passages, not the main idea.

Sample 2.   A Pulitzer Prize is a U.S. award given in newspaper journalism, literature, and musical composition. It was established by Joseph Pulitzer, a Hungarian American journalist and newspaper publisher. Upon his death in 1911, he bequeathed a sum of money to Columbia University that was used to fund the school's journalism department. The first Pulitzer Prize was awarded in 1917. Awards are given to U.S. newspapers and news organizations for reports and photographs. Some of the recipients of past Pulitzer Prizes were Robert Frost, John F. Kennedy, William Faulkner, John Updike, and Ernest Hemingway.

The best title for the above passage is

1-A "Who was Joseph Pulitzer?"

1-B "What is the Pulitzer Prize?"

1-C "Awards for Newspaper Journalism."

1-D "Past Pulitzer Prize Winners."

1-B   The best title is choice B, "What is the Pulitzer Prize?" Notice that the main topic of the passage is the definition of the Pulitzer Prize. The passage tells how the prize began, who can receive it, and who has received it in the past. Choice A is not a good answer because the passage only mentions that Joseph Pulitzer established the prize. Choice C is not a good answer because the passage only discusses one award for newspaper journalism: the Pulitzer Prize. Choice D gives a detail in the passage, not the main idea.

Sample 3.   Robert William "Bobby" Flay, who was born in 1964, is an American chef, a restaurateur, and a television personality from New York City. Flay dropped out of high school and first started to work in the restaurant industry at the age of seventeen. He graduated from the first graduating class of the French Culinary Institute in 1984 and has held many positions at different restaurants, honing his Southwestern cooking style. Flay is the owner and executive chef of restaurants Mesa Grill, Bar Americain, Bobby Flay Steak, and Bobby's Burger Palace. He has hosted seven television shows on the Food Network and has served as a guest, competitor, and judge on many other programs, including *Iron Chef America*. He is also the author of several cookbooks.

The main point expressed in this passage is that Bobby Flay

3-A owns several large restaurants.

3-B has become famous in the cooking world.

3-C dropped out of high school when he was seventeen.

3-D is a frequent guest on television shows.

3-B   The best answer is that Bobby Flay has become famous in the cooking world. Most, if not all, of the details in this passage support this idea—that Bobby Flay is a famous chef, restaurateur, and television personality. The other choices give only details in the passage that support the main idea.

EXERCISES: FINDING MAIN IDEAS 1

Directions: Now try the exercises below. Choose the best answer to each question. As you finish each exercise, check your answers with the answer key and explanations that follow.

1. The Great Fire of London burned the great English city for three days in September of 1666. It gutted the city, destroying more than 13,000 homes, 80 churches, including St. Paul's Cathedral, and most of the city's other buildings. It left 70,000 of the city's 80,000 residents homeless. The death toll is unknown as there were no recognizable remains, but it is thought to be small. The fire started in a bakery, and high winds helped it spread quickly to other structures. People used gunpowder to create explosions to keep the fire from spreading.

    The general idea in this passage is that the Great Fire of London

    1-A   happened in England many years ago.

    1-B   spread quickly and caused a great deal of damage.

    1-C   had a small death toll and left no recognizable remains.

    1-D   destroyed St. Paul's Cathedral in London.

2. French toast is an easy breakfast to make for those who don't have much time in the morning. First, gather the ingredients: two slices of bread, one egg, two tablespoons of milk, one teaspoon of vanilla extract, one teaspoon of cinnamon, butter, and syrup. Spray a pan with nonstick cooking spray, and place the pan on a stovetop over medium-high heat. Whisk together the egg, milk, vanilla, and cinnamon. Dip the bread into the egg mixture, and place it in the pan. Flip the bread over when it is golden brown. When the French toast is done, transfer it to a plate and serve with butter and syrup.

    Which of the following statements is best supported by the passage?

    2-A   Most people don't have time to eat breakfast.

    2-B   French toast tastes better with lots of butter.

    2-C   Making French toast is simple and quick.

    2-D   Making French toast requires many ingredients.

QUESTIONS 3 AND 4 REFER TO THE PASSAGE BELOW.

A lemur is a primate native to the island of Madagascar and surrounding islands. These animals are known for their large, reflective eyes that enhance night vision, and long tails that aid in balance and communication with one another. Lemurs range in size from 1 ounce to 22 pounds. Some species once weighed more than 100 hundred pounds, but these species have since become extinct. The smaller lemurs are nocturnal, and the larger ones roam during the day. Lemurs exist in a matriarchal structure where the females dominate the males. Some lemurs are herbivores, and others are omnivores, sometimes eating insects.

3. This passage is mainly about
   3-A   species of large lemurs that are now extinct.
   3-B   primates that use their tails for balance and communication.
   3-C   the size of lemurs, which ranges from an ounce to twenty-two pounds.
   3-D   interesting primates called lemurs that are native to the island of Madagascar.

4. The best title for this selection is
   4-A   "Facts About Lemurs."
   4-B   "A Lemur's Eyes."
   4-C   "Matriarchal Primates."
   4-D   "Omnivores and Herbivores."

5. Marie Curie (1867–1934) was born in Warsaw, Poland. She was an influential physicist who was famous for her research in radioactivity. She explored the source of radiation and discovered the elements radium and polonium. Curie won a Nobel Prize in physics in 1903 for her discovery, the first woman ever to do so. After her husband's death in 1906, she continued her work in radioactivity and won the 1911 Nobel Prize in chemistry. She invented the first portable X-ray unit during World War I and founded the Radium Institute in Paris.

   What is the main message of this passage?
   5-A   In 1903, Marie Curie became the first woman to win a Nobel Prize.
   5-B   Marie Curie was born in Warsaw, Poland, in 1867.
   5-C   Marie Curie was a famous physicist known for her research in radioactivity.
   5-D   Known for her remarkable memory, Marie Curie did well in school.

6. The Great Lakes are the largest group of freshwater lakes on Earth. The lakes of Michigan, Huron, Erie, Superior, and Ontario are located on the border of the United States and Canada. Lake Superior is considered the largest of the lakes, and the combined surface area of the lakes is about the same size as the United Kingdom. The region is surrounded by 35,000 islands and many other bodies of water such as minor lakes and rivers. The Great Lakes contain 22 percent of the world's supply of fresh surface water, but because of human use, the water levels have been decreasing over the past years.

   The main idea above is that
   6-A   Lake Superior is the largest of the Great Lakes.
   6-B   the Great Lakes are the largest group of freshwater lakes.
   6-C   the water levels of the Great Lakes have decreased over the years.
   6-D   the Great Lakes are surrounded by islands and other bodies of water.

7. Iceland is a European island located in the North Atlantic Ocean. During the twentieth century, the country's economy exploded, moving from fishing to services and finance industries. The country has low taxes and a Nordic welfare system, which provides universal health care and educational opportunities past high school. In 2007, the country was ranked as the most developed country in the world and the fourth most productive country. By 2008, though, Iceland's banking system had failed, as did the U.S. banking system, causing economic hardship and political unrest.

exercises

The best title for this passage would be

7-A   "The Economy of Iceland."

7-B   "A Famous European Island."

7-C   "Iceland's Low Taxes."

7-D   "The Island of Iceland."

8. *Good Housekeeping* is a woman's magazine that has been in production since 1885. It was bought by the Hearst Corporation, its current owner, in 1911. The magazine produces articles pertinent to women's interests about topics such as diet, health, recipes, home, beauty, and product testing. It is well-known for its Good Housekeeping Seal of Approval, which is given to products tested by the Good Housekeeping Research Institute. Each product that is tested is given a two-year warranty. More than 5,000 products have been given this seal.

This passage is mainly about

8-A   a magazine with articles of interest to women.

8-B   the Good Housekeeping Seal of Approval.

8-C   topics of interest to women, such as diet and exercise.

8-D   products that are tested and given a two-year warranty.

9. The Dead Sea Scrolls are historical documents that were discovered in 1947 and 1948 in caves near the ruins of the ancient settlement of Khirbet Qumran in the West Bank of Palestine. About 900 documents comprise the scrolls, and some are the only surviving copies of biblical documents made before 100 BCE. The manuscripts are written in Hebrew, Aramaic, and Greek on papyrus and parchment. About 40 percent of the scrolls are copies of texts from the Hebrew Bible, 30 percent are non-canonical psalms, and the rest are sectarian writings.

The author's most important message is that

9-A   historical documents are often discovered in caves.

9-B   the Dead Sea Scrolls are written in several languages.

9-C   the Dead Sea Scrolls are an important part of history.

9-D   the ancient settlement of Khirbet Qumran is in the West Bank.

QUESTIONS 10 AND 11 REFER TO THE PASSAGE BELOW.

Stephen King, born in 1947 in Maine, is one of the greatest American writers in the horror, science fiction, and fantasy genres. He has written novels, screenplays, and short story collections. Many of his works have been adapted into movies and television series. His most famous books include his first novel *Carrie*, *The Shining*, *The Stand*, *The Tommyknockers*, and *Thinner*, which he wrote under the pseudonym Richard Bachman. He also wrote a novel under the name John Swithen. He has sold more than 350 million copies of his books and has received many awards, including the Medal for Distinguished Contribution to American Letters in 2003 by the National Book Foundation. King has most recently published *Under the Dome* and has begun work on a comic book series.

10. What is the author's main message?

10-A   Stephen King writes under different names.

10-B   Stephen King writes screenplays for movies.

10-C   Stephen King's first novel is *Carrie*.

10-D   Stephen King is a great American writer.

11. This passage is mainly about
    11-A Stephen King's life.
    11-B Stephen King's writings.
    11-C the National Book Foundation.
    11-D the novel *Under the Dome*.

12. Haiku is a style of Japanese poetry that has roots in the religion of Buddhism. It is a short, seventeen-syllable poem traditionally written in one line in Japanese, or in three lines in English, with a five-seven-five syllable count. It uses simple words and grammar to convey themes of nature, feelings, or experiences. Originally called hokku, this form of poetry has been around since the ninth to twelfth centuries. It was renamed Haiku at the end of the nineteenth century by a Japanese writer named Masaòka Shiki.

The best title here would be
12-A "Japanese Nature Poems."
12-B "Haiku Poetry."
12-C "The Religion of Buddhism."
12-D "How to Write Haiku Poetry."

exercises

ANSWER KEY AND EXPLANATIONS

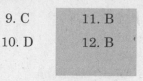

1. B	4. A	7. A	9. C	11. B
2. C	5. C	8. A	10. D	12. B
3. D	6. B			

1-B The main idea of this passage is that the Great Fire of London was enormous, spread quickly, and destroyed most of the city. Choice B is the best answer.

2-C The opening sentence of this paragraph says that French toast is an easy breakfast to make for those who don't have much time in the morning. The rest of the passage teaches the reader how to make French toast. Therefore, the statement "Making French toast is simple and quick" is the best answer.

3-D The passage gives general information about lemurs. The author is trying to explain to readers what a lemur is and what makes it interesting. Therefore, the passage is mainly about "interesting primates called lemurs that are native to the island of Madagascar." Choices A, B, and C give details that support the main idea of the passage.

4-A Since this passage gives general information about lemurs, the best title is "Facts About Lemurs." The entire passage is not about a lemur's eyes (choice B), matriarchal primates (choice C), or animals that are omnivores and herbivores (choice D).

5-C The main message of this passage is that Marie Curie was a famous physicist known for her research in radioactivity. Choices A and B give details in the passage, and choice D is not mentioned in the passage.

6-B The opening sentence gives the main idea of this passage: the Great Lakes are the largest group of freshwater lakes on Earth. Therefore, choice B is correct. The other answer choices are details in the passage that tell about the Great Lakes.

7-A Most of this passage discusses Iceland's economy. It does not give general information about Iceland. Choice A gives the best title for this passage.

8-A This passage is mainly about *Good Housekeeping*, a magazine that publishes articles of interest to women. Therefore, choice A is the best answer.

9-C The author's most important message is that the Dead Sea Scrolls are an important part of history. The author explains that some scrolls are the only surviving copies of biblical documents made before 100 BCE.

10-D The author's main message is that Stephen King is an important American writer. Therefore, choice D is correct. Choices A, B, and C give details in the passage that support the main idea.

11-B The passage is mostly about Stephen King as a writer, so choice B is correct. The passage does not discuss Stephen King's life (choice A), and it only mentions the National Book Foundation (choice C) and King's novel *Under the Dome* (choice D).

12-B The passage explains what Haiku is and offers general information about it. Therefore, choice B is the best answer.

answers exercises

EXERCISES: FINDING MAIN IDEAS 2

Directions: Now try the exercises below. Choose the best answer to each question. As you finish each exercise, check your answers with the answer key and explanations that follow.

1. Flag Day is a U.S. holiday celebrated on June 14 every year to honor the adoption of the American flag. President Woodrow Wilson established the holiday in 1916, and it was recognized by Congress in 1949. Americans observe the holiday by displaying the American flag during what is called National Flag Week, and some cities and towns host parades and celebrations. Flag Day is not considered a federal holiday.

    The main message above is that

    1-A President Woodrow Wilson established Flag Day in 1916.

    1-B Flag Day is a holiday in honor of the adoption of the American flag.

    1-C Flag Day was recognized by Congress in 1949.

    1-D Americans observe Flag Day by displaying the American flag.

2. The world's rainforests are disappearing at an alarming rate. Rainforests once covered 14 percent of the earth's surface. Today, they cover only 6 percent. Scientists predict that in forty years, rainforests may be gone altogether. Rainforests are home to many plants that are an important source for pharmaceuticals. More than 100 prescriptions come from plants that grow in the rainforest, and 3,000 rainforest plants have been identified as being active in fighting cancer cells. If the plants in the rainforest are lost, human beings may never find cures to some diseases and illnesses.

    This passage best supports the statement that

    2-A people must work together to stop the destruction of rainforests.

    2-B many species of plants and animals live in rainforests throughout the world.

    2-C people need the plants in the rainforests to make medicine to fight diseases and illnesses.

    2-D human beings may never be able to treat and cure some diseases and illnesses.

QUESTIONS 3 AND 4 REFER TO THE FOLLOWING PASSAGE.

While Clara Barton is best known as the founder of the American Red Cross, she was also a teacher and a nurse who dedicated her life to helping others. When she was only fifteen, Barton began teaching at a private school in Bordentown, New Jersey. There she saw the city's need for public education and established a free public school. After the Battle of Bull Run during the Civil War, Barton established an agency that transported goods such as bandages and socks to soldiers. Barton even received permission to go behind enemy lines to administer first aid to wounded soldiers. After the Civil War, Barton received permission from President Lincoln to begin a letter-writing campaign to help find soldiers who were missing in action.

3. What is the main idea of this paragraph?

   3-A Clara Barton was the founder of the American Red Cross.

   3-B Clara Barton became both a teacher and a nurse.

   3-C Clara Barton established the first free public school in Bordentown, New Jersey.

   3-D Clara Barton spent her life finding ways to help others in need.

4. This passage is mainly about

   4-A the Battle of Bull Run during the Civil War.

   4-B Barton's many accomplishments.

   4-C Barton's free public school.

   4-D a letter-writing campaign to find missing soldiers.

5. Opening Day at the Philadelphia Zoo was a spectacular event. More than 3,000 visitors flocked on foot, in streetcars, in horse-drawn carriages, and by steamboat to go to the zoo that day. These visitors were welcomed by a brass band and numerous flags blowing in the breeze. The price of admission was a meager 25 cents for adults and 10 cents for children. July 1, 1874, the day the Philadelphia Zoo first opened its gates, was a day that would be remembered throughout history. During its first year of operation, the Philadelphia Zoo acquired 813 animals and welcomed more than 200,000 visitors. Today, the zoo boasts more than 1,300 rare and exotic animals and more than 1 million visitors per year.

This passage is mainly about the

   5-A rare and exotic animals at the Philadelphia Zoo.

   5-B day the Philadelphia Zoo opened.

   5-C ways in which people traveled to the Philadelphia Zoo.

   5-D cost of admission to the Philadelphia Zoo.

6. Gardening is a rewarding hobby that starts with soil, seeds, and water. Gardeners plant flowers, foliage, or edible plants, such as herbs, vegetables, and fruits, and tend to those plants by watering and weeding. They watch their crops grow, and when they are ready, reap their returns. Gardeners can pick and display beautiful flowers and eat harvested fruits and vegetables. Gardens can be grown in a variety of places outside and inside, such as window boxes, ponds, greenhouses, containers, rooftops, patios, or balconies. Gardening can also be enjoyed many months of the year outside depending on the weather, and year-round inside.

The best title for this passage is

   6-A "How to Become a Gardener."

   6-B "Outdoor Gardening."

   6-C "How to Grow Plants."

   6-D "The Joys of Gardening."

7. The ancient Sumerians lived in 3000 BCE in a fertile valley between the Tigris and Euphrates rivers, an area that is modern-day Iraq. Even though they lived thousands of years ago, the ancient Sumerians' way of life was remarkably similar to our own. They had their own language and learned to write. They lived in large city-states with temples. They created bricks out of mud and used them to build walls surrounding their cities. To water their crops, the ancient Sumerians dug large canals from the rivers to their fields. This ancient civilization had its own government and was responsible for advances in early technology such as the invention of the wheel and the sailboat. Sumerian children played with toys and even enjoyed a game similar to checkers.

Which of the following would the author most likely agree with?

7-A The Sumerian civilization was much like a modern civilization.

7-B The Sumerian civilization was the most advanced of all time.

7-C Little is known about the way in which the Sumerians lived.

7-D Sumerian children were raised and educated like U.S. children.

QUESTIONS 8 AND 9 ARE BASED ON THE FOLLOWING PASSAGE.

The Brooklyn Bridge in New York spans the East River, connecting the boroughs of Manhattan and Brooklyn. The beautiful bridge took thirteen years to build and is more than 1,595 feet long. At the time of its opening, the Brooklyn Bridge was the longest suspension bridge in the United States. The bridge officially opened on May 24, 1883, with 1,800 vehicles and more than 150,000 people crossing it. While people were excited about the Brooklyn Bridge, it also made them nervous. The bridge took longer than expected to build, which made people doubt its stability. A few days after the opening, a rumor circulated that the bridge was going to collapse, which caused a terrible stampede on the bridge. To show people that the bridge was safe, P.T. Barnum had his famous elephant Jumbo lead a parade of twenty-one elephants across it.

8. This passage is mainly about

8-A the construction of the Brooklyn Bridge.

8-B opening day on the Brooklyn Bridge.

8-C how people first felt about the Brooklyn Bridge.

8-D a parade of elephants on the Brooklyn Bridge.

9. This passage best supports the statement that

9-A the Brooklyn Bridge was not safe when it first opened.

9-B people were afraid that the Brooklyn Bridge might collapse.

9-C the Brooklyn Bridge is still the longest bridge in the country.

9-D too many people were on the Brooklyn Bridge at one time.

10. Historians and Egyptologists believe they have finally discovered what killed King Tut, Egypt's famous boy king. For many years, they speculated that someone close to the king, such as an advisor or a relative, may have murdered him. An X-ray taken in 1968 seemed to confirm their suspicions; it revealed a possible crack in the back of Tut's skull, which meant that he could have been struck from behind with a heavy object. Modern technology has led them to a different conclusion, however. A CT scan performed on Tut's mummy revealed that the boy had suffered a badly broken leg a few days before his death, perhaps from a fall. The bone broke through the skin and likely caused an infection that killed the king.

The best title for this passage is

10-A "What Really Killed King Tut."

10-B "Who Killed King Tut."

10-C "King Tut, the Boy King."

10-D "The World's Most Famous King."

11. Mount Everest is the highest point on Earth. It is part of the Himalayas in Asia and is located on the border between Nepal and Tibet. It is more than 29,000 feet tall, and experienced climbers from all over the world flock to conquer it. Even though Mount Everest is not a difficult mountain to climb, its altitude poses many risks, and climbers should be aware of weather, wind, avalanches, sickness, and oxygen depletion. Climbers are required to obtain a permit that costs $25,000 per person to scale Mount Everest.

Which of the following would the author most likely agree with?

11-A Mount Everest is one of the most difficult mountains to climb.

11-B The winter is the best time to climb Mount Everest.

11-C The cost for a permit to climb Mount Everest is too expensive.

11-D Only experienced climbers should attempt to climb Mount Everest.

12. The northern cardinal is one of the most beloved birds in America. The cardinal is known for both its sharp crest and beautiful color. The male's bright red plumage is easily recognizable while the female's warm brown color with red accents is also appreciated. The northern cardinal is a large bird, nearly eight inches long, with a beautiful song that sounds like "cheer, cheer, cheer" or "purty, purty, purty." Cardinals don't migrate, and both the male and female sing nearly year-round, which makes them a welcome addition to any backyard birdfeeder.

The main message above is that

12-A many people like to see and hear the northern cardinal.

12-B the male cardinal is red, and the female is warm brown.

12-C the cardinal has a sharp crest on top of its head.

12-D cardinals enjoy eating at backyard birdfeeders.

exercises

ANSWER KEY AND EXPLANATIONS

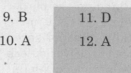

1. B	4. B	7. A	9. B	11. D
2. C	5. B	8. C	10. A	12. A
3. D	6. D			

1-B The main idea of the passage is that Flag Day is celebrated to honor the adoption of the American flag. Choices A, C, and D present details about Flag Day that support the main idea.

2-C While all the answer choices about the rainforest are true, this particular passage mainly discusses the importance of the plants in the rainforest because they are needed to make pharmaceuticals. Therefore, the main idea of the passage is choice C.

3-D This passage focuses on Clara Barton's contributions to humankind in addition to establishing the Red Cross. Choice D gives the main idea: Clara Barton spent her life finding ways to help others in need. Her establishment of a free public school (choice C) and the fact that she became both a teacher and a nurse (choice B) are details supporting this idea.

4-B This passage is mainly about Clara Barton's many accomplishments, so choice B is correct. Choices C and D give details that support the main idea.

5-B This passage is mainly about the celebration that was held on the day the Philadelphia Zoo opened. While the passage mentions how people traveled to the zoo that day (choice C) and the cost of admission (choice D), these are not the main idea. The passage does not discuss the rare and exotic animals that were at the zoo (choice A).

6-D The passage explains that gardeners grow herbs, vegetables, fruits, flowers, and foliage and then reap their rewards. It also tells how gardeners sometimes grow plants both indoors and outdoors and the ways in which they do this. The passage gives general information about gardening, so choice D is the best title: "The Joys of Gardening."

7-A The passage explains that even though the Sumerians lived thousands of years ago, their life was remarkably similar to our own. This is the main idea of the passage, so choice A is the correct answer.

8-C This passage is mainly about how people felt about the Brooklyn Bridge at first. The author explains that even though people were excited about the bridge, the bridge also made them nervous and that a rumor that the bridge was collapsing caused a stampede. Therefore, choice C is correct.

9-B This passage best supports the idea that people were afraid that the Brooklyn Bridge might collapse (choice B). The Brooklyn Bridge was safe, however, so choices A and D are incorrect.

10-A The main idea of this passage is that modern technology has led historians to believe that a broken leg followed by an infection killed King Tut. Therefore, the best title is "What Really Killed King Tut?"

11-D The passage says that while Mount Everest is not a difficult mountain to climb, its altitude makes it challenging. Therefore, the author would most likely agree that only experienced climbers should attempt to climb it.

12-A The opening sentence of this paragraph gives the main idea: "The northern cardinal is one of the most beloved birds in America." Choice A is closest to this idea.

LOOKING FOR DETAILS

In addition to being asked to find the main idea, questions on the Paragraph Comprehension subtest of the ASVAB will ask you about details in the passage. These details provide specific facts and information. Once again, it's a good idea to read the question *before* you read the passage. Look at the key words in the question, and then find these words in the passage. For example, if a question asks you about the length of a sailboat, look for the words *length* and *sailboat* in the passage.

Looking-for-details questions often begin with specific key words from the passage, as in the following:

William Shakespeare was _____.

The Great Depression was _____.

The weather in Alaska in the summer is _____.

You can spot a cumulous cloud by _____.

The three sample questions that follow illustrate typical looking-for-details questions.

Sample 1.   A trumpet is one of the oldest musical instruments. It is part of the brass family of instruments and dates back to 1500 BCE. It is made of brass tubing bent into an oblong shape with three valves on top and is played by blowing air into its mouthpiece using closed lips. There are many different types of trumpets, and the older versions did not have valves. The trumpet is used in all forms of musical styles, such as classical, rock, jazz, blues, and funk. Louis Armstrong and Miles Davis are two of the most famous trumpeters of the twentieth century.

The older versions of trumpets were different because they

1-A were made of brass.

1-B did not have valves.

1-C were used to play blues.

1-D were not in an oblong shape.

1-B   To find the answer to this looking-for-details question, look for the key words *older versions* in the passage. You'll see that right after these words it says *did not have valves.* This is what made older trumpets different from modern ones. Choice A is not correct because all trumpets are made of brass. Choice C is not correct because the passage does not say older trumpets were used to play the blues. Choice D is also incorrect because all trumpets are made in an oblong shape.

Sample 2. Alaska is the 49th and largest state in the United States. It is also the least densely populated state in the country. Alaska, like Hawaii, is completely separated from the lower forty-eight states. Its landscape is peppered with volcanoes, and it contains half of the world's glaciers. Alaska's economy depends on its oil and gas reserves. The Trans-Alaska Pipeline produces about 2.1 million barrels of oil per day and the state produces about 20 percent of the country's oil.

Alaska contains half of the world's

2-A oil supply.

2-B volcanoes.

2-C glaciers.

2-D population.

2-C The key words in this looking-for-details question are *half of the world's*. If you look for these words in the passage, you'll see that Alaska contains half of the world's glaciers, so choice C is correct. Choice A is not correct; Alaska produces about 20 percent of America's oil. Choice B is not correct because the passage says that Alaska is peppered with volcanoes. Choice D is not correct because the passage says Alaska is the least densely populated state. Therefore, it can't contain half the world's population.

Sample 3. Sea glass is a smooth, colorful glass found on beaches throughout the world. It is formed from littered glass left on beaches that has been smoothed by sand and water. The color of the sea glass is determined by the color of the glass from which it was formed. The most popular colors are green, clear, and brown, while purple, blue, and pink are less commonly found. Collecting sea glass is considered a hobby. Sea glass can be used to make a variety of objects, including jewelry.

Sea glass is made smooth by sand and

3-A water.

3-B wind.

3-C rocks.

3-D sun.

3-A The passage says that sea glass is made smooth by sand and water, so choice A is correct. Wind (choice B), rocks (choice C), and sun (choice D) are not mentioned in the passage.

EXERCISES: LOOKING FOR DETAILS 1

Directions: Now try the exercises below. Choose the best answer to each question. As you finish each exercise, check your answers with the answer key and explanations that follow.

1. Because of the surge in the use of computers in recent years, Web blogging has become a popular hobby. Hundreds of thousands of blogs are posted on the Internet. A blog is a Web site maintained and updated by a blogger, the author of a blog. A blog can focus on a range of different subjects from hobbies, such as cooking, reading, writing, decorating, or photography, to life events, such as a baby on the way, family life, or buying a home, to diary blogs that record a blogger's life. The blogger adds content—text, photographs, images, videos, and links—to the blog in a timely manner and interacts with readers, also called followers, who can leave comments for the blogger and others to read.

   Who updates a blog?

   1-A   a follower

   1-B   a blogger

   1-C   a reader

   1-D   a poster

2. The Day of the Dead is a Mexican holiday celebrated each year on the first two days of November in Mexico and parts of the United States. On this holiday, families and friends gather to remember loved ones who have passed away. They honor the deceased using traditional sugar skulls, marigolds, photos, memorabilia, and favorite foods and drinks. Family and friends bring these gifts to a deceased person's grave, where they dance and hold a celebration of the deceased person's life. The Day of the Dead dates back more than 3,000 years in Mexico.

   On the Day of the Dead, family and friends bring gifts to a deceased person's

   2-A   place of birth.

   2-B   former home.

   2-C   favorite place.

   2-D   grave site.

3. Dental floss is a thin ribbon of nylon used to clean between teeth. Dental floss removes food particles and plaque. The floss is inserted between teeth near the gum line and is used to scrape between teeth and under the gums. Many varieties of floss are available—from mint- and cinnamon-flavored to wax-coated. Levi Spear Parmly invented silk dental floss in 1815. In 1898, Johnson & Johnson received the first patent for silk floss. Dental floss is now made of nylon, which is stronger than silk.

   The first dental floss was made of

   3-A   silk.

   3-B   nylon.

   3-C   ribbon.

   3-D   wax.

4. The Tower of London, a historic fortress and monument, is considered one of the most famous tourist attractions in the world. Also called the Tower or Her Majesty's Royal Palace and Fortress, the Tower—which is actually a set of buildings—is still in use by the British government. The Tower contains several buildings, protective walls, and a moat. It was originally built as a palace, fortress, and prison, having housed royal prisoners such as Queen Elizabeth I, Henry VI, and Anne Boleyn. Throughout the years,

it has been used as a treasury, a zoo, a mint, an observatory, a public office, and a home to the Crown Jewels.

The Tower of London is still used today by

4-A   Queen Elizabeth I.

4-B   the British government.

4-C   her majesty's royal palace.

4-D   the city of London, England.

QUESTIONS 5 AND 6 ARE BASED ON THE FOLLOWING PASSAGE.

The Kentucky Derby is an annual horse race held on the first Saturday of May at Churchill Downs in Louisville, Kentucky. Held since 1875, it is one of the oldest horse races in the United States. It is known as "the most exciting two minutes in sports," because the one-and-a-quarter-mile race lasts only about two minutes. It is the first race of the Triple Crown followed by the Preakness and Belmont. The Kentucky Derby is the most popular and most attended of the three races. Spectators can be seen drinking mint juleps and wearing brightly colored dresses and large ornate hats.

5. Which of the following is TRUE according to this passage?

    5-A   The Kentucky Derby is the second race of the Triple Crown.

    5-B   The race is held in Bowling Green, Kentucky.

    5-C   The race is known as "the most exciting five minutes in sports."

    5-D   The Kentucky Derby is held on the first Saturday of May.

6. The Kentucky Derby takes place

    6-A   each year.

    6-B   twice a year.

    6-C   every two years.

    6-D   every five years.

QUESTIONS 7 AND 8 ARE BASED ON THE FOLLOWING PASSAGE.

Henry Ford, founder of the Ford Motor Company, revolutionized transportation with the invention of the assembly line that enabled mass production of his Model T automobile in 1908. The Model T was considered the first affordable automobile in America. Ford was born to farming parents in 1863, and as he grew up, he became interested in mechanics. In 1891, he gained employment with the Edison Illuminating Company as an engineer. During this time, he was able to experiment with engines and built a self-propelled vehicle in 1896. Throughout his life, Ford amassed 161 patents for products. The Ford Motor Company catapulted him from an inventor to one of the richest and most well-known people in the world.

7. Henry Ford worked at the Edison Illuminating Company as

    7-A   an assembly line worker.

    7-B   a mechanic.

    7-C   an engineer.

    7-D   a manager.

8. Henry Ford's Model T was considered the

    8-A   first affordable automobile in America.

    8-B   first automobile in America.

    8-C   fastest automobile in the world.

    8-D   most comfortable automobile in the world.

exercises

QUESTIONS 9 AND 10 ARE BASED ON THE FOLLOWING PASSAGE.

Brewing a good cup of tea is an easy way to warm the body and soothe the soul. First, gather what you will need: a teapot, a tea bag or loose tea leaves packed into an infuser, and a mug. Fill the teapot with cold water. Glass, clay, or ceramic teapots yield the best results. Bring the water to a boil and allow it to cool for a few minutes before adding it to your tea. For black or oolong teas, use hotter water. For green or white teas, use cooler water. Do not overfill the infuser with tea, so the water can circulate between the tea leaves. Allow the tea bag or infuser to sit for at least two to five minutes. Then, remove the tea bag or diffuser, and add milk, sugar, or honey to taste.

9. When making green or white teas, you should use
   9-A hotter water.
   9-B a glass teapot.
   9-C cooler water.
   9-D a ceramic teapot.

10. You should use hotter water when you make
    10-A green tea.
    10-B black tea.
    10-C diffused tea.
    10-D white tea.

QUESTIONS 11 AND 12 ARE BASED ON THE FOLLOWING PASSAGE.

The Nobel Prize is an international award given to recipients for achievements in five areas: physics, chemistry, physiology or medicine, literature, and peace. It was established in 1895 by Swedish inventor Alfred Nobel, who is the inventor of dynamite, and was first awarded in 1901. A medal and monetary prize accompany the award. Selected individuals are asked to nominate candidates. Of those chosen, fifteen make it to the final round. Nominees are not announced or notified that they have been considered.

11. Alfred Nobel is known as the inventor of
    11-A physics.
    11-B chemistry.
    11-C modern medicine.
    11-D dynamite.

12. Who nominates candidates for the Nobel Prize?
    12-A the public
    12-B a special committee
    12-C selected individuals
    12-D Alfred Nobel

ANSWER KEY AND EXPLANATIONS

1. B	4. B	7. C	9. C	11. D
2. D	5. D	8. A	10. B	12. C
3. A	6. A			

1-B According to the passage, a blog is a Web site maintained and updated by a blogger. This is the author of the blog.

2-D The passage explains that on the Day of the Dead, family and friends bring gifts to the deceased person's grave. Therefore, choice D is correct.

3-A The passage says that Levi Spear Parmly invented silk dental floss in 1815 and that Johnson & Johnson received the first patent for silk floss in 1898. Therefore, the first dental floss was made of silk. Dental floss today is made of nylon (choice D).

4-B The passage says the British government still uses the Tower of London.

5-D The only answer choice that is true is choice D. The Kentucky Derby is held on the first Saturday of May. Choice A is incorrect; the Kentucky Derby is the first race of the Triple Crown. Choice B is also incorrect; the Kentucky Derby is held in Louisville, Kentucky. Choice C is incorrect; the Kentucky Derby is known as "the most exciting two minutes in sports."

6-A The passage says the Kentucky Derby is an annual horse race. This means that it takes place once a year.

7-C The passage says Henry Ford worked at the Edison Illuminating Company as an engineer.

8-A Henry Ford's automobile was not the first automobile made (choice B), but it was considered the first affordable automobile. Choice A is correct.

9-C According to the passage, when making green or white teas, use cooler water.

10-B The passage says that you should use hotter water when making black or oolong teas.

11-D According to the passage, Alfred Nobel invented dynamite.

12-C Selected individuals nominate candidates for the Nobel Prize.

EXERCISES: LOOKING FOR DETAILS 2

Directions: Now try the exercises below. Choose the best answer to each question. As you finish each exercise, check your answers with the answer key and explanations that follow.

1. An alpaca is an animal used for herding in South America. Alpacas are similar to llamas, but the two animals differ in size, temperament, and ear shape. Alpacas were once bred for their meat, but the species has since been protected. Alpacas are now domesticated animals that are mainly bred for their fiber, which is similar to wool and used to make knitted and woven items, such as sweaters, hats, blankets, coats, ponchos, and bedding. Alpaca fiber comes in 52 natural colors.

   Today, alpacas are bred mainly for their

   1-A meat.

   1-B fiber.

   1-C temperament.

   1-D herding abilities.

2. The United Nations Children's Fund (UNICEF) is an intergovernmental humanitarian organization that assists children and mothers in more than 190 countries plagued by poverty, violence, disease, and discrimination. It promotes equal education for boys and girls, provides vaccinations to protect against disease, works to prevent the spread of HIV and AIDS through education, and creates a safe environment for children to live during emergencies and natural disasters. UNICEF relies on support from governments and private donors. It's headquartered in New York and its distribution center is located in Copenhagen, Denmark.

   UNICEF relies on support from governments and

   2-A public associations.

   2-B other countries.

   2-C private donors.

   2-D private organizations.

QUESTIONS 3 AND 4 ARE BASED ON THE FOLLOWING PASSAGE.

Each year, thousands of tourists visit Ernest Hemingway's house in Key West, which is now a museum. For more than ten years, the Nobel Prize-winning author lived in the home, where he wrote in the mornings when the temperature was coolest. Visitors of the Hemingway House and Museum can see Hemingway's furniture and the studio in which he penned his famous novel, *Farewell to Arms*. The house is adorned with the many antiques the author collected on his excursions in Europe and Africa. The home boasts the first swimming pool in Key West, which at sixty-five feet long, is still the largest. Descendants of Hemingway's beloved six-toed cats still inhabit the home and greet its many guests.

3. While living in Key West, Hemingway wrote in the mornings because

   3-A he was at his best.

   3-B it was quieter.

   3-C he swam at noon.

   3-D it was cooler.

4. Which novel did Hemingway write while living in his home in Key West?

4-A *The Sun Also Rises*

4-B *The Old Man and the Sea*

4-C *Farewell to Arms*

4-D *For Whom the Bell Tolls*

QUESTIONS 5 AND 6 ARE BASED ON THE FOLLOWING PASSAGE.

The practice of yoga began more than 3,000 years ago in India. Yoga is a form of exercise that uses breathing techniques, poses, and meditation to connect the mind, body, and spirit. There are many different forms of yoga, including hatha, which uses poses to develop strength and flexibility. Some of the different forms of hatha yoga are ashtanga, bikram, gentle, and vinyasa. Ashtanga is a fast-paced form that builds flexibility, strength, and concentration. Bikram or "hot yoga" is practiced in rooms heated to more than 100 degrees. Gentle yoga focuses on slow stretches and deep breathing. Vinyasa, the most popular form, is used to improve stamina, strength, and flexibility.

5. What type of yoga is practiced in rooms heated to more than 100 degrees?

5-A gentle

5-B bikram

5-C vinyasa

5-D ashtanga

6. What type of yoga is the most popular?

6-A vinyasa

6-B asthanga

6-C bikram

6-D gentle

7. Dorothea Lange (1895–1965) was an American photographer and photojournalist known for her work with the Farm Security Administration during the Great Depression. She studied photography in New York City and moved to San Francisco, where she operated a portrait studio. During the Depression, she left her studio to capture the faces of the unemployed and homeless. Lange and her husband, Paul Schuster Taylor, worked as a team documenting poverty and the plight of the poor migrant laborers and farm families. She also is known for her controversial photographs of Japanese Americans being sent to internment camps, which were seized by the U.S. Army.

Dorothea Lange is known for her controversial photographs of

7-A Japanese Americans being sent to internment camps.

7-B poor migrant families traveling from place to place.

7-C unemployed and homeless Americans.

7-D persons who posed in her studio in San Francisco.

8. Natural pearls are found inside a mollusk, such as an oyster, a mussel, or a clam, and are formed by the mollusk's ability to protect itself from a foreign substance. When an object such as a grain of sand gets trapped in the shell of a mollusk, it irritates its mantle, the organ that produces the mollusk's shell. The mantle tries to cover the irritation with layers of the same material it uses to make its shell, and this forms a pearl. Because natural pearls are very rare, most of the world's pearls are now cultured. Natural pearls can still be found in the seas near the island of Bahrain, and Australia still uses pearl diving ships. An X-ray can show if a pearl is natural or cultured because the layers of natural pearl are formed in a different way.

A mantle is

8-A   a type of mollusk.

8-B   an organ in a mollusk.

8-C   a type of natural pearl.

8-D   a cultured pearl.

9. With fossil fuel reserves being depleted at a faster rate than new ones can form, much research is being done on alternative energy sources such as wind energy from wind turbines. A wind turbine is a large rotating machine similar to a windmill that converts wind energy into electricity. Wind turbines are made of steel, and their blades are usually painted gray to blend in with clouds. The blades rotate using motors controlled by computers and can surpass 200 miles per hour. Groups of turbines are being built on many U.S. mountaintops in what are known as wind farms. Wind farms can contain a dozen to more than several hundred wind turbines generating electricity.

A wind turbine converts wind energy into

9-A   heat.

9-B   water.

9-C   electricity.

9-D   fossil fuels.

10. Eliezer "Elie" Wiesel survived the Holocaust and became a writer and an activist. He is the author of fifty-seven books. In his book *Night,* he recounts his experiences in the German concentration camps at Auschwitz and Buchenwald during World War II. For the ten years following the war, Wiesel refused to write or even talk about his experiences in the camps that claimed the lives of his mother, father, and sister. His other two sisters survived and were reunited after the war. Wiesel has been given many awards for educating the public about the Holocaust. He was awarded the Nobel Peace Prize in 1986 and was granted knighthood in the United Kingdom.

Wiesel has received many awards for teaching the public about

10-A   the United Kingdom.

10-B   World War II.

10-C   his family.

10-D   the Holocaust.

11. Ice hockey is a team sport in which players skate on ice using sticks to hit a puck into the opposing team's goal. It was once widely popular in areas with cold climates such as Canada, Sweden, Russia, and the northern United States, but the invention of indoor ice rinks has enabled the sport to be played year-round in warmer climates. Ice hockey's history dates back to the mid-1800s in Windsor, Nova Scotia, but developed into a modern sport in Montreal, Canada. It is Canada's official national winter sport and continues to be immensely popular throughout the country. Despite the fact that only six of the thirty National Hockey League franchises are in Canada, Canadians comprise most of the teams.

Ice hockey developed into a modern sport in

11-A   Nova Scotia.

11-B   Canada.

11-C   the United States.

11-D   Sweden.

12. Buddhism is a religion, a philosophy, and a way of life based on the teachings of Siddhartha Gautama, more commonly known as Buddha. An estimated 350- to 1,500-million people are followers of Buddhism, the fourth largest religion in the world. The religion was founded by Buddha in the sixth century BCE in India. Buddhism teaches suffering, rebirth, and karma and does not recognize the worship of a deity or the existence of a human soul. Six forms of Buddhism

are practiced in various countries throughout the world: Theravada, Mahayana, Vajrayana, Tibetan, Zen, and Modern Buddhism.

How many forms of Buddhism are practiced throughout the world?

12-A three

12-B four

12-C five

12-D six

exercises

ANSWER KEY AND EXPLANATIONS

1. B	4. C	7. A	9. C	11. B
2. C	5. B	8. B	10. D	12. D
3. D	6. A			

1-B The passage explains that alpacas were once bred for their meat (choice A), but today they are bred mainly for their fiber, which is used to make knitted and woven items such as clothing and bedding.

2-C If you look for the key words "support from governments," you'll see that UNICEF relies on support from governments and private donors. Therefore, choice C is correct.

3-D The passage says that Hemingway wrote in the mornings when the temperature was coolest. Choice D is the correct answer.

4-C Hemingway wrote the novels in all the answer choices, but the passage explains that he wrote *Farewell to Arms* while living in his house in Key West.

5-B If you look for the key words "more than 100 degrees," you'll see that bikram yoga, also called "hot yoga," is the correct answer.

6-A The last sentence of the passage states that vinyasa is the most popular type of hatha yoga.

7-A According to the passage, Dorothea Lange's photos of Japanese Americans being sent to internment camps, which were seized by the U.S. Army, were controversial. Choice A is the correct answer.

8-B A mantle is the organ that produces the mollusk's shell. Choice B is the correct answer.

9-C The passage explains that a wind turbine is similar to a windmill and converts wind energy into electricity.

10-D According to the passage, Wiesel has been given many awards for educating the public about the Holocaust.

11-B The passage explains that ice hockey dates back to the mid-1800s in Windsor, Nova Scotia, but developed into a modern sport in Montreal, Canada.

12-D Six forms of Buddhism are practiced throughout the world: Theravada, Mahayana, Vajrayana, Tibetan, Zen, and Modern Buddhism.

MAKING INFERENCES

When you make an *inference*, you make an educated guess based on the information at hand. Some questions on the Paragraph Comprehension subtest of the ASVAB will ask you to make an inference about a passage. You won't find the answer to an inference question in the passage. Rather, you have to use the information in the passage to make the inference. This requires careful reading, logic, and reasoning.

Inference questions are often stated as follows:

From this passage, it is reasonable to infer that _____.

The author probably believes that _____.

Which of the following is implied by this passage?

It can be inferred from this passage that _____.

The following three sample questions are typical inference questions.

Sample 1.   The American crocodile, which inhabits South Florida, is an endangered species largely because of human beings. The urban sprawl in Florida has encroached upon the crocodile's habitat, making encounters between crocodiles and humans more frequent. While people often think of crocodiles as ferocious creatures, they are actually shy and reserved. Crocodiles will avoid conflicts with human beings unless provoked. Those who discover a crocodile on their land should contact the Florida Fish and Wildlife Conservation Commission to move the crocodile to a safe location away from people.

Which of the following can be assumed from this passage?

1-A Crocodiles have many places to live.

1-B Crocodiles rarely attack human beings.

1-C Crocodiles are rarely seen in South Florida.

1-D Crocodiles in South Florida are often kept as pets.

1-B   The author says that while most people think of crocodiles as ferocious creatures, they are actually shy and avoid conflicts with humans unless provoked. From this, you can infer that crocodiles rarely attack people, so choice B is correct. Choice A is incorrect because the passage says that urban sprawl has encroached upon the crocodile's habitat. This statement also makes choice C incorrect. Nothing in the passage should lead you to believe that people in South Florida keep crocodiles as pets (choice D).

Sample 2. Dolley Madison was the wife of James Madison, the fourth president of the United States. Dolley was known for her outgoing personality and flamboyant style of décor and dress. She relished her position as hostess of White House functions, and guests adored her. However, it was in August of 1814, during the War of 1812, that Dolley showed her country just how special and strong she was. When Washington, D.C., was about to be invaded by British troops, Dolley was ordered to immediately evacuate the White House. She refused, however, until she had secured important government documents and a famous portrait of George Washington and had them transported to a safe location. When Dolley and James returned to Washington, they learned that the White House had been burned down and that Dolley had saved the day.

From this passage, you might infer that

2-A Dolley's actions got her into trouble.

2-B Dolley was involved in politics.

2-C Dolley enjoyed helping people.

2-D Dolley was a brave person.

2-D Dolley stayed in the White House even though British troops were approaching. From this, you can infer that she was very brave. Nothing in the passage suggests that she got into trouble for doing this, so choice A is incorrect. The passage also does not mention her involvement in politics (choice B). While she may have enjoyed helping others, nothing in the passage suggests this, so choice C is also incorrect.

Sample 3. Before the days of the U.S. Postal Service, a group of 80 to 100 young men rode on horses to transport mail from Missouri to California. These riders were part of the legendary Pony Express. They rode from station to station, quickly passing their mail bag to the next rider. While riders enjoyed good pay, not everyone met the requirements of the job. Riders could not be older than 20 or weigh more than 120 pounds. They had to be comfortable riding a horse—fast—for a long period of time. Riders rode through rough terrain with raging rivers, scorching deserts, and blinding snowstorms. They sometimes faced hostile Native Americans who were angry over the recent loss of their land.

Based on the passage, the reader may conclude that Pony Express riders had to be young and small because they

3-A needed to ride quickly.

3-B had to face Native Americans.

3-C had to travel a great distance.

3-D needed less pay.

3-A The passage mentions that Pony Express riders had to ride fast from station to station. This is the most likely reason that they had to be young and light. Heavier men would cause a horse to ride more slowly. Their age and weight had nothing to do with them having to face Native Americans (choice B), having to travel far (choice C), or needing less pay (choice D).

EXERCISES: MAKING INFERENCES 1

Directions: Now try the exercises below. Choose the best answer to each question. As you finish each exercise, check your answers with the answer key and explanations that follow.

1. Chesley Burnett "Sully" Sullenberger is an American airline pilot from California, who is best-known for his emergency landing of US Airways Flight 1549 in the Hudson River, New York, on January 15, 2009. All 150 people aboard the plane survived. The flight had taken off from LaGuardia Airport in New York and was destined for the Charlotte/Douglas International Airport in North Carolina, when an impact with a flock of birds damaged the aircraft's engines. With not enough time to return to LaGuardia or make it to another airport, Sullenberger quickly decided that his best bet was to land the plane in the Hudson River. He and his crew have been honored for their bravery on that day. He also wrote the book *Highest Duty,* a memoir of the events surrounding the Flight 1549 landing.

   The author probably believes that Sully Sullenberger

   1-A has many years' experience.

   1-B makes good decisions under pressure.

   1-C enjoys dealing with people.

   1-D has been in this situation before.

2. For hundreds of years, people tried to decode the Egyptian hieroglyphics found in ancient tombs and at other archeological sites. Although many people tried to determine the pictographs' meanings, it would take another archeological find to finally crack the code. The Rosetta Stone was first discovered in 1799 in Egypt. The stone is important because it includes text that is written in both hieroglyphics and Greek. Scholars used the Greek translation to decipher the meanings of the hieroglyphics. The Rosetta Stone is currently on display at the British Museum so that everyone can study this amazing artifact.

   The author suggests that the Rosetta Stone

   2-A helped people understand Greek.

   2-B was large and heavy.

   2-C helped people understand the past.

   2-D was found in a tomb.

3. On March 28, 1979, a cooling malfunction at the Three Mile Island Unit 2 nuclear plant in Dauphin County, Pennsylvania, caused the Unit 2 core to melt and release radioactive gases into the air. Even though there were no deaths or injuries, it is considered the most serious nuclear accident in U.S. history. The accident brought to light many other nuclear-power-plant operation issues, such as emergency-response planning, radiation protection, and reactor-operator training. It took nearly twelve years and cost more than $900 million to clean up the damage. Unit 2 has since been deactivated. An eighteen-year study by the Pennsylvania Department of Health proved that there were no health problems caused by the accident.

   It can be implied by reading this passage that the accident at Three Mile Island

   3-A resulted in many people eventually becoming sick.

   3-B caused people to use less nuclear energy.

3-C caused damage throughout most of the United States.

3-D resulted in nuclear power plants operating more safely.

4. Carl Jung was a Swiss psychiatrist who lived during the turn of the twentieth century. Many consider him to be the father of modern psychology. Jung worked very closely with Sigmund Freud, but the two men had a disagreement and never reconciled. Jung's most famous idea was that all human beings share a collective unconscious. In other words, all human beings share some of the same ideas. We fit people into archetypes—types that all humans recognize. For instance, all humans associate certain personality traits, such as selflessness and honor, with the archetypal hero. When we see someone act out those traits, we assume he or she is heroic.

From this passage, you might infer that Carl Jung

4-A believed most people think in the same way.

4-B eventually made up with Sigmund Freud.

4-C thought most people were selfish and cruel.

4-D thought most people were selfless and honorable.

5. Sakura is the Japanese name for the cherry blossom tree, which does not produce fruit, but displays beautiful pink blossoms that often find their way into backyards and home décor. In ancient Japan, cherry blossom trees most often graced the grounds of the richest and most respected families in the country, but today they can be found around most public buildings. The blossom is a traditional symbol of love and the rebirth of spring. As an earlier gesture of friendship, in 1912, Japan gave 3,020 cherry blossom trees to the United States and then repeated the gesture in 1956 with another 3,800 trees. These trees can be found in many of the country's major cities, including Washington D.C.'s West Potomac Park and New York City's Sakura Park.

The author suggests that today cherry blossom trees

5-A are a gesture of friendship.

5-B is fairly common.

5-C produce fruit.

5-D grow mainly in Japan.

6. Chichen Itza is a world-famous archeological site in Mexico. Chichen Itza was once a Mayan city that served as a religious and cultural center for the Mayan civilization. The Mayans began building Chichen Itza in the seventh century CE. Later during that century, many people left the city and inhabited the surrounding farmland. By the tenth century, however, the city was again filled with people. During its prime, Chichen Itza was a bastion of religion, art, and culture for the Mayans. Although Chichen Itza once contained hundreds of standing structures, now only about thirty remain. Today, thousands of people visit the ruins every year.

According to this passage, it can be inferred that

6-A archeologists have more to discover in Chichen Itza.

6-B Chichen Itza is no longer a popular place.

6-C the ruins at Chichen Itza extend into nearby farmlands.

6-D Chichen Itza has changed a great deal over time.

7. Long before skiing became a popular winter sport, humans used skis to travel. The oldest skis were created in Sweden more than 4,500 years ago. For thousands of years, people in countries such as Russia, Denmark, and Norway used skis as their primary mode of transportation during the long winter months. Skiing did not become a leisure activity until the

nineteenth century, a time when the distinction between alpine (downhill) skiing and cross-country skiing became clear. Alpine skiers race down snowy mountains, while cross-country skiers gently propel themselves across a primarily flat landscape using skis and poles. Cross-country skiing was one of seven sports featured at the first Winter Olympics in 1924. Since then, Scandinavian athletes have dominated the sport. Norway holds the record for winning the most cross-country skiing gold medals with a total of thirty.

From this passage, you might infer that alpine skiing

7-A   is more fun than cross-country skiing.

7-B   takes place most often in Norway.

7-C   is more dangerous than cross-country skiing.

7-D   is the most popular part of the Olympics.

QUESTIONS 8 AND 9 ARE BASED ON THE FOLLOWING PASSAGE.

What do investigators do when they discover the badly decomposed body of a crime victim? When investigators have little more than skeletal remains to work with, they may call in forensic anthropologists to help them determine the victim's characteristics. By studying and measuring a victim's bones, forensic anthropologists can often determine physical traits such as gender, age, height, weight, and race. Investigators can use this information to narrow their search for missing persons and identify the victim. In addition to helping with criminal investigations, however, forensic anthropologists study ancient skeletons to learn about the past.

8. The author suggests that forensic anthropologists

8-A   take a great deal of time when examining bones.

8-B   cannot determine hair and eye color.

8-C   cannot differentiate males from females.

8-D   prefer to study ancient skeletons.

9. The author probably believes that the job of a forensic anthropologist

9-A   is more important than the job of an investigator.

9-B   requires more skill than the job of an investigator.

9-C   is difficult and dangerous.

9-D   is interesting and worthwhile.

QUESTIONS 10 AND 11 ARE BASED ON THE FOLLOWING PASSAGE.

In golf, each stroke a person takes while playing a hole counts as one point. Each hole indicates its par, or the number of strokes it *should* take to get the ball from the tee box to the hole. Pars on most standard golf courses range from three to five points, depending on the difficulty of the hole. A "birdie" is one stroke below par, while an "eagle" is two strokes below par. If a golfer puts the ball in the hole on the first stroke, he or she scores a "hole in one," or an "ace." Golfers do their best to avoid scoring "bogeys," which are additional strokes above par. The goal in golf, unlike other sports, is to score the least points.

10. According to this passage, a golfer who scores an eagle

10-A   is not doing as well as par.

10-B   is playing very well.

10-C   has made a hole in one.

10-D   is not doing as well as a birdie.

11. According to this passage, a golfer who scores an ace has

11-A made a hole in one.

11-B not made par.

11-C not scored as well as an eagle.

11-D won the game.

12. Women first used vacuum cleaners set on the exhaust function to dry their wet hair. The first electric hairdryer was invented in 1890 by a French man named Alexandre Godefoy. It was not popular because of its noisy motor. In 1920, the first handheld hairdryer was introduced, but this model was heavy and cumbersome and usually overheated. In 1951, the first user-friendly and safe hairdryer was made. It was a handheld model connected to a plastic bonnet that fit over a woman's head. Most hairdryers today are fashioned after this model, but without the bonnet.

The author probably believes that early hair dryers were

12-A not warm.

12-B too expensive.

12-C not practical.

12-D too light.

ANSWER KEY AND EXPLANATIONS

1. B	4. A	7. C	9. D	11. A
2. C	5. B	8. B	10. B	12. C
3. D	6. D			

1-B　Choice B is the best answer. Because Sullenberger quickly decided to land the plane in the Hudson River, he saved the lives of all 150 passengers. Therefore, you can infer that the author probably believes that Sullenberger makes good decisions under pressure. The passage does not mention that he has many years' experience (choice A) or that he enjoys dealing with people (choice C). Nothing in the passage leads you to believe that this has happened to him before (choice D).

2-C　Before the discovery of the Rosetta Stone, people could not determine the meaning of hieroglyphics found in ancient tombs. Because the Rosetta Stone had text in both hieroglyphics and Greek, scholars used it to understand the meaning of the hieroglyphics. Therefore, choice C is the best answer, since the hieroglyphics helped scholars learn about the ancient world.

3-D　The passage says that the accident brought to light many other nuclear-power-plant operation issues, so you can infer that it resulted in nuclear power plants operating more safely. People did not get sick from the accident (choice A). There is not enough information in the passage to infer that the accident caused people to use less nuclear energy or that it caused damage throughout most of the United States.

4-A　You can infer from the passage that Carl Jung believed that most people think in the same way, since he believed all human beings associate certain personality traits with the archetypal hero. The passage says he and Freud never reconciled, so choice B is incorrect. The passage does not contain information that would lead you to conclude that either choice C or D is correct.

5-B　The author says that today cherry blossom trees can be found around most public buildings. Therefore, the author suggests that the trees are now fairly common. They are not a gesture of friendship (choice A), and they don't produce fruit (choice C). They also are not grown mainly in Japan, since they are now common in the United States (choice D).

6-D　The passage says that Chichen Itza once contained hundreds of structures, but today only about thirty remain. Therefore, you can infer that the city has changed a great deal over time. We don't know if archaeologists have more to discover there (choice A). Since thousands of people visit Chichen Itza each year, it is a popular place, so choice B is incorrect. Nothing in the passage leads you to believe that the city extends into nearby farmlands, so choice C is also incorrect.

7-C　The only inference you can make from the passage is that alpine skiing is more dangerous than cross-country skiing, since alpine skiers race down snowy mountains. Therefore, choice C is the best answer.

8-B The passage states that forensic anthropologists can often determine physical traits such as gender, age, height, weight, and race. It does not seem that they can identify hair and eye color, as they only deal with skeletal remains. Therefore, choice B is the best answer.

9-D The author seems to think that forensic anthropologists have a fascinating job that helps people. Therefore, choice D is the best answer.

10-B According to the passage, an eagle is two strokes below par, which means it's two strokes better than par. Therefore, choice B is correct.

11-A If a golfer scores a hole in one, he or she has only done this on one hole; it doesn't mean that the golfer has won the game (choice D). The golfer has done better than par (choice B) and has scored better than an eagle (choice C). The golfer has made a hole in one. Choice A is correct.

12-C The passage says that early hairdryers were noisy, heavy, and cumbersome. Therefore, they were not practical. Choice C is correct.

answers exercises

EXERCISES: MAKING INFERENCES 2

Directions: Now try the exercises below. Choose the best answer to each question. As you finish each exercise, check your answers with the answer key and explanations that follow.

1. When Helen Keller (1880–1968) was nineteen months old, an illness left her without sight and hearing. With the help of a patient teacher, Anne Sullivan, she learned how to communicate. Sullivan, also blind, taught Keller by spelling out words into her hand. Sullivan and Keller shared a forty-nine-year-long relationship. Keller eventually received a bachelor's degree and went on to become a writer and an activist. She campaigned for the rights of women, workers, the blind, and the handicapped. She wrote a series of autobiographies, including *The Story of My Life,* and helped raise funds for the American Foundation for the Blind.

   Which of the following can be assumed from this passage?

   1-A   Sullivan and Keller were friends.

   1-B   Sullivan and Keller were the same age.

   1-C   Sullivan taught at a school for blind children.

   1-D   Sullivan also lost her sight because of an illness.

2. Making pasta from scratch takes time and patience, but is a satisfying and delicious way to enjoy Italian cuisine. To start, place two cups of flour, three eggs, and one teaspoon each of water, olive oil, and salt into a food processor, running the machine until a ball of dough forms. To hand-roll the dough, divide it into several balls and work with one ball at a time, covering the waiting balls to keep them moist. Using a rolling pin, roll the ball until it is about one-eighth of an inch thick. Then, fold it and roll it again. Repeat this action several times. On the final roll, make the dough paper thin and hang the sheet to dry. When it is dry but still soft, cut it into the shape of your choice and cook for about four minutes. Then, add sauce and enjoy!

   The author probably believes that

   2-A   most people don't roll the ball enough.

   2-B   most people aren't skilled enough to make pasta.

   2-C   pasta made from scratch tastes best.

   2-D   pasta from a box takes longer to cook.

3. Parrots are famous for their ability to "speak"—or, at least, mimic the sounds of words. Parrots have many more distinctive traits than just that, however. The macaw parrot, for instance, is one of the world's largest and most colorful parrots. Despite its elegance, it has one strange and distasteful habit: It eats dirt! Macaws regularly dine on various kinds of soil, particularly clay. Scientists believe that the clay helps parrots by calming their stomachs. At certain times of year, macaws eat unripe fruit. This fruit upsets their stomachs, and its seeds even carry a kind of poison. Special materials in the clay, however, may neutralize the poison, keep the birds safe, and make them feel better.

   The author probably believes that macaws eat clay because it

   3-A   looks like seeds.

   3-B   is like medicine.

   3-C   tastes very good.

   3-D   is like vitamins.

QUESTIONS 4 AND 5 ARE BASED ON THE FOLLOWING PASSAGE.

Though located in the sparkling blue Caribbean Sea, St. Thomas, one of the Virgin Islands, is a U.S. territory. Its scenery suggests paradise, and adding to that beauty are the island's mangrove forests. Mangrove trees grow along the shoreline, but their roots extend above water, suspending the trees in the air. This space between the roots creates a safe haven for fish and crabs. The roots also hold the shoreline in place, preventing erosion, and act as a filter for debris, helping to keep the water crystal clear. Above ground, mangrove forests are home to many unique birds and lizards. These havens have taken a hard hit, though, as tourism and the resident population continue to grow. In an attempt to lessen the human impact, some owners of tourist-attracting businesses designed mangrove forest tours where tourists learn about the ecosystem and plant mangrove sprouts.

4. Based on the passage, the reader may conclude that mangroves in St. Thomas have been harmed because

4-A there are too many fish there.

4-B the shoreline has eroded.

4-C the water has become polluted.

4-D there are too many people there.

5. The author probably believes that if the mangrove trees in St. Thomas are gone

5-A the tourists will stop visiting.

5-B the water will become murky.

5-C fish will reproduce too quickly.

5-D birds will become ill.

6. New York City is well-known for its urban transportation system. In the early 1800s, the city's multi-passenger stagecoaches and horse-drawn carriages clogged and tore up city streets. When an above-ground railroad did not provide the necessary relief, city planners decided to look higher and lower for their transportation solutions. The first "el" train, suspended above the city, was built in 1868, though it was shaky and unsafe. After many improvements, the railway line expanded, as did the city. As bridges and apartment buildings were erected, it was clear that the city transportation must move underground. The first subway opened to city residents in 1904 and soon carried more than 580,000 passengers each day. More subway train lines were built across the city, and the Transit Authority brought the routes together in 1939. Before long, about one-tenth of the country's urban population was traveling on New York City's trains.

From this passage, it is reasonable to infer that subways were built underground because

6-A people could travel more quickly underground.

6-B it was unsafe to travel above ground.

6-C there was not room for trains above ground.

6-D people wanted to travel in trains underground.

QUESTIONS 7 AND 8 ARE BASED ON THE FOLLOWING PASSAGE.

Bred in Portugal thousands of years ago, Portuguese water dogs were valued for their loyalty and fierce protection of their owners. As the companions of fishermen, the dogs had to have excellent swimming skills. Owners trained the highly intelligent dogs to dive under the water and retrieve lost fishing gear.

Though the breed was popular in Europe for centuries, it did not arrive in the United States until the 1960s. The American Kennel Club (AKC) accepted the Portuguese water dog for registration in 1983, allowing the breed to participate in AKC-sponsored events. In recent years, the breed's hypoallergenic coat has made it a popular choice among people with allergies. This is one reason that President Barack Obama selected a Portuguese water dog as the first pet; his daughter Malia is allergic to most dogs. Portuguese water dogs are extremely friendly and get along well with children. The breed is people-orientated, and the dogs do not like being alone for long periods.

7. Based on the passage, the reader may conclude that the Portuguese water dog

   7-A   is sometimes hard to train.

   7-B   prefers the company of adults.

   7-C   needs to live near water.

   7-D   makes an excellent family pet.

8. From this passage, you might infer that the Portuguese water dog is a good choice for people with allergies because its coat

   8-A   stays cleaner than most dogs' coats.

   8-B   is different from other dogs' coats.

   8-C   is shorter than most other dogs' coats.

   8-D   dries more quickly than other dogs' coats.

9. Changing your oil is one of the easiest things you can do to keep your car running smoothly. First, position your car on a ramp and engage the parking brake. Chock the tires to prevent the car from rolling. Next, place a bucket beneath your car's oil pan, and remove the drain plug. Allow the old oil to drain completely, and remove the old oil filter. Next, return the drain plug to the oil pan, and tighten it into place. Then, screw the new oil filter into place. Finally, open the hood of your car, locate the oil cap, and remove it. Add fresh oil to your engine, and replace the cap. When you finish, be sure to properly dispose of your old oil and oil filter.

The author probably believes that

9-A   changing oil is a simple task.

9-B   removing the old oil filter is tricky.

9-C   changing oil takes much practice.

9-D   removing the drain plug is difficult.

10. When she was nineteen years old, Susan Bucher moved to Alaska's Wrangell Mountains, where she hunted for food and learned how to work with sled dogs, a practice called mushing. She trained for the famous Iditarod Trail Sled Dog Race, traveling a course spanning more than 1,150 miles through the harsh and beautiful Alaskan wilderness over a duration of ten to seventeen days. With so much time alone, Bucher's sled dogs became her best friends, and she and the dogs took care of each other during their time in the wild. Together, they won four Iditarod races, an unparalleled accomplishment for a female racer.

Which of the following is implied by this passage?

10-A   Nineteen is a good age to begin training for racing.

10-B   Susan Bucher has retired from sled dog racing.

10-C   The Iditarod Trail Sled Dog Race is extremely difficult to win.

10-D   Alaska's Wrangell Mountains are a nice place to live.

11. Long ago, Britain was invaded and conquered by a group called the Normans. The Normans were descendents of the Vikings who lived in northern France. In 1066, their leader William, Duke of Normandy, was insulted by the behavior of the English king, Harold. When the English Army was occupied with other battles, William took his own army across the English Channel. Members of the Norman Army landed at the village of Hastings, where they built a fort. By the time Harold and his army arrived, the Normans were ready for battle. On October 14, 1066, the Normans outfought the English Army. King Harold was killed, and William proclaimed himself the ruler of Britain. After that, he would be remembered as "William the Conqueror."

From this passage, you can assume that

11-A William changed the course of history.

11-B people thought William was a good ruler.

11-C Harold once again took control after the battle.

11-D the Norman Army won many other battles.

12. Born in the Netherlands in 1853, Vincent Van Gogh had a quiet childhood with his five brothers and sisters. His uncles were respected art dealers, and Van Gogh's love for art blossomed at the age of sixteen, when he and his brother Theo started working for them. Van Gogh had an indefinable illness, however, which caused him to leave the business in 1876. After a few teaching stints, Van Gogh felt that his place was to help the poor, and he became a missionary. On his missions, he sketched his surroundings and eventually realized that painting was his true calling. He moved to The Hague and began studying with famous artists and later became one of them. He then moved to Provence, a seaside region of France, where he painted many of the nature-inspired scenes that would become a big force in the Impressionist Movement, featuring thick brushstrokes and natural light. In 1889, he painted what was perhaps his most famous work, *Starry Night*.

The passage suggests that Van Gogh

12-A started the Impressionist Movement.

12-B preferred to paint outdoors rather than indoors.

12-C passed away from an illness at a young age.

12-D was one of the world's most talented artists.

exercises

ANSWER KEY AND EXPLANATIONS

1. A	4. D	7. D	9. A	11. A
2. C	5. B	8. D	10. C	12. D
3. B	6. C			

1-A The passage says that Sullivan and Keller shared a forty-nine-year relationship. This means that they were most likely friends. Choice A is the best answer. Sullivan was Keller's teacher, so she was likely older than Keller, so choice B is not correct. The passage does not contain enough information to conclude that Sullivan also taught other blind children (choice C) or that she lost her sight because of an illness (choice D).

2-C The author describes homemade pasta as delicious, so you can infer that the author thinks it's better than boxed pasta. Choice C is best.

3-B The author says that scientists believe materials in the clay calm the birds' stomachs. Therefore, it is like medicine.

4-D The passage says that mangroves have taken a hard hit as tourism and resident populations continue to grow. This means that mangroves have been harmed because of too many people visiting and living in St. Thomas. Choice D is correct.

5-B The author says that the mangroves act as a filter for debris and help keep the water crystal clear. Therefore, if the mangroves are gone, debris will get into the water and change its color. Choice B is the correct answer.

6-C The passage says that when bridges and apartment buildings were erected, the city transportation system had to move underground. This means that there was not enough room for a subway system above ground. Choice C is the correct answer.

7-D The passage says that Portuguese water dogs are very friendly, get along well with children, are loyal, and intelligent. This information leads you to the conclusion that these dogs make excellent family pets. Choice D is correct.

8-D The passage says a Portuguese water dog's coat is hypoallergenic. This means that its coat is different from that of most other dogs. Choice B is the best answer.

9-A The opening sentence of this passage states that changing your oil is one of the easiest things you can do keep your car running smoothly. Therefore, choice A is the correct answer.

10-C The passage said the course for the Iditarod Trail Sled Dog Race is more than 1,150 miles long and extends through harsh Alaskan wilderness. This makes it seem as if the race is very difficult to win. Choice C is the correct answer. There isn't enough information in the passage to know if nineteen is a good age to begin training (choice A) or if Susan Bucher has retired (choice B). And, the Wrangell Mountains sounds as if it is a difficult place to live (choice D).

11-A Harold would have continued as King of England if William had not taken it upon himself to overthrow him. Therefore, William changed the course of history. Choice A is correct.

12-D The passage says that Van Gogh became a famous artist and that he was a big force in the Impressionist Movement. This suggests that he was a very talented artist. Choice D is the best answer.

answers exercises

FINDING WORD MEANINGS

The final type of question you will encounter on the Paragraph Comprehension subtest will assess your vocabulary skills. Word meaning questions ask you to determine the definition of a word as used in the context of the paragraph. You can use *context clues*, nearby words or phrases, in the paragraph to help you figure out the meaning of the unknown word. Read the entire paragraph carefully to get an idea of what the author is trying to say. This will help you eliminate obviously incorrect choices first. Remember to read the question first before reading the paragraph. This helps you understand what you must look for as you read.

Questions that ask you to find the meaning of a word will often begin like this:

> In this passage, the word <u>rowdy</u> means_____.

> As used above, <u>tedious</u> means_____.

> The word <u>fraternize</u> as used in the last sentence means _____.

Review the following three samples of word meaning questions before you move on to the exercise.

Sample 1. With more than 50 million participants, birding has become the number-one hobby in the United States. Birding is the observation of birds in their natural habitats. Birders use their ears and eyes and sometimes binoculars to detect birds. This challenging-yet-rewarding activity can be enjoyed solo or with a group. Birdwatchers usually consult a field guide that contains pictures and information about the different species of birds to aid in identifying the birds they come across.

In this context, <u>solo</u> means

1-A alone.

1-B quickly.

1-C easily.

1-D before.

1-A The word *solo* means without companion or *alone*. The context clue is the phrase *or with a group*. This tells you that *solo* means the opposite of *or with a group*. Choices B, C, and D are unrelated to the passage.

Sample 2. The first Earth Day was recognized on April 22, 1970, as a day of appreciation of the environment, and it has continued every year since in many countries throughout the world. Many U.S. cities participate in a full week of events prior to Earth Day. The events focus on educating the public about recycling, energy efficiency, global warming, and waste reduction and urge people to do their part to clean up Earth's environment.

As used above, the word <u>focus</u> means

2-A view.

2-B carry.

2-C center.

2-D prevent.

2-C The correct answer is *center*. When you *focus* on something, you *center* your attention on a specific person or project. The Earth Day events *center* on educating people about protecting the environment. *View* and *focus* are related, but you could not substitute *view* for *focus* in the paragraph. *Carry* and *prevent* are unrelated to the topic.

Sample 3. Puerto Vallarta is a tropical port city in the state of Jalisco in Mexico. It was thrust into the light as a tourist destination during the 1960s with the release of the U.S. film *The Night of the Iguana*, starring Elizabeth Taylor, Richard Burton, Ava Gardner, and Deborah Kerr. *The Love Boat* television series of the 1970s and 1980s also made the city famous. The show used the city as a port of call for the *Pacific Princess*. Since then, many other television shows and movies have been filmed there. Today, nearly 50 percent of the city's economy is based on tourism.

The word <u>thrust</u> in the second sentence means

3-A removed.

3-B finished.

3-C knocked.

3-D propelled.

3-D The word *thrust* means to *push with force*. *Propelled* is an acceptable synonym for *thrust*. The author is trying to tell you how a movie *propelled* Puerto Vallarta into the spotlight. Choices A, B, and C could not be substituted for thrust and maintain the integrity of the sentence.

EXERCISES: FINDING WORD MEANINGS

Directions: Now try the exercises below. Choose the best answer for each question. As you finish each exercise, check your answers with the answer key and explanations that follow.

QUESTIONS 1 AND 2 ARE BASED ON THE FOLLOWING PASSAGE.

The bald eagle is the national bird and symbol of the United States. This species is only found in North America, and about half of the bird's population lives in Alaska. A large bird of prey, the bald eagle is twenty-eight to forty inches tall and can weigh up to fifteen pounds. Bald eagles have brown bodies, white heads and tails, yellow eyes, hooked beaks, and talons on their feet. Males and females look identical, except for size; females are usually larger than males. Bald eagles survive on a diet of mostly fish, which they can snatch right out of the water with their talons. This species builds the largest nest of any other North American bird. At one time, the bald eagle was on the brink of extinction but has since been removed from the endangered species list.

1. The word _identical_ in the fifth sentence means
   - **1-A** alike.
   - **1-B** tiny.
   - **1-C** scary.
   - **1-D** angry.

2. In this context, _snatch_ means
   - **2-A** swim.
   - **2-B** fly.
   - **2-C** grasp.
   - **2-D** drop.

3. Coffee makers collect residues and other impurities over time that can make your morning cup of coffee hard to swallow. Cleaning your coffee pot and coffee maker is easy and can greatly improve the taste of your coffee. To clean your coffee maker, you need only two ingredients: white vinegar and water. First, make a mixture of one part white vinegar to two parts water to fill the pot. Pour the mixture into the coffee maker, and add a filter. Turn on the coffee maker, and let it run through a cycle. Discard the liquid and filter. Rinse the coffee pot, and repeat twice using water only. If you still smell vinegar, repeat the process one more time.

In the first sentence, _collect_ means
   - **3-A** restore.
   - **3-B** overtake.
   - **3-C** refill.
   - **3-D** build up.

QUESTIONS 4 AND 5 ARE BASED ON THE FOLLOWING PASSAGE.

Paul Jackson Pollock was an American abstract expressionist painter of the early twentieth century. Pollock shied away from people, preferring the life of a recluse. He had an eccentric painting style that consisted of dripping paint onto enormous canvases that covered the floor. He used the flow of the paint and his body's movements to creatively fling and pour paint on canvases. He didn't stop until he believed the piece was finished. After his death, his work was honored at many art exhibits. He was even the subject of the biographical film _Pollock_ starring Ed Harris.

4. As used in the third sentence, <u>enormous</u> means
   4-A blank.
   4-B huge.
   4-C dirty.
   4-D oval.

5. In this context, the word <u>subject</u> means
   5-A cause.
   5-B check.
   5-C topic.
   5-D spirit.

6. The Taj Mahal in Agra, India, is regarded as one of the most beautiful masterpieces in the world. It consists of a white marble mausoleum decorated with flowers and calligraphy surrounded by other structures. It was commissioned by Mughal Emperor Shah Jahan for his third and favorite wife, Mumtaz Mahal. It took more than 20,000 artisans 22,000 years to build the grand structure. The mausoleum was completed in 1648, while the surrounding buildings were finished a few years later. The Taj Mahal is a tourist attraction that draws more than 2 million visitors each year.

   In this context, the word <u>regarded</u> means
   6-A imagined.
   6-B considered.
   6-C categorized.
   6-D determined.

QUESTIONS 7 AND 8 ARE BASED ON THE FOLLOWING PASSAGE.

Phineas Taylor (P.T.) Barnum was an American showman from the nineteenth century who founded the circus that went on to become Ringling Bros. and Barnum & Bailey Circus. He opened the Barnum Museum to showcase hoaxes and human oddities, such as a mermaid and General Tom Thumb, a dwarf. Barnum then established a traveling circus that he called "P.T. Barnum's Grand Traveling Museum, Menagerie, Caravan and Hippodrome," complete with performers and animals. The show was the first of its kind to tour America by train. Today, it is known as "The Greatest Show on Earth."

7. In this context, <u>established</u> means
   7-A fixed.
   7-B purchased.
   7-C founded.
   7-D rebuilt.

8. As used above, the word <u>tour</u> means
   8-A reviewed.
   8-B discovered.
   8-C travelled.
   8-D concluded.

9. Ruth Handler (1916–2002) is credited with creating Barbie, a doll that has become a symbol of girlhood in America. Handler's husband, Elliot, and his business partner, Harold Matson, formed a small picture-frame business called Mattel, which later branched out into toys. Ruth Handler came up with the idea for Barbie after watching her daughter Barbara play with paper dolls. Barbie debuted at a toy fair in 1959, where the doll garnered much fame and fortune for Mattel.

   In the last sentence, <u>garnered</u> means
   9-A gained.
   9-B proved.
   9-C bought.
   9-D faced.

QUESTIONS 10 AND 11 ARE BASED ON THE FOLLOWING PASSAGE.

Sandpainting is an art form in which sand and other powdered pigments are poured onto a canvas to make a painting. Most sandpaintings are made by medicine men who believe the paintings help people heal. Once a sandpainting fulfills its purpose, it is discarded. The colors in the paintings come from natural sources such as yellow ochre, cornmeal, charcoal, red sandstone, pollen, bark, and gypsum. Different colors are created by mixing sources.

10. As used above, discarded means
    10-A picked up.
    10-B taken home.
    10-C thrown away.
    10-D hung out.

11. In this context, natural means
    11-A new.
    11-B organic.
    11-C safe.
    11-D studied.

12. Rock climbing not only requires strength, balance, and grace, but also great concentration. Rock climbing is a physically and mentally taxing sport. Climbers scale rock formations or rock walls and then rappel (descend from a rope) back down. A climber must use his or her legs and hands for balance and weight support. Specialized gear, such as harnesses, ropes, and pulleys, is also used. Because rock climbing can be dangerous, only those with proper training should pursue this sport.

As used above, gear means
    12-A component.
    12-B basis.
    12-C force.
    12-D equipment.

ANSWER KEY AND EXPLANATIONS

1. A	4. B	7. C	9. A	11. B
2. C	5. C	8. C	10. C	12. D
3. D	6. B			

1-A The word *identical* means *alike*. The author is telling you that male and female eagles look almost exactly *alike*, except for their size. From the paragraph, you can tell that the eagles are not *tiny*. The context of the sentence doesn't allow you to determine whether the eagles look *scary* or *angry*.

2-C From the sentence, you can tell that eagles use their talons to pick up fish. This helps you recognize that *snatch* means *grasp*. Choices A, B, and D don't make sense in the context of the sentence.

3-D In the context of this sentence, *collect* means *build up*. When you use a coffee pot repeatedly without cleaning it, residue will *build up*. The author is explaining how you can prevent residue by cleaning the pot regularly. The other choices don't fit the context of the sentence.

4-B To cover the floor, the canvas would need to be quite large. In the context of this sentence, you can assume that *enormous* means *huge*. The other choices could not be substituted for the word *enormous* and still have the sentence make sense.

5-C In this context, the word *subject* means *topic*. The context clue *biographical* helps you determine the meaning of the word. A biography is a written history of a person's life. Logically, this means that Pollack is the *topic* of a movie about his life.

6-B *Regard* means attention or *consideration*. In this sentence, the author is explaining that the Taj Mahal is *considered* one of the most beautiful masterpieces in the world. The other choices don't fit the context of the sentence.

7-C In this context, *established* means *founded*. Barnum *founded* his own travelling circus that toured across America for many years. *Fixed*, *purchased*, and *rebuilt* cannot be substituted for *established*.

8-C In this sentence, *tour* means *travelled*. The circus *travelled* across America, performing in many cities. *Reviewed*, *discovered*, and *concluded* don't make sense in this sentence.

9-A *Garnered* means *gained*. The sentence is telling you that the Barbie doll helped Mattel gain a fair amount of fame and money. The other choices don't fit the context of this sentence.

10-C In the context of this sentence, *discarded* means *thrown away*. Because there are not harmful ingredients in sandpaintings, they are *thrown away* once they have served their purpose. *Picked up*, *taken home*, and *hung out* don't fit the context of the sentence.

11-B As used in this paragraph, *natural* means *organic*, or coming from nature. *New* is not a synonym for *natural* and there is no way to tell if the sources are *safe* based on the context of this sentence. *Studied* is also incorrect because it would not make sense in the sentence.

12-D The context clues in this sentence are *harnesses*, *ropes*, and *pulleys*. These words tell you that *gear* must mean *equipment*. Though *gear* can also refer to a *component*, this doesn't fit the context of the sentence. *Basis* and *force* are unrelated to the topic.

SUMMING IT UP

- When answering main idea questions, choose the answer option that states what the entire passage is about.

- When answering looking-for-details questions, use key words in the question to help you choose the correct answer.

- Remember that you won't find the answer to inference questions in the passage. You have to use the information in the passage to make an educated guess as to the correct answer.

- To answer word meaning questions, use context clues to help you determine the meaning of the word.

PART V

THREE PRACTICE TESTS

ARITHMETIC REASONING

1. Ⓐ Ⓑ Ⓒ Ⓓ   7. Ⓐ Ⓑ Ⓒ Ⓓ   13. Ⓐ Ⓑ Ⓒ Ⓓ   19. Ⓐ Ⓑ Ⓒ Ⓓ   25. Ⓐ Ⓑ Ⓒ Ⓓ
2. Ⓐ Ⓑ Ⓒ Ⓓ   8. Ⓐ Ⓑ Ⓒ Ⓓ   14. Ⓐ Ⓑ Ⓒ Ⓓ   20. Ⓐ Ⓑ Ⓒ Ⓓ   26. Ⓐ Ⓑ Ⓒ Ⓓ
3. Ⓐ Ⓑ Ⓒ Ⓓ   9. Ⓐ Ⓑ Ⓒ Ⓓ   15. Ⓐ Ⓑ Ⓒ Ⓓ   21. Ⓐ Ⓑ Ⓒ Ⓓ   27. Ⓐ Ⓑ Ⓒ Ⓓ
4. Ⓐ Ⓑ Ⓒ Ⓓ   10. Ⓐ Ⓑ Ⓒ Ⓓ   16. Ⓐ Ⓑ Ⓒ Ⓓ   22. Ⓐ Ⓑ Ⓒ Ⓓ   28. Ⓐ Ⓑ Ⓒ Ⓓ
5. Ⓐ Ⓑ Ⓒ Ⓓ   11. Ⓐ Ⓑ Ⓒ Ⓓ   17. Ⓐ Ⓑ Ⓒ Ⓓ   23. Ⓐ Ⓑ Ⓒ Ⓓ   29. Ⓐ Ⓑ Ⓒ Ⓓ
6. Ⓐ Ⓑ Ⓒ Ⓓ   12. Ⓐ Ⓑ Ⓒ Ⓓ   18. Ⓐ Ⓑ Ⓒ Ⓓ   24. Ⓐ Ⓑ Ⓒ Ⓓ   30. Ⓐ Ⓑ Ⓒ Ⓓ

MATHEMATICS KNOWLEDGE

1. Ⓐ Ⓑ Ⓒ Ⓓ   6. Ⓐ Ⓑ Ⓒ Ⓓ   11. Ⓐ Ⓑ Ⓒ Ⓓ   16. Ⓐ Ⓑ Ⓒ Ⓓ   21. Ⓐ Ⓑ Ⓒ Ⓓ
2. Ⓐ Ⓑ Ⓒ Ⓓ   7. Ⓐ Ⓑ Ⓒ Ⓓ   12. Ⓐ Ⓑ Ⓒ Ⓓ   17. Ⓐ Ⓑ Ⓒ Ⓓ   22. Ⓐ Ⓑ Ⓒ Ⓓ
3. Ⓐ Ⓑ Ⓒ Ⓓ   8. Ⓐ Ⓑ Ⓒ Ⓓ   13. Ⓐ Ⓑ Ⓒ Ⓓ   18. Ⓐ Ⓑ Ⓒ Ⓓ   23. Ⓐ Ⓑ Ⓒ Ⓓ
4. Ⓐ Ⓑ Ⓒ Ⓓ   9. Ⓐ Ⓑ Ⓒ Ⓓ   14. Ⓐ Ⓑ Ⓒ Ⓓ   19. Ⓐ Ⓑ Ⓒ Ⓓ   24. Ⓐ Ⓑ Ⓒ Ⓓ
5. Ⓐ Ⓑ Ⓒ Ⓓ   10. Ⓐ Ⓑ Ⓒ Ⓓ   15. Ⓐ Ⓑ Ⓒ Ⓓ   20. Ⓐ Ⓑ Ⓒ Ⓓ   25. Ⓐ Ⓑ Ⓒ Ⓓ

WORD KNOWLEDGE

1. Ⓐ Ⓑ Ⓒ Ⓓ   8. Ⓐ Ⓑ Ⓒ Ⓓ   15. Ⓐ Ⓑ Ⓒ Ⓓ   22. Ⓐ Ⓑ Ⓒ Ⓓ   29. Ⓐ Ⓑ Ⓒ Ⓓ
2. Ⓐ Ⓑ Ⓒ Ⓓ   9. Ⓐ Ⓑ Ⓒ Ⓓ   16. Ⓐ Ⓑ Ⓒ Ⓓ   23. Ⓐ Ⓑ Ⓒ Ⓓ   30. Ⓐ Ⓑ Ⓒ Ⓓ
3. Ⓐ Ⓑ Ⓒ Ⓓ   10. Ⓐ Ⓑ Ⓒ Ⓓ   17. Ⓐ Ⓑ Ⓒ Ⓓ   24. Ⓐ Ⓑ Ⓒ Ⓓ   31. Ⓐ Ⓑ Ⓒ Ⓓ
4. Ⓐ Ⓑ Ⓒ Ⓓ   11. Ⓐ Ⓑ Ⓒ Ⓓ   18. Ⓐ Ⓑ Ⓒ Ⓓ   25. Ⓐ Ⓑ Ⓒ Ⓓ   32. Ⓐ Ⓑ Ⓒ Ⓓ
5. Ⓐ Ⓑ Ⓒ Ⓓ   12. Ⓐ Ⓑ Ⓒ Ⓓ   19. Ⓐ Ⓑ Ⓒ Ⓓ   26. Ⓐ Ⓑ Ⓒ Ⓓ   33. Ⓐ Ⓑ Ⓒ Ⓓ
6. Ⓐ Ⓑ Ⓒ Ⓓ   13. Ⓐ Ⓑ Ⓒ Ⓓ   20. Ⓐ Ⓑ Ⓒ Ⓓ   27. Ⓐ Ⓑ Ⓒ Ⓓ   34. Ⓐ Ⓑ Ⓒ Ⓓ
7. Ⓐ Ⓑ Ⓒ Ⓓ   14. Ⓐ Ⓑ Ⓒ Ⓓ   21. Ⓐ Ⓑ Ⓒ Ⓓ   28. Ⓐ Ⓑ Ⓒ Ⓓ   35. Ⓐ Ⓑ Ⓒ Ⓓ

PARAGRAPH COMPREHENSION

1. Ⓐ Ⓑ Ⓒ Ⓓ   4. Ⓐ Ⓑ Ⓒ Ⓓ   7. Ⓐ Ⓑ Ⓒ Ⓓ   10. Ⓐ Ⓑ Ⓒ Ⓓ   13. Ⓐ Ⓑ Ⓒ Ⓓ
2. Ⓐ Ⓑ Ⓒ Ⓓ   5. Ⓐ Ⓑ Ⓒ Ⓓ   8. Ⓐ Ⓑ Ⓒ Ⓓ   11. Ⓐ Ⓑ Ⓒ Ⓓ   14. Ⓐ Ⓑ Ⓒ Ⓓ
3. Ⓐ Ⓑ Ⓒ Ⓓ   6. Ⓐ Ⓑ Ⓒ Ⓓ   9. Ⓐ Ⓑ Ⓒ Ⓓ   12. Ⓐ Ⓑ Ⓒ Ⓓ   15. Ⓐ Ⓑ Ⓒ Ⓓ

answer sheet

Practice Test 1

ARITHMETIC REASONING

TIME: 36 Minute • 30 Questions

> **Directions:** This test has 30 arithmetic questions followed by four possible answers. Decide which answer is correct and then mark the space on your answer form with the same number and letter as your choice. Don't forget to use scrap paper to work out problems and organize your thoughts.
>
> Your score on this test will be based on the number of questions you answer correctly. You should try to answer every question. Do not spend too much time on any one question.

1. Seth bought 100 shares of stock at $16 per share. If the value of the stock increased by 30%, how many dollars would his stock be worth?

   1-A $20.80

   1-B $480.00

   1-C $2,080.00

   1-D $4,800.00

2. Two identical buses are parked bumper-to-bumper along a curb. The first bus is 30 feet from the corner. How many feet is the farthest part of the second bus from the corner, if each bus is 20 feet long?

   2-A 70 ft.

   2-B 60 ft.

   2-C 50 ft.

   2-D 20 ft.

3. A 15-foot 5-inch radio tower stands on a 3-foot base on top of a 30-foot building. How far is the top of the radio tower from the ground?

   3-A 45 ft. 8 in.

   3-B 48 ft.

   3-C 48 ft. 5 in.

   3-D 53 ft.

4. Kevin is training to try out for the track team. For his 2-hour daily workout, he spends $\frac{1}{2}$ of the time running, $\frac{1}{8}$ of the time stretching, $\frac{1}{4}$ of the time lifting weights, and the rest of the time jumping and exercising. How much time does he spend stretching and lifting weights?

   4-A $\frac{1}{8}$ hr.

   4-B $\frac{1}{4}$ hr.

   4-C $\frac{1}{2}$ hr.

   4-D $\frac{3}{4}$ hr.

5. Members of the art club sold poinsettias to raise money for a nearby soup kitchen. It cost $1.25 to buy each plant, which they sold for $5.00. How much did the art club make on 32 plants sold?

  5-A $18.85

  5-B $40.00

  5-C $120.00

  5-D $160.00

6. Socks that cost $8.60 for three pairs to manufacture are sold for $12.20 for three pairs. How much profit is made on each pair of socks?

  6-A $1.20

  6-B $1.40

  6-C $1.80

  6-D $3.60

7. Four-hundred-and-twenty-high school seniors entered the gymnasium for the senior prom by 6:00 p.m. If 120 left by 9:00 p.m., how many couples still remained? Assume that only couples entered or left.

  7-A   120

  7-B   150

  7-C   300

  7-D   540

8. A birthday cake has 25 servings, but only 16 servings are eaten. What percent of the cake is left?

  8-A   20%

  8-B   36%

  8-C   42%

  8-D   64%

9. The McCall Theater sold tickets for its weekly show each week of June as follows:

       Week 1: 250 tickets

       Week 2: 200 tickets

       Week 3: 200 tickets

       Week 4: 350 tickets

What fraction of the tickets were sold during the third week?

  9-A $\frac{1}{3}$

  9-B $\frac{1}{4}$

  9-C $\frac{1}{5}$

  9-D $\frac{1}{8}$

10. Rami asked his father at 6:30 p.m. on Sunday how much time he had until school the next morning at 8:45 a.m. What should his father's reply be?

  10-A   12 hr. 15 min.

  10-B   13 hr.

  10-C   14 hr.

  10-D   14 hr. 15 min.

11. Megan wanted to make a piñata for a school project. Her register receipt from the craft store showed the following:

       Tissue paper $6.75

       Glue $2.10

       Balloons $3.25

       Ribbons $5.40

How much change should Megan get back if she hands the clerk a $20 bill?

  11-A $1.25

  11-B $2.50

  11-C $7.90

  11-D $17.50

12. A farmer had 312.40 pounds of grain but sold some. After the sale, he had 246.50 pounds of grain. Approximately, how many pounds of grain did the farmer sell?

  12-A   247

  12-B   69

  12-C   66

  12-D   55

13. An empty bus started out from the terminal and picked up 8 passengers on Main Street, unloaded 2 passengers on High Street, and picked up 3 passengers on Center Street. How many passengers were on the bus after Center Street?

13-A 13

13-B 9

13-C 7

13-D 5

14. At the vet last year, Rachel's dog Owen weighed 62 pounds 8 ounces. This year, he weighed 70 pounds 2 ounces. How much weight did he gain?

14-A 7 lbs. 4 oz.

14-B 7 lbs. 10 oz.

14-C 8 lbs. 4 oz.

14-D 8 lbs. 6 oz.

15. A waffle recipe called for 3 cups of milk, but Jonathan accidentally added 4 cups of milk. He then added 1 cup of flour to thicken the batter. However, his mother said the batter was too thick and added 1 more cup of milk. How many total cups of milk were in the waffle batter?

15-A 4

15-B 5

15-C 7

15-D 8

16. "How long until we get there?" Rick asked. "I told you 15 minutes ago that we would be there in 25 minutes," replied his father. In how many minutes will Rick arrive at his destination?

16-A 40 min.

16-B 25 min.

16-C 15 min.

16-D 10 min.

17. Diana scored 5, 6, 2, 2, 2, 8, 4, and 3 points during her last 8 basketball games. What was the average number of points she scored per game?

17-A 2

17-B 4

17-C 6

17-D 8

18. Jamie has a board that is 8 feet 2 inches long. He wants to cut the board into 7-inch-long pieces that have the same width as the board. How many pieces can he cut?

18-A 14

18-B 16

18-C 98

18-D 686

19. Sarah works for Roy's Furniture Store. She gets a 7% commission on all sales. If her sales were $5,700 in June and $4,200 in July, how much commission did she earn for June and July?

19-A $294

19-B $399

19-C $693

19-D $6,930

20. It takes $\frac{1}{2}$ lb. of cheese to make a macaroni-and-cheese casserole dish. How many pounds of cheese are needed to make 8 casserole dishes of macaroni and cheese?

20-A 2 lb.

20-B 4 lb.

20-C 8 lb.

20-D 16 lb.

21. If each sandwich requires 2 slices of bread, how many slices of bread will be needed to serve 75 people if each person eats 2 sandwiches?

21-A 125

21-B 150

21-C 200

21-D 300

22. How many pieces of 3-inch pipe can be cut from a pipe that is 6 feet long?

22-A 24

22-B 18

22-C 6

22-D 2

23. Twee weighs 130 pounds. About how many kilograms does she weigh? (*Note:* 2.2 pounds = 1 kilogram)

23-A 59.1

23-B 65.2

23-C 260

23-D 286

24. Dan is a waiter with a book of 150 checks. For the first three days of the week, he wrote the following checks:

Monday   31

Tuesday   26

Wednesday   40

How many checks did he have left when he started work on Thursday?

24-A 97

24-B 93

24-C 84

24-D 53

25. Tablets that normally sell for $3 each were on sale for 2 for $5. How much would Cheryl save if she purchased 10 tablets at the sale price?

25-A $2

25-B $5

25-C 10

25-D $25

26. Kendra paid for a 44-cent stamp with a $10 bill. How much change should she get?

26-A $5.60

26-B $9.56

26-C $9.66

26-D $10.06

27. Calculate: 2×14^3

27-A 84

27-B 392

27-C 2,744

27-D 5,488

28. Calculate: $\dfrac{3^2}{3^3}$

28-A $\dfrac{1}{9}$

28-B $\dfrac{1}{6}$

28-C $\dfrac{1}{3}$

28-D $\dfrac{1}{2}$

$3^2 \times 3^3 = 3^{-1} = \dfrac{1}{3}$

QUESTIONS 29 AND 30 REFER TO THE FOLLOWING GRAPH.

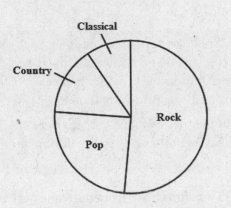

Favorite Type of Music:

Rock	52%
Pop	28%
Country	12%
Classical	8%

29. How many people chose country music if 500 people were surveyed?
    - **29-A** 6
    - **29-B** 12
    - **29-C** 24
    - **29-D** 60

30. If 200 people were surveyed, how many more chose pop than chose classical?
    - **30-A** 16
    - **30-B** 40
    - **30-C** 56
    - **30-D** 72

MATHEMATICS KNOWLEDGE

TIME: 24 Minutes • 25 Questions

Directions: This is a test of your ability to solve 25 general mathematical problems. Select the correct response from the choices given and then mark the space on your answer form that has the same number and letter as your choice. Don't forget to use scrap paper to work out problems and organize your thoughts.

Your score on this test will be based on the number of questions you answer correctly. You should try to answer every question. Do not spend too much time on any one question.

1. The sum of two numbers is 258. If one number is 114, how much is the other?
   - 1-A   134
   - 1-B   144
   - 1-C   224
   - 1-D   378

2. If the owner of a store is required to collect a 6% sales tax, what was the total sales for a day in which she collected $360 in taxes?
   - 2-A $21.60
   - 2-B $366.00
   - 2-C $3,600.00
   - 2-D $6,000.00

3. Add: $(5x^2 + 3x + 8) + (x^2 - 3x + 10)$
   - 3-A $4x^2 + 2x + 18$
   - 3-B $5x^2 + 2x + 8$
   - 3-C $6x^2 + 2x + 18$
   - 3-D $6x^2 + 4x + 18$

4. The value of $[6 - (1-2)] + [(3-9) - (5-4)]$ is
   - 4-A   0
   - 4-B   13
   - 4-C   14
   - 4-D   −14

5. If $2x + 2x - 2x = 10$, find $2x + 1$.
   - 5-A   2
   - 5-B   5
   - 5-C   10
   - 5-D   11

6. Two ships leave from the same port at 10:30 p.m. If one sails due east at 15 miles per hour, and the other sails due south at 20 miles per hour, how many miles apart are they at 2:30 p.m.?
   - 6-A   54
   - 6-B   80
   - 6-C   100
   - 6-D   375

7. What is the next term in the following sequence: 16, 8, 4, 2, ___
   - 7-A   −2
   - 7-B   −1
   - 7-C   1
   - 7-D $\frac{1}{4}$

8. A clerk's weekly salary is $210 after a 25% raise. What was his weekly salary before the raise?
   - 8-A $105.00
   - 8-B $157.50
   - 8-C $168.00
   - 8-D $262.50

9. $(5x - 2) + (2x^2 - 2x + 6) + (3x^2 + 6x + 3) =$
   - 9-A $5x^2 + 9 - 7$
   - 9-B $5x^4 + 13x - 11$
   - 9-C $5x^2 + 9x + 7$
   - 9-D $6x^2 + 9x - 7$

10. If the area of each circle enclosed in rectangle $ABCD$ is 4π, the area of $ABCD$ is

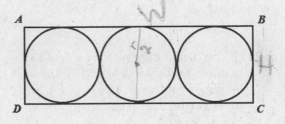

10-A 16
10-B 48
10-C 144
10-D 151

11. If $3x + 8 = 10$, then x equals

11-A $-\dfrac{2}{3}$

11-B $\dfrac{2}{3}$

11-C $-\dfrac{1}{6}$

11-D $\dfrac{1}{6}$

12. If the area of a square of side x is 5, what is the area of a square of side $2x$?

12-A 10
12-B 15
12-C 20
12-D 25

13. From 8 a.m. to 1 p.m. the temperature rose at a constant rate from $-10°$ to $25°$. What was the average temperature at noon?

13-A 6°
13-B 18°
13-C 24°
13-D 35°

14. If $4x = 3x + 7$, the $2x + 6 =$

14-A $\dfrac{7}{12}$

14-B 8
14-C 15
14-D 20

15. If a discount of 25% off the marked price of a pair of boots saves a woman $20, how much did she pay for the boots?

15-A $20
15-B $25
15-C $60
15-D $80

16. Divide: $\dfrac{2xy^2 - 3x^2y}{xy}$

16-A $2y - 3x$
16-B $2x^2y - 3x$
16-C $2y - 3x^2$
16-D $2x^2y^3 - 3x^2y^2$

17. If the diameter of a circle is increased by 100%, the area is increased by

17-A 50%
17-B 100%
17-C 200%
17-D 300%

18. If $a = x^2$ and $x = \left(\sqrt{9}\right)^2$, then $a =$

18-A $2\sqrt{3}$
18-B 3
18-C 9
18-D 81

19. What number added to 20% of itself is equal to 72?

19-A 12.8
19-B 60
19-C 62
19-D 72.6

20. Mr. Miller takes his wife and three children to the county fair. If the price of a child's ticket is $\frac{1}{3}$ the price of an adult ticket, and Mr. Miller pays a total of $10.80, find the price of a child's ticket.

   20-A $1.20

   20-B $1.80

   20-C $3.60

   20-D $5.40

21. The value of $(-4) + (-1)(-6) \div (-2) + (-2)$ is

   21-A -9

   21-B -4

   21-C 4

   21-D 9

22. If $2x + y = 8$, what is the value of y when $x = -2$?

   22-A   8

   22-B   10

   22-C   12

   22-D   24

23. If $3n^{-3} = 27$, then $n =$

   23-A   3

   23-B   4

   23-C   6

   23-D   9

24. If the cost of digging a trench is $3.14 a cubic yard, what would be the cost of digging a trench 2 yards by 4 yards by 2 yards?

   24-A $16.00

   24-B $25.12

   24-C $50.24

   24-D $150.72

25. $(3y + 1)(2y - 1) =$

   25-A $6y^2 - y - 1$

   25-B $6y^2 - 6y - 1$

   25-C $6y^2 - y - 2$

   25-D $6y^2 - 1$

WORD KNOWLEDGE

TIME: 11 Minute • 35 Questions

Directions: This test has 35 questions about the meanings of words. Each question has an underlined word. Select the answer choice that is closest in meaning to the underlined word and then mark the space on your answer form with the same number and letter as your choice.

Your score on this test will be based on the number of questions you answer correctly. You should try to answer every question. Do not spend too much time on any one item.

1. Ensnare most nearly means
   - 1-A injure.
   - 1-B trap.
   - 1-C shake.
   - 1-D tip.

2. The show went on a hiatus for the summer.
   - 2-A break
   - 2-B term
   - 2-C trip
   - 2-D run

3. Simulate most nearly means
   - 3-A tackle.
   - 3-B shorten.
   - 3-C imitate.
   - 3-D battle.

4. The water on the still lake was serene.
   - 4-A peaceful
   - 4-B gray
   - 4-C wavy
   - 4-D wintry

5. The sick girl had an ashen appearance.
   - 5-A glowing
   - 5-B pale
   - 5-C pretty
   - 5-D unusual

6. Vie most nearly means
   - 6-A buy.
   - 6-B win.
   - 6-C drop.
   - 6-D contend.

7. The scouts went on an excursion.
   - 7-A journey
   - 7-B boat
   - 7-C deviation
   - 7-D campus

8. The rules of the class were stringent.
   - 8-A free
   - 8-B rigid
   - 8-C easy
   - 8-D nice

9. The desert is arid.
   - 9-A warm
   - 9-B sunny
   - 9-C dusty
   - 9-D dry

10. Fraudulent most nearly means
    - 10-A false.
    - 10-B busy.
    - 10-C true.
    - 10-D honest.

11. The boy felt <u>jovial</u> on his birthday.
11-A   sour
11-B   merry
11-C   older
11-D   mad

12. The <u>hideous</u> mask horrified the guests.
12-A   large
12-B   bright
12-C   ugly
12-D   plastic

13. The SAT is <u>requisite</u> for college.
13-A   luxury
13-B   essential
13-C   supportive
13-D   excess

14. There was an <u>aroma</u> coming from the kitchen.
14-A   pleasant odor
14-B   scary sight
14-C   pungent taste
14-D   white smoke

15. <u>Loathe</u> most nearly means
15-A   treasure.
15-B   hate.
15-C   welcome.
15-D   love.

16. There were flowers <u>galore</u> in the meadow.
16-A   colorful
16-B   varied
16-C   planted
16-D   abundant

17. The <u>mishap</u> left her with a broken leg.
17-A   accident
17-B   vacation
17-C   miracle
17-D   boon

18. It was a <u>bleak</u> rainy day.
18-A   happy
18-B   cold
18-C   sunny
18-D   windy

19. <u>Safeguard</u> most nearly means
19-A   hunt.
19-B   confine.
19-C   protect.
19-D   bother.

20. The inauguration ceremony marked the <u>genesis</u> of his term.
20-A   difficulty
20-B   celebration
20-C   happiness
20-D   beginning

21. Palm trees are <u>endemic</u> to tropical climates.
21-A   native
21-B   imported
21-C   lively
21-D   abandoned

22. The package arrived in an <u>expeditious</u> manner.
22-A   steady
22-B   strange
22-C   dull
22-D   speedy

23. The <u>benign</u> man gave his money to charity.
23-A   powerful
23-B   kind
23-C   humorous
23-D   rough

24. His <u>erratic</u> behavior was difficult to follow.
24-A   uninteresting
24-B   severe
24-C   unpredictable
24-D   enjoyable

25. <u>Complex</u> most nearly means
    25-A continual.
    25-B effortless.
    25-C natural.
    25-D complicated.

26. <u>Seclusion</u> most nearly means
    26-A isolation.
    26-B social.
    26-C together.
    26-D beside.

27. He is a <u>merciless</u> competitor who wants to win.
    27-A cruel
    27-B fierce
    27-C polite
    27-D clever

28. The <u>discord</u> between the two led to their breakup.
    28-A discussion
    28-B mandate
    28-C conflict
    28-D party

29. An <u>obstruction</u> in the pipe made the water back up.
    29-A crack
    29-B block
    29-C hole
    29-D break

30. He was able to <u>salvage</u> a few mementos after the fire.
    30-A lift
    30-B burn
    30-C return
    30-D save

31. The editor found a <u>blunder</u> in the book.
    31-A paper
    31-B error
    31-C meaning
    31-D correctness

32. He gets a <u>quarterly</u> bonus for his hard work.
    32-A large
    32-B trimonthly
    32-C regular
    32-D secured

33. The dog <u>plodded</u> through the snow.
    33-A skipped
    33-B trudged
    33-C moved
    33-D hopped

34. <u>Defiance</u> most nearly means
    34-A agreeable.
    34-B approval.
    34-C resistance.
    34-D extension.

35. Composure most nearly means
    35-A calmness.
    35-B reputation.
    35-C popularity.
    35-D presence.

PARAGRAPH COMPREHENSION

TIME: 13 Minute • 15 Questions

Directions: This test contains 15 items measuring your ability to obtain information from written passages. You will find one or more paragraphs of reading material followed by incomplete statements or questions. You are to read the paragraph(s) and then mark the lettered choice that best completes the statement or answers the question on your answer form.

Your score on this test will be based on the number of questions you answer correctly. You should try to answer every question. Do not spend too much time on any one item.

1. Though people have used personal hygiene products since ancient times, modern staples such as detergents and toothpaste were not always as effective as they are today. Toothpaste was invented in 1850 by Dr. Washington Wentworth Sheffield. Before this time, people used harsh substances such as sand, salt, and acid to scrub stains from their teeth. Dr. Sheffield, a dentist and chemist, started with a paste that his patients loved. He improved on the product and eventually sold it in tubes. By the end of the nineteenth century, many companies were producing toothpaste. Within the next century, they began to add fluoride, a material that protects and strengthens teeth, and began experimenting with tooth-whitening chemicals.

The most recent addition to toothpaste is

   1-A   acid.

   1-B   fluoride.

   1-C   detergents.

   1-D   salt.

2. Fires fall into four general categories: Class A, B, C, or D. Class A fires involve ordinary flammable materials such as wood, plastic, or paper. Fires involving gasoline, oil, alcohol, or other combustible liquids are Class B fires. Fires that consume energized electrical equipment, such as computers, household appliances, or transformers, are Class C fires. Class D fires involve combustible metals such as aluminum and magnesium. When responding to a fire, firefighters must determine the type of materials involved so they can classify the fire. These classifications help firefighters determine which extinguishing agent—for example, water, carbon dioxide, or dry chemical agents—will smother the flames.

From this passage, you can infer that

   2-A   Class C fires are the most dangerous.

   2-B   not all fires can be put out with water.

   2-C   Class D fires are easily extinguished.

   2-D   metals cannot be set on fire.

3. Benjamin Franklin is famous for his many inventions such as bifocal eyeglasses and the lightning rod. One Franklin's favorite inventions, however, is also one of his least famous. After hearing a performer play music by rubbing his fingers around the moistened edges of a drinking glass, Franklin decided to invent an instrument, which he called the glass armonica, that would make the same sound. Franklin had a glassblower make thirty-seven rounded pieces of glass, through which he inserted a

rod. The rod was laid horizontally and placed in a wooden case so it resembled a piano. Although Mozart composed a piece of music specifically for the glass armonica, the instrument fell out of popularity by the early 1800s. Even so, a few people still play the instrument today.

The glass armonica looked most like

3-A lightning rods.

3-B eyeglasses.

3-C a drinking glass.

3-D a piano.

4. No one enjoys changing a flat tire, but it's a good skill to know. To change a flat, locate your vehicle's spare tire, jack, and tire iron. Use the tire iron to loosen the lug nuts, or lugs, on the flattened tire *before* you jack up the vehicle. Next, turn the lever on the jack until it lifts the flat tire off the ground. Remove the lugs, and pull off the flat tire. Place the spare tire over the wheel studs and screw the lugs into place, tightening them first by hand and then with the tire iron. Return to the jack to lower the car, and then finish tightening the lugs with the tire iron once the car is securely on the ground. Put the flat tire and your tools in your car and continue on your way.

This paragraph is mainly about

4-A what to carry in your car.

4-B how to drive safely.

4-C what makes tires go flat.

4-D how to perform a car repair.

5. Swamps are a type of wetland ecosystem. Many people see them as smelly, mosquito-ridden detriments filled with stagnant water and mushy ground, but swamps play an important role in our lives. In addition to serving as a home to various forms of plant and animal life, swamps also help drain water from floods. These floodwaters supply swamps with plenty of nutrients, which has actually created a problem for swamps. Because swamps contain such healthy, nutrient-rich soil, many have been drained and cleared for agricultural use. According to estimates by the Environmental Protection Agency, more than 70 percent of America's floodplain forested swamps have been destroyed.

As used above, the word <u>detriments</u> means

5-A harmful things.

5-B rich soils.

5-C wet regions.

5-D severe damages.

6. Julia Child (1912–2004), born Julia Carolyn McWilliams, was a renowned American chef best known for her 1961 cookbook *Mastering the Art of French Cooking*. She penned numerous other cookbooks and starred on cooking television programs, including *The French Chef* in 1963. She married Paul Cushing Child, whom she met during her stint with the U.S. government's Office of Strategic Services in 1946. The couple moved to Paris, and Child attended Le Cordon Bleu cooking school and studied privately with master chefs. Child's goal was to make French cuisine appeal to Americans. Child was recently brought back into the limelight with the movie *Julie & Julia*, which intertwines Child's life with that of Julie Powell, a food blogger who cooked and blogged about the recipes in Child's *Mastering the Art of French Cooking*. The movie starred Meryl Streep as Child and Amy Adams as Powell.

This paragraph is mainly about

6-A what food bloggers have done.

6-B a popular recent movie.

6-C the life of a famous chef.

6-D what makes French food special.

QUESTIONS 7 AND 8 ARE BASED ON THE FOLLOWING PASSAGE.

On January 28, 1969, an oil-drilling platform six miles off the coast of Santa Barbara, California, experienced a blowout after a failed attempt to replace a drill bit. Over the course of the next ten days, about 100,000 barrels of crude oil spilled into the Santa Barbara Channel, affecting California beaches and coastlines. Seabirds were drenched in oil and unable to fly. Fish, seals, and other aquatic life were also affected by the pollution. The oil spill sparked a grassroots environmental movement and eventually led to the halt of oil exploration off the Atlantic and Pacific coasts.

7. What does the word <u>aquatic</u> mean as used above?
   - 7-A   threatened
   - 7-B   living on land
   - 7-C   common
   - 7-D   living in water

8. This paragraph is mainly about
   - 8-A   how to clean up the environment.
   - 8-B   an environmental disaster.
   - 8-C   the many uses of crude oil.
   - 8-D   the wildlife of California beaches.

9. Imagine waking up one morning and seeing a dinosaur in your yard. This was similar to what happened in 1938, when a fisherman in South Africa caught a coelacanth. A coelacanth is a monstrous fish that lived during the age of the dinosaurs. Most scientists considered it long extinct. Nobody expected that a live specimen would still be swimming in the ocean until this amazing discovery. After 1938, people became more aware of the rare animal, and more coelacanths have emerged. Coelacanths have been found in Kenya, Tanzania, Mozambique, and Madagascar. Scientists have worked hard to examine this fascinating animal and study the clues about prehistoric life that it offers. The coelacanth has also proven that the oceans are places of great mystery.

A coelacanth was first caught in
   - 9-A   South Africa.
   - 9-B   Kenya.
   - 9-C   Madagascar.
   - 9-D   Tanzania.

10. Baking a cake is easy if you follow the directions. First, wash your hands. Next, gather the supplies you will need: the recipe, a bowl, measuring cups and spoons, a cake pan, ingredients, and a hand mixer. Preheat the oven according to directions. Grease and flour the sides and bottom of the cake pan and set it aside. Following the recipe, measure the ingredients into a bowl and beat them well with a mixer. Pour the cake batter into the pan and bake according to the directions. Test the center of the cake with a toothpick to determine if it is done. If the toothpick comes out clean, the cake is ready. If not, continue baking the cake for a few more minutes. Remove the finished cake from the oven and place it on a wire rack to cool. After ten minutes, invert the pan onto the wire rack to remove the cake from the pan. Because it has a smoother surface for icing, the bottom of the cake will become the top. After the cake has cooled, top with your favorite icing.

From this passage, you can infer that
   - 10-A   cakes are removed from the pan while hot.
   - 10-B   the toothpick test is not important to baking.
   - 10-C   cakes require very high oven temperatures.
   - 10-D   icing works best on a smooth surface.

11. In the 1700s, colonizers from France and England claimed much of North America. However, many Native Americans contested these claims. The Iroquois Confederacy, an alliance of native tribes in the Northeast, worked hard to keep the French and English at bay. One of the most influential figures among the Iroquois was Chief Joseph Brant, a dynamic young man from the Mohawk tribe. Brant had strong ties within his own tribe and built alliances and friendships with many English people as well. He became an important figure in negotiating deals between the groups, and he helped to keep the groups in a state of peace for many years. When the American Revolutionary War started, Brant sided with England. He helped lead Iroquois warriors and English soldiers in battle. After the war, Brant moved to Canada, where he continued working for Native American rights.

Which of the following is the best title for this passage?

11-A "Native Americans Today"

11-B "A Native American Leader"

11-C "The Colonization of America"

11-D "The Revolutionary War"

QUESTIONS 12 TO 14 ARE BASED ON THE FOLLOWING PASSAGE.

At more than 3,000 feet tall, Angel Falls is the highest waterfall in the world. Angel Falls is located in the Canaima National Park in Venezuela and is part of the Churun River. The falls became famous during the 1930s when American pilot and adventurer Jimmie Angel crashed his airplane near the waterfall. He and his passengers had to travel by foot for eleven days to reach civilization. Angel Falls received its name after the group's harrowing experience.

12. From this passage, you can infer that

12-A Jimmie Angel was popular in Venezuela.

12-B many American pilots traveled to Angel Falls.

12-C Angel Falls is far away from civilization.

12-D the Churun River is the longest in South America.

13. What does the word <u>harrowing</u> mean as used in this passage?

13-A beautiful

13-B famous

13-C brief

13-D frightening

14. This paragraph is mainly about

14-A a special waterfall.

14-B a well-known pilot.

14-C national parks.

14-D airplane safety.

15. Audio books allow people to listen to books while leaving their hands and eyes free to work on something else. Students who learn better when they can simultaneously see and hear information find these books especially helpful. Some audio books feature an actor simply reading the text, while others include sound effects and an entire cast of performers who act out the story. Audio books were first produced in the 1930s as reading material for blind people. They grew more popular with the invention of the walkman, the CD, and downloadable formats.

Audio books were first produced to help

15-A students.

15-B inventors.

15-C actors.

15-D blind people.

ANSWER KEY AND EXPLANATIONS

Arithmetic Reasoning

1. C	6. A	11. B	16. D	21. D	26. B
2. A	7. B	12. C	17. B	22. A	27. D
3. C	8. B	13. B	18. A	23. A	28. C
4. D	9. C	14. B	19. C	24. D	29. D
5. C	10. D	15. B	20. B	25. B	30. B

1-C Value of stock = original cost + increase in original cost

$16 + ($16 · 0.30) = $16 + $4.80 = $20.80

Multiplying by 100 gives the total worth:
100 × $20.80 = $2,080

2-A Sketch the parked buses.

30'	20'	20'	20'

30 + (2 × 20) = 30 + 40 = 70 feet

3-C Make a sketch.

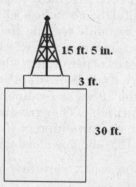

To find the total distance, line up the feet and inches and add:

Radio tower:	15 ft.	5 in.
Base	3 ft.	
+ Building	30 ft.	
	48 ft.	5 in.

4-D   Draw a circle graph.

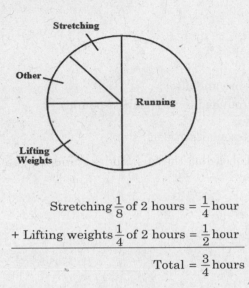

$$\text{Stretching } \tfrac{1}{8} \text{ of 2 hours} = \tfrac{1}{4} \text{ hour}$$

$$+ \text{ Lifting weights } \tfrac{1}{4} \text{ of 2 hours} = \tfrac{1}{2} \text{ hour}$$

$$\overline{\hspace{5cm}}$$

$$\text{Total} = \tfrac{3}{4} \text{ hours}$$

5-C   Individual Profit = Selling Price − Cost

$$32 \times [\$5.00 - \$1.25] = 32 \times 3.75 = \$120$$

6-A   For three pairs of socks, the profit is $12.20 − $8.60 = $3.60

To find the profit on each pair of socks, divide by 3:
$3.60 ÷ 3 = $1.20

7-B   420 − 120 = 300 remained. Be sure to answer the question that is asked. Here, you are asked for the number of couples, which is half the total number of students remaining, or $\dfrac{300}{2} = 150$ couples.

8-B   Use this formula:

$$\text{Fraction} = \frac{\text{number of pieces eaten}}{\text{total number of pieces}} = \frac{16}{25} = 0.64 \times 100 = 64\%$$

Be careful! This is the percentage of cake that was eaten; the question asks for the percentage left over: 100% − 64% = 36%.

9-C $\text{Fraction} = \dfrac{\text{number sold week 3}}{\text{total number sold}}$

$$\frac{200}{250 + 200 + 200 + 350} = \frac{200}{1000} = 0.20 = \frac{1}{5}$$

10-D   Break down the problem into different time segments:

6:30 p.m. Sunday to 6:30 a.m. Monday = 12 hours
6:30 a.m. Monday to 8:45 a.m. Monday = 2 hours 15 minutes

Add the hours and minutes = 14 hours 15 minutes

11-B   Add the prices of the supplies Megan bought at the craft store:
6.75 + 2.10 + 3.25 + 5.40 = $17.50

Subtract the total from $20:
$20.00 − $17.50 = $2.50

12-C   Find the difference between before and after:
312.40 − 246.50 = 65.90 or 66 (rounded to the nearest pound)

13-B   You must account for all the passengers at each stop.

Let + stand for passengers who boarded the bus, and − stand for passengers who got off the bus:

Before the terminal	0
On Main Street	+8
On High Street	−2
+ On Center Street	+3
After Center Street	+9

14-B   16 ounces (oz.) = 1 pound (lb.); 70 lb. 2 oz. = 69 lb. 18 oz. (In subtracting, borrow 1 pound from the 70 lb., making it 69 lb., and add 16 oz. to the 2 oz., making it 18 oz.)

     69 lb. 18 oz.
   − 62 lb. 8 oz.
      7 lb. 10 oz.

15-B   Add the cups of water, but don't add the cup of flour:

     Jonathan   4 cups
   + His mother   1 cup
                    5 cups

16-D   Read the dialogue carefully.

Rick's father said 15 minutes ago that they would be there in 25 minutes. Now, they are closer to their destination.

25 − 15 = 10

They will arrive at their destination in 10 minutes.

17-B $$\text{Average} = \frac{\text{the sum}}{\text{the number of values}}$$

$$\text{Average} = \frac{(5 + 6 + 2 + 2 + 2 + 8 + 4 + 3)}{8} + \frac{32}{8} = 4$$

18-A Multiply: Length of board × $\frac{1}{7}$

Change the length into inches: 8 ft. 2 in. = (12 × 8) + 2 = 98 in.

$98 \times \frac{1}{7} = 14$ pieces

19-C "7% commission on all sales" is 0.07 × (each) sale.

June: 0.07 × 5,700 = 399
July: 0.07 × 4,200 = 294

Total commission is $399 + $294 = $693.

20-B Make a ratio to solve this problem. Let P be the number of pounds of cheese required for 8 casserole dishes.

$$\frac{\frac{1}{2}\,\text{lb.}}{1\,\text{casserole}} = \frac{P\,\text{lb.}}{8\,\text{casseroles}}$$

Cross multiply:

$\frac{1}{2} \times 8 = P \times 1$

$4 \text{ lb.} = P$

21-D If each sandwich uses 2 slices of bread, and each person orders 2 sandwiches, then each person gets 4 slices of bread total. Therefore, 75 people need 75 × 4 = 300 slices of bread.

22-A Draw a picture.

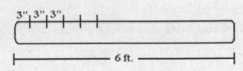

Convert 6 feet into inches:
6 × 12 = 72 in.

Divide:
72 ÷ 3 = 24 pieces

23-A   **Method 1:** 2.2 pounds is 1 kilogram.

1 pound is $\frac{1}{2.2}$ kilograms.

130 pounds is $130 \times \frac{1}{2.2} = 59.1$ kilograms.

Method 2: Using unit cancellations:

$$130 \text{ (pounds)} \times \frac{1 \text{ (kilogram)}}{2.2 \text{ (pounds)}}$$

After canceling all units, we arrive at 59.1 kilograms.

24-D   The total number of tickets Dan used was $31 + 26 + 40 = 97$. The number left on Thursday was $150 - 97 = 53$.

25-B   Normally, tablets would cost $10 \times \$3 = \$30$. On sale, they would cost $5 \times \$5 = \$25$, since Cheryl would buy 5 sets of two tablets to get 10 tablets. Therefore, $\$30 - \$25 = \$5$. Cheryl would save $5 by buying 10 tablets at the sale price.

26-B $\$10.00 - 0.44 = \$9.56$

27-D $2(14 \times 14 \times 14) = 2 \times (2{,}744) = 5{,}488$

28-C   Calculate: $\frac{3 \times 3}{3 \times 3 \times 3} = \frac{1}{3}$

29-D   To find the number of people who chose country music, multiply (percentage) × (total number of people).

$12\% \times 500 = 0.12 \times 500 = 60$

30-B   Pop: $28\% \times 200 = 0.28 \times 200 = 56$
Classical: $8\% \times 200 = 0.08 \times 200 = 16$

$56 - 16 = 40$

Mathematics Knowledge

1. B	6. C	11. B	16. A	21. A
2. D	7. C	12. C	17. D	22. C
3. C	8. C	13. B	18. D	23. C
4. A	9. C	14. D	19. B	24. C
5. D	10. B	15. C	20. A	25. A

1-B　　Let n = missing number.

$$n + 114 = 258$$
$$n = 258 - 114$$
$$n = 144$$

2-D　　Let x = total sales.

6% of total sales = \$360

$$0.06x = 360$$
$$x = 360 \div 0.06$$
$$x = 6,000$$

3-C　　Add like terms:　$5x^2 + 3x + 8$
　　　　　　　　　　　　$+\ \ x^2 - \ x + 10$　←
　　　　　　　　　　　　$\overline{6x^2 + 2x + 18}$

4-A　　$= [6 - (-1)] + [(-6) - 1]$
　　　　$= 7 + (-7)$
　　　　$= 0$

5-D　　　　$2x = 10$
　　　　　　　$x = 5$
　　　　$2x + 1 = 11$

6-C　　10:30 a.m. to 2:30 p.m. = 4 hours. In 4 hours, one ship went 60 miles and the other went 80 miles. This is a 3-4-5 right triangle as 60 = 3(20), 80 = 4(20). The hypotenuse will be 5(20), or 100.

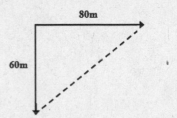

7-C The sequence is geometric with a common ratio of $\frac{8}{16} = \frac{1}{2}$. The term after 2 is

$2 \times \frac{1}{2} = \frac{2}{2} = 1$.

8-C $210 is 125% of his former salary.

$$210 = 1.25x$$
$$21,000 = 125x$$
$$\$168 = x$$

9-C Add like terms:

$$5x - 2$$
$$2x^2 - 2x + 6$$
$$\underline{3x^2 + 6x + 3}$$
$$5x^2 + 9x + 7$$

10-B The area of a circle is $\pi r2 = 4\pi$. The radius of each circle is $\sqrt{4} = 2$. Therefore, $AB = 6 \times 2$ and $AD = 2 \times 2 = 4$. The area of rectangle $ABCD = 12 \times 4 = 48$.

11-B $3x + 8 = 10$
$$3x = 10 - 8$$
$$3x = 2$$
$$x = \frac{2}{3}$$

12-C Area $= s^2$
Area$_1 = x^2$
Area$_2 = (2x)^2 = 4x^2$
$x^2 : 4x^2 = 1 : 4$
$4 \times 5 = 20$

13-B Total rise in temperature:
$25 - (-10) = 25 + 10 = 35$

8 a.m. to 1 p.m. = 5 hours

Hourly rise in temperature $= \frac{35}{5} = 7°F$ per hour

At noon temperature $= -10 + 4(7) = -10 + 28 = +18$

14-D Solve for x.

$$4x = 3x + 7$$
$$x = 7$$
$$2(7) + 6 = 20$$

15-C Let x = the amount of marked price.

$$\frac{1}{4}x = 20$$

$$x = 80$$

$$x - 20 = \$60$$

16-A $\dfrac{2xy^2 - 3x^2y}{xy} = \dfrac{2xy^2}{xy} - \dfrac{3x^2y}{xy} = 2y - 3x$

17-D If the linear ratio is 1:2, then the area ratio is $(1)^2:(2)^2$ or 1:4. The increase is 3 or 300% of the original area.

18-D $x = \left(\sqrt{9}\right)^2 = 9$

$a = x^2$

$a = (9)^2$

$a = 81$

19-B $x + 0.20x = 72$

$1.20x = 72$

$12x = 720$

$x = 60$

20-A $3a = \$10.80$

$a = \$3.60$

$\dfrac{1}{3}(3.60) = \$1.20$

21-A $-4 + (-1)(-6) \div (-2) + (-2)$

$-4 + 6 \div (-2) + (-2)$

$-4 + (-3) + (-2)$

-9

22-C $2(-2) + y = 8$

$-4 + y = 8$

$y = 8 + 4$

$y = 12$

23-C $3n^{-3} = 27 = 3^3$

$n - 3 = 3$

$n = 6$

24-C The trench contains:

2 yd. × 4 yd. × 2 yd. = 16 cubic yards

$16 \times \$3.14 = \$50.24$

25-A $(3y + 1)(2y - 1) =$

$6y^2 - 3y + 2y - 1 =$

$6y^2 - y - 1$

Word Knowledge

1. B	8. B	15. B	22. D	29. B
2. A	9. D	16. D	23. B	30. D
3. C	10. A	17. A	24. C	31. B
4. A	11. B	18. B	25. D	32. B
5. B	12. C	19. C	26. A	33. B
6. D	13. B	20. D	27. A	34. C
7. A	14. A	21. A	28. C	35. A

1-B *Ensnare* means to catch or hold something in a net. Therefore, the best synonym for *ensnare* is *trap*.

2-A *Hiatus* means a *break* in the continuity of an action, a work, a series, etc. Therefore, in this sentence *hiatus* means the show took a *break* from production for the summer.

3-C *Simulate* means to create a likeness, or to *imitate*, something. For example, there are cosmetics that *simulate*, or *imitate*, a suntan on skin.

4-A *Serene* means free from disruption. Therefore, *peaceful* is the best synonym to describe a lake that is still, undisrupted, and *serene*.

5-B *Ashen* means lacking a healthy color in the skin. Therefore, *pale* is a good synonym to describe a person who has an *ashen* appearance.

6-D *Vie* means to engage in a contest. Therefore, *contend* is a good synonym choice for *vie*. The other choices are not synonyms for *vie*.

7-A *Excursion* means a brief pleasure trip. In this sentence, an *excursion* refers to a *journey*. The scouts may be on a *journey* through the forest or to a special place, such as a museum.

8-B *Stringent* means strict or severe. *Rigid* is considered a synonym for *stringent* since *rigid* means inflexible and unyielding. The other choices are not synonyms for *stringent*.

9-D *Arid* means excessively *dry*. Deserts have little rainfall to support life and crops, therefore deserts are *arid* environments.

10-A *Fraudulent* activities or actions are based on dishonesty and deceit. Crooked, dishonest, and *false* are good synonyms for *fraudulent*.

11-B *Jovial* means characterized as good-humored and joyous. For children, birthdays are joyous occasions; therefore, *merry* is a good synonym for jovial.

12-C *Hideous* means horrible or frightening to the senses. A *hideous* mask is one that would be difficult to look at or *ugly*. The other choices don't fit the context of the sentence.

13-B *Requisite* means something that is necessary, required, or *essential*. Students must take the SATs in order to enroll in college.

14-A   *Aroma* means a savory or *pleasant odor*. It comes from the French word *aromat*, which means sweet spice.

15-B   *Loathe* means to dislike something greatly. An appropriate synonym for *loathe* would be *hate*. The other choices aren't related to *loathe*.

16-D   *Galore* means in plentiful amounts or *abundant. Galore* originated from the Irish *go leor*, which means enough or plenty. This sentence implies that there were many flowers in the meadow.

17-A   *Mishap* means bad luck or an unfortunate *accident*. The prefix *mis-* means bad or wrong, which suggests something unfavorable. The root word *hap* means a happening. Therefore, *mishap* means an unfavorable happening or an *accident*.

18-B   *Bleak* means *cold* and piercing, lacking in warmth. A *bleak* day would be one that was raw, *cold*, or chilly.

19-C   The verb *safeguard* means to defend or *protect*. The compound word is made up of *safe,* which means free from harm, and *guard*, which means to watch over. Therefore, *safeguard* means *protect*.

20-D   *Genesis* means the origin, start, or *beginning*. It is originated in the Greek word *genos,* which means birth. The other choices don't fit the context of the sentence.

21-A   *Endemic* means belonging to a particular people, area, or environment. Because palm trees naturally grow in warm, tropical climates, they are *endemic,* or *native,* to the area. Choices B, C, and D are not synonyms for *endemic*.

22-D   *Expeditious* means characterized by promptness. Therefore, *speedy* is good synonym for *expeditious*.

23-B   *Benign* means showing kindness or gentleness. Therefore, a *benign* person is a *kind* person who does good things for others, such as giving to charities.

24-C   *Erractic* means irregular or having no fixed course. Something that is *erratic* is *unpredictable*. The context clues *difficult to follow* help in understanding that *erratic* behavior is unstable and difficult to understand.

25-D   The adjective *complex* means difficult to analyze or separate. Therefore, the best answer choice is *complicated*. The other choices are not appropriate synonyms for *complex*.

26-A   *Seclusion* means a state of solitude or aloneness. The words *social, together,* and *beside* all imply the idea of more than one person, which is the opposite of *seclusion*. Therefore, *isolation*, which means separation from others, is the best answer choice.

27-A   *Merciless* means having or showing no compassion. A competitor who is *merciless* is difficult to defeat. The suffix *-less* means devoid of or without. Therefore, *cruel* is the best answer choice, since the competitor is without mercy for his opponent.

28-C   *Discord* means a lack of agreement or harmony. The prefix *dis-* means opposite or absence of and *cord* means a moral or spiritual bond. Therefore, *discord* means the opposite or absence of a bond, or *conflict*.

29-B *Obstruction* means a condition of being clogged or *blocked*. Therefore, an *obstruction* or a *block* in a drain would cause the water to back up. The other choices don't fit the context of the sentence.

30-D The verb *salvage* means to rescue from destruction. Therefore, *save* is the best answer.

31-B *Blunder* means an *error* or mistake because of carelessness. It is derived from the Middle English word *blunderen,* which means *to go blindly.* The other choices don't fit the context of the sentence.

32-B *Quarterly* means payable in three-month intervals. Therefore, if someone gets a *quarterly* bonus, it means that he gets a bonus every three months, or *trimonthly*.

33-B *Plodded* means to walk heavily or *trudged*. The answer choices *skipped*, *moved*, and *hopped* are not synonyms of *plodded*.

34-C *Defiance* means open disregard, contempt, or *resistance*. The word defiance originated from the Latin *dis*, meaning away, and *fidus*, meaning faithful. *Defiance* originally had the meaning to be disloyal, but the meaning shifted to challenge or *resistance*.

35-A *Composure* means a tranquil state of mind or appearance. Therefore, *calmness* is a good synonym for composure.

Paragraph Comprehension

1. B	4. D	7. D	10. D	13. D
2. B	5. A	8. B	11. B	14. A
3. D	6. C	9. A	12. C	15. D

1-B The author mentions people using things such as acid and salt to clean teeth before toothpaste was invented. Detergents are not related to toothpaste. Fluoride, a material that helps teeth, was the most recent addition to toothpaste.

2-B This passage lists several materials used to put out fires. These materials include water, carbon dioxide, and dry chemical agents. Some of these materials work better with different kinds of fire. You can infer that not all fires can be put out with water.

3-D This passage mentions lightning rods and eyeglasses as other inventions of Ben Franklin. It also says that drinking glasses provided the inspiration for the glass armonica. However, the actual glass armonica instrument looked most like a piano.

4-D The author of this passage presents a lot of information, but it all has to do with changing a flat tire, which is a kind of car repair. The main idea of this paragraph, therefore, is how to perform a car repair.

5-A The author uses the word *detriment* to describe what many people think about swamps. This word is paired with words and phrases such as *smelly*, *mosquito-ridden*, and *stagnant*. These words have bad connotations and make all swamps sound like harmful environments. You can use these context clues to determine

that *detriments* means harmful things.

6-C This is the correct answer, because all of the information the author presents in this passage has to do with Julia Child and her life. Child was a famous chef. Therefore, the main idea of the paragraph deals with the life of a famous chef.

7-D Consider the context clues in the passage to determine the meaning of *aquatic*. The author writes that fish and seals are examples of aquatic life. In addition, the passage deals with water. You can use these clues to determine that *aquatic* means "living in water."

8-B The author gives much information in this passage, but the main idea of the passage is that an oil spill caused great damage to an environment and its animal life. Therefore, you can say that the paragraph is mainly about an environmental disaster.

9-A You read about several places in this passage, including South Africa, Kenya, Madagascar, and Tanzania. Coelacanths have been seen in each of these places. However, the passage explains that the first coelacanth was caught in South Africa. That is the correct answer.

10-D Consider each of the inferences in these answer choices. Only one is correct. The correct answer is that icing works best on a smooth surface. You can make this inference because the author tells you that a person making a cake should ice the bottom of the cake because it is smoother.

11-B The title of a passage usually refers to the main idea of the passage. To find the best title for this passage, consider its main idea. It does not deal with Native Americans today. It does mention the colonization of America and the Revolutionary War, but these are not the most important ideas in the passage. This passage is mostly about a Native American leader, Joseph Brant.

12-C You read that Jimmie Angel had to walk for eleven days to find civilization. Eleven days is a long time to walk, which suggests that Angel Falls is far away from civilization. That is the correct answer.

13-D You may not be familiar with the word *harrowing*, but you can determine its meaning using clues from the passage. The author writes that Jimmie Angel and his crew had a harrowing experience. That experience included a plane crash and being stranded for eleven days. That would be a frightening experience.

14-A This passage deals with several topics: a famous pilot, a plane crash, and a national park. Each of these topics, however, serves to support a description of Angel Falls. You can determine that this passage is mostly about a special waterfall.

15-D This passage about audio books mentions several groups of people. The author writes that students often use audio books to learn. Inventors made audio books and actors record the audio book text. You learn in this passage, however, that audio books were first produced to help blind people.

ARITHMETIC REASONING

1. Ⓐ Ⓑ Ⓒ Ⓓ 7. Ⓐ Ⓑ Ⓒ Ⓓ 13. Ⓐ Ⓑ Ⓒ Ⓓ 19. Ⓐ Ⓑ Ⓒ Ⓓ 25. Ⓐ Ⓑ Ⓒ Ⓓ
2. Ⓐ Ⓑ Ⓒ Ⓓ 8. Ⓐ Ⓑ Ⓒ Ⓓ 14. Ⓐ Ⓑ Ⓒ Ⓓ 20. Ⓐ Ⓑ Ⓒ Ⓓ 26. Ⓐ Ⓑ Ⓒ Ⓓ
3. Ⓐ Ⓑ Ⓒ Ⓓ 9. Ⓐ Ⓑ Ⓒ Ⓓ 15. Ⓐ Ⓑ Ⓒ Ⓓ 21. Ⓐ Ⓑ Ⓒ Ⓓ 27. Ⓐ Ⓑ Ⓒ Ⓓ
4. Ⓐ Ⓑ Ⓒ Ⓓ 10. Ⓐ Ⓑ Ⓒ Ⓓ 16. Ⓐ Ⓑ Ⓒ Ⓓ 22. Ⓐ Ⓑ Ⓒ Ⓓ 28. Ⓐ Ⓑ Ⓒ Ⓓ
5. Ⓐ Ⓑ Ⓒ Ⓓ 11. Ⓐ Ⓑ Ⓒ Ⓓ 17. Ⓐ Ⓑ Ⓒ Ⓓ 23. Ⓐ Ⓑ Ⓒ Ⓓ 29. Ⓐ Ⓑ Ⓒ Ⓓ
6. Ⓐ Ⓑ Ⓒ Ⓓ 12. Ⓐ Ⓑ Ⓒ Ⓓ 18. Ⓐ Ⓑ Ⓒ Ⓓ 24. Ⓐ Ⓑ Ⓒ Ⓓ 30. Ⓐ Ⓑ Ⓒ Ⓓ

MATHEMATICS KNOWLEDGE

1. Ⓐ Ⓑ Ⓒ Ⓓ 6. Ⓐ Ⓑ Ⓒ Ⓓ 11. Ⓐ Ⓑ Ⓒ Ⓓ 16. Ⓐ Ⓑ Ⓒ Ⓓ 21. Ⓐ Ⓑ Ⓒ Ⓓ
2. Ⓐ Ⓑ Ⓒ Ⓓ 7. Ⓐ Ⓑ Ⓒ Ⓓ 12. Ⓐ Ⓑ Ⓒ Ⓓ 17. Ⓐ Ⓑ Ⓒ Ⓓ 22. Ⓐ Ⓑ Ⓒ Ⓓ
3. Ⓐ Ⓑ Ⓒ Ⓓ 8. Ⓐ Ⓑ Ⓒ Ⓓ 13. Ⓐ Ⓑ Ⓒ Ⓓ 18. Ⓐ Ⓑ Ⓒ Ⓓ 23. Ⓐ Ⓑ Ⓒ Ⓓ
4. Ⓐ Ⓑ Ⓒ Ⓓ 9. Ⓐ Ⓑ Ⓒ Ⓓ 14. Ⓐ Ⓑ Ⓒ Ⓓ 19. Ⓐ Ⓑ Ⓒ Ⓓ 24. Ⓐ Ⓑ Ⓒ Ⓓ
5. Ⓐ Ⓑ Ⓒ Ⓓ 10. Ⓐ Ⓑ Ⓒ Ⓓ 15. Ⓐ Ⓑ Ⓒ Ⓓ 20. Ⓐ Ⓑ Ⓒ Ⓓ 25. Ⓐ Ⓑ Ⓒ Ⓓ

WORD KNOWLEDGE

1. Ⓐ Ⓑ Ⓒ Ⓓ 8. Ⓐ Ⓑ Ⓒ Ⓓ 15. Ⓐ Ⓑ Ⓒ Ⓓ 22. Ⓐ Ⓑ Ⓒ Ⓓ 29. Ⓐ Ⓑ Ⓒ Ⓓ
2. Ⓐ Ⓑ Ⓒ Ⓓ 9. Ⓐ Ⓑ Ⓒ Ⓓ 16. Ⓐ Ⓑ Ⓒ Ⓓ 23. Ⓐ Ⓑ Ⓒ Ⓓ 30. Ⓐ Ⓑ Ⓒ Ⓓ
3. Ⓐ Ⓑ Ⓒ Ⓓ 10. Ⓐ Ⓑ Ⓒ Ⓓ 17. Ⓐ Ⓑ Ⓒ Ⓓ 24. Ⓐ Ⓑ Ⓒ Ⓓ 31. Ⓐ Ⓑ Ⓒ Ⓓ
4. Ⓐ Ⓑ Ⓒ Ⓓ 11. Ⓐ Ⓑ Ⓒ Ⓓ 18. Ⓐ Ⓑ Ⓒ Ⓓ 25. Ⓐ Ⓑ Ⓒ Ⓓ 32. Ⓐ Ⓑ Ⓒ Ⓓ
5. Ⓐ Ⓑ Ⓒ Ⓓ 12. Ⓐ Ⓑ Ⓒ Ⓓ 19. Ⓐ Ⓑ Ⓒ Ⓓ 26. Ⓐ Ⓑ Ⓒ Ⓓ 33. Ⓐ Ⓑ Ⓒ Ⓓ
6. Ⓐ Ⓑ Ⓒ Ⓓ 13. Ⓐ Ⓑ Ⓒ Ⓓ 20. Ⓐ Ⓑ Ⓒ Ⓓ 27. Ⓐ Ⓑ Ⓒ Ⓓ 34. Ⓐ Ⓑ Ⓒ Ⓓ
7. Ⓐ Ⓑ Ⓒ Ⓓ 14. Ⓐ Ⓑ Ⓒ Ⓓ 21. Ⓐ Ⓑ Ⓒ Ⓓ 28. Ⓐ Ⓑ Ⓒ Ⓓ 35. Ⓐ Ⓑ Ⓒ Ⓓ

PARAGRAPH COMPREHENSION

1. Ⓐ Ⓑ Ⓒ Ⓓ 4. Ⓐ Ⓑ Ⓒ Ⓓ 7. Ⓐ Ⓑ Ⓒ Ⓓ 10. Ⓐ Ⓑ Ⓒ Ⓓ 13. Ⓐ Ⓑ Ⓒ Ⓓ
2. Ⓐ Ⓑ Ⓒ Ⓓ 5. Ⓐ Ⓑ Ⓒ Ⓓ 8. Ⓐ Ⓑ Ⓒ Ⓓ 11. Ⓐ Ⓑ Ⓒ Ⓓ 14. Ⓐ Ⓑ Ⓒ Ⓓ
3. Ⓐ Ⓑ Ⓒ Ⓓ 6. Ⓐ Ⓑ Ⓒ Ⓓ 9. Ⓐ Ⓑ Ⓒ Ⓓ 12. Ⓐ Ⓑ Ⓒ Ⓓ 15. Ⓐ Ⓑ Ⓒ Ⓓ

answer sheet

Practice Test 2

ARITHMETIC REASONING

TIME: 36 Minute • 30 Questions

Directions: This test has 30 arithmetic questions followed by four possible answers. Decide which answer is correct and then mark the space on your answer form with the same number and letter as your choice. Don't forget to use scrap paper to work out problems and organize your thoughts.

Your score on this test will be based on the number of questions you answer correctly. You should try to answer every question. Do not spend too much time on any one question.

1. How many cups of punch can be served from a 4-gallon punch bowl? (4 cups = 1 quart)
   - 1-A   16
   - 1-B   32
   - 1-C   64
   - 1-D   128

2. A shipment consists of 260 one-foot pieces of conduit with a coupling on each piece. If the conduit weighs 0.55 pounds per foot and the coupling weighs 0.12 pounds per piece, the total weight of the shipment is
   - 2-A   1,461.2 lbs.
   - 2-B   174.2 lbs.
   - 2-C   56.2 lbs.
   - 2-D   46.26 lbs.

3. Emile drove from his family's house to his grandmother's house in 3 hours and 32 minutes. His sister Santina also drove from the family's house to her grandmother's house, but she traveled a different route. Santina made the trip in 2 hours and 54 minutes. What was the difference in their times?
   - 3-A   8 min.
   - 3-B   38 min.
   - 3-C   1 hr. 18 min.
   - 3-D   1 hr. 22 min.

4. Mike sold 62 rolls of wrapping paper at $5.80 per roll, making a profit of $2.10 per roll. What was his profit on all 62 rolls?
   - 4-A $12.28
   - 4-B $130.20
   - 4-C $233.00
   - 4-D $359.00

5. The road in front of Carl's house is 330 yards long. How many feet is this?
   - 5-A   100
   - 5-B   660
   - 5-C   990
   - 5-D   1,980

6. Admission to the museum costs $4.50, but schools can buy a book of 10 tickets for $40.00. What percentage of the regular cost is saved by buying the book?

6-A $\frac{1}{9}$%

6-B $\frac{1}{4}$%

6-C   10%

6-D $11\frac{1}{9}$%

7. Tina wants to buy a scarf for $8.50, earrings for $5.20, and a pair of socks for $3.20. She gives the cashier a $10 bill. How much more money does she need for her purchase?

7-A $6.90

7-B $7.90

7-C $16.90

7-D $26.90

8. Latisha recorded the amount of time she spent playing the piano after school for a week:

Monday	32 minutes
Tuesday	23 minutes
Wednesday	35 minutes
Thursday	30 minutes
Friday	25 minutes

What was the average time she spent playing the piano per day over the five days?

8-A   29 min.

8-B   30 min.

8-C   31 min.

8-D   145 min.

9. Calculate: $\frac{3^3}{3^2}$

9-A 3^5

9-B 3^2

9-C   3

9-D   9

10. A furniture store marked down the price of a sofa to $420, which was 30% off the regular price. What was the regular price of the sofa?

10-A $126.00

10-B $546.00

10-C $600.00

10-D $1,400.00

11. If it is 9:40 a.m. and George has to take a history test at 2:30 p.m., how much time does he have until he takes the test?

11-A   4 hrs. 10 min.

11-B   4 hrs. 50 min.

11-C   5 hrs. 10 min.

11-D   5 hrs. 50 min.

12. Megan and Randy ordered the following for lunch at a restaurant:

1 tuna melt	$4.95
2 slices of pizza	$4.50
2 glasses of milk	$2.50
1 slice of pie	$2.25

If they left a 15% tip, what was the total amount that they spent?

12-A $14.20

12-B $16.20

12-C $16.33

12-D $17.33

13. Miranda counted the cars in the parking lot of her apartment building. There were 6 blue cars, 4 black cars, and 2 red cars. What percentage of the cars was NOT blue?

13-A   30%

13-B   40%

13-C   50%

13-D   60%

14. A scene of a play takes $16\frac{1}{4}$ minutes to perform. If the scene has $2\frac{1}{2}$ minutes left, how many minutes of the scene have already been performed?

14-A $13\frac{1}{2}$ min.

14-B $13\frac{3}{4}$ min.

14-C $14\frac{1}{4}$ min.

14-D $14\frac{1}{2}$ min.

15. Admission to the zoo is $10.00 for adults and $5.50 for children. How much does it cost for 3 adults and 2 children to go to the zoo?

15-A $26.50

15-B $36.50

15-C $40.00

15-D $41.00

16. An average basketball game at Northwest High lasts 2 hours and 15 minutes. How long would 4 average basketball games last?

16-A 10 hrs.

16-B 10 hrs. 15 min.

16-C 9 hrs.

16-D 9 hrs. 45 min.

QUESTIONS 17 TO 19 REFER TO THE FOLLOWING GRAPH, WHICH ILLUSTRATES THE NUMBER OF PROPERTY CRIME RATES IN A TOWN OVER A PERIOD OF SIX YEARS.

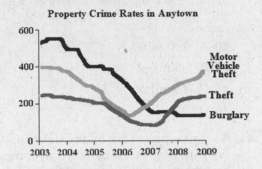

Property Crime Rates in Anytown

17. According to the graph, in which year was the number of burglaries the highest?

17-A 2003

17-B 2005

17-C 2007

17-D 2009

18. What is the approximate difference in the number of burglaries and the number of thefts in 2005?

18-A 100

18-B 200

18-C 300

18-D 400

19. According to the graph, in which year was the number of motor vehicle thefts the highest?

19-A 2003

19-B 2005

19-C 2007

19-D 2009

20. The scale on a map is $\frac{1}{4}$ inch equals 10 miles. How many miles does it take to get from one town to another if the distance on the map measures $2\frac{3}{8}$ inches?

20-A 100 miles

20-B 95 miles

20-C 45 miles

20-D 25 miles

21. Kevin has plans to go hiking and camping with friends. He bought a sleeping bag for $56.00, 10 water bottles for $1.25 each, boots for $32.50, 2 shirts for $21.99 each, and 3 pairs of socks for $3.50 each. If Kevin gave the clerk two $100 bills, how much change did he receive?

21-A $44.52

21-B $51.52

21-C $84.86

21-D $155.48

22. A bag of nickels and dimes contains $15.50. If there are 85 dimes, how many nickels are there?

22-A 7

22-B 140

22-C 700

22-D 1,465

23. If stickers are purchased for $2.10 per dozen and sold for 2 for $0.50, what is the total profit on $4\frac{1}{2}$ dozen?

23-A $13.50

23-B $9.45

23-C $4.05

23-D $3.05

24. Ronald receives a 15% commission for each magazine subscription of $12.50 that he sells. If he sells 30 magazine subscriptions, how much will he earn?

24-A $55.00

24-B $56.25

24-C $375.50

24-D $450.00

25. The newspaper advertised the following airfares:

New York to London
$525 each way

New York to San Francisco
$379 each way

How much will Christine save if she buys a round-trip ticket to San Francisco instead of a round-trip ticket to London?

25-A $73.00

25-B $146.00

25-C $292.00

25-D $438.00

26. How many 1-inch slices can be cut from an 8-foot hero sandwich?

26-A 80

26-B 96

26-C 108

16-D 128

27. How many round trips must a shuttle bus make to transport 678 passengers if the bus can carry 48 passengers at a time?

27-A 8

27-B 11

27-C 14

27-D 15

28. Normal daily mean temperatures for January to June in Daytona Beach, Florida, are as follows:

January	57.4°
February	58.9°
March	64.3°
April	69.3°
May	74.7°
June	79.4°

The average daily mean temperature in Daytona Beach for the first six months of the year is approximately

28-A 64.3°

28-B 66.5°

28-C 67.3°

28-D 69.3°

29. Connor, who is 5 feet 8 inches tall, is standing next to his younger brother Nick. Connor's shadow is 40 inches long, and Nick's shadow is 30 inches long. How tall is Nick?

29-A 58 inches

29-B 51 inches

29-C 48 inches

29-D 46 inches

30. A recipe calls for $2\frac{1}{2}$ cups of flour. It is necessary to make 4 times the recipe for a graduation party. If 2 cups of flour equal 1 pound, how many pounds of flour will be needed to make the recipe for the party?

30-A 3

30-B 4

30-C 5

30-D 6

MATHEMATICS KNOWLEDGE

TIME: 24 Minutes • 25 Questions

Directions: This is a test of your ability to solve 25 general mathematical problems. Select the correct response from the choices given and then mark the space on your answer form that has the same number and letter as your choice. Don't forget to use scrap paper to work out problems and organize your thoughts.

Your score on this test will be based on the number of questions you answer correctly. You should try to answer every question. Do not spend too much time on any one question.

1. Door *ABCD* is to be reinforced by 2 metal wires, *AC* and *BD*. If the dimensions of the door are 8 feet by 15 feet, how many feet of wire will be required to reinforce the door?

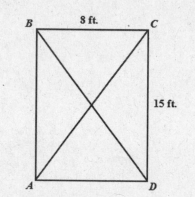

1-A   13 ft.
1-B   17 ft.
1-C   34 ft.
1-D   120 ft.

2. Solve for *C*: *C* + 3 = *Y* and *Y* = 6.
2-A   −3
2-B   0
2-C   2
2-D   3

3. What's the next number in the following series? 41, 39, 42, 38, 43, ____
3-A   37
3-B   38
3-C   41
3-D   47

4. Subtract: $(2x^2 + 2x + 4) - (3x^2 + 3x + 5)$
4-A $-(x^2 + x + 1)$
4-B $x^2 + x$
4-C $-x^2 + x + 1$
4-D $x^2 - 1$

5. At an average speed of 55 miles per hour, how many hours will it take a train to travel 385 miles?
5-A   6 hrs.
5-B   7 hrs.
5-C   8 hrs.
5-D   9 hrs.

6. Find the value of $\left(2\sqrt{3}\right)^2$.
6-A $4\sqrt{3}$
6-B   6
6-C   12
6-D   18

7. Solve for *p*: $\frac{p}{2} + \frac{p}{3} = 1$
7-A $\frac{7}{5}$
7-B $\frac{5}{7}$
7-C $\frac{5}{6}$
7-D $\frac{6}{5}$

8. If the angles of a triangle are in the ratio 3: 6: 9, the triangle is
   8-A right.
   8-B acute.
   8-C isosceles.
   8-D obtuse.

9. The surface area of a cube is 24 square feet. How many cubic feet are there in the volume of the cube?
   9-A 4
   9-B 8
   9-C 16
   9-D 24

10. The Falcons played 32 games last season. If they won 12 games more than they lost, how many games did they lose?
    10-A 10
    10-B 20
    10-C 24
    10-D 40

11. $\sqrt{8} + \sqrt{32} =$
    11-A $\sqrt{40}$
    11-B $2\sqrt{2}$
    11-C $6\sqrt{2}$
    11-D $4\sqrt{2}$

12. The perimeter of a rectangle is 60 feet. The length is 2 feet more than 3 times the width. Find the width of the rectangle.
    12-A 4.6 ft.
    12-B 7 ft.
    12-C 8 ft.
    12-D 9 ft.

13. If $0.14m = 0.0028$, $m =$
    13-A 2
    13-B 0.2
    13-C 0.02
    13-D 0.002

14. As shown in the figure, a circular metal disc wears down to one-fifth of its original radius. What percent of the original area remains?

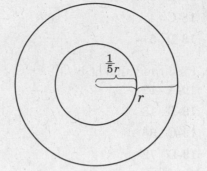

    14-A 1%
    14-B 4%
    14-C 40%
    14-D 50%

15. Multiply: $(2x^2y)(3x^3y^2)$
    15-A $5x^5y^3$
    15-B $6xy^8$
    15-C $6x^5y^3$
    15-D $6x^6y^3$

16. A train traveled 120 miles in $1\frac{3}{4}$ hours. At the same rate, how long will it take for the train to travel 360 miles?
    16-A 4 hrs.
    16-B $4\frac{1}{2}$ hrs.
    16-C $5\frac{1}{4}$ hrs.
    16-D $5\frac{1}{2}$ hrs.

17. If $\frac{a}{b} = \frac{1}{2}$, then $20a =$
    17-A $5b$
    17-B $10b$
    17-C $15b$
    17-D $40b$

18. How many digits are in the square root of 194,481?

  18-A   2

  18-B   3

  18-C   4

  18-D   5

19. Find the value of $6\sqrt{3}^{2}$.

  19-A   12

  19-B   18

  19-C   36

  19-D   72

20. Multiply: $(x + 5)(x - 5)$

  20-A $x^2 - 25$

  20-B $(x - 25)^2$

  20-C $x + 5$

  20-D $x - 5$

21. A rectangular door that is 7 feet tall and 3 feet wide has 6 indents, each 2 feet by 1 foot. How many square feet of the door is not indented?

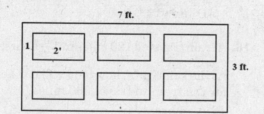

  21-A   2 ft²

  21-B   9 ft²

  21-C   12 ft²

  21-D   21 ft²

22. Nine is 9% of what number?

  22-A   81

  22-B   1

  22-C   10

  22-D   100

23. The area of circle Q is 36π. The perimeter of square $ABCD$ is

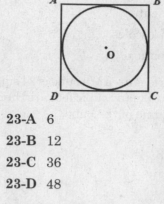

  23-A   6

  23-B   12

  23-C   36

  23-D   48

24. If $x = -2$, then $x^2 + 4x - 2 =$

  24-A   0

  24-B   -6

  24-C   -8

  24-D   -14

25. At the end of one year, a $4,000 savings certificate earning $5\frac{1}{2}\%$ simple interest per year will be worth

  25-A $220

  25-B $4,055

  25-C $4,220

  25-D $5,500

WORD KNOWLEDGE

TIME: 11 Minute • 35 Questions

Directions: This test has 35 questions about the meanings of words. Each question has an underlined word. Select the answer choice that is closest in meaning to the underlined word and then mark the space on your answer form with the same number and letter as your choice.

Your score on this test will be based on the number of questions you answer correctly. You should try to answer every question. Do not spend too much time on any one item.

1. "Mark Twain" was the <u>pseudonym</u> of Samuel Clemens.
   - 1-A   assumed name
   - 1-B   best work
   - 1-C   great idea
   - 1-D   best friend

2. <u>Substandard</u> most nearly means
   - 2-A   below a standard.
   - 2-B   above a standard.
   - 2-C   after a standard.
   - 2-D   without a standard.

3. The army kept its supplies in a huge <u>depot</u>.
   - 3-A   battlefield
   - 3-B   sailing ship
   - 3-C   unfair ruler
   - 3-D   warehouse

4. Mom yelled at Lilly for her <u>unkempt</u> room.
   - 4-A   appealing
   - 4-B   messy
   - 4-C   missing
   - 4-D   costly

5. It was ironic that the poor man's father was a <u>tycoon</u>!
   - 5-A   unkind parent
   - 5-B   great leader
   - 5-C   rich businessperson
   - 5-D   good athlete

6. The farmers in the area lost crops in the recent <u>drought</u>.
   - 6-A   lack of rain
   - 6-B   nearby region
   - 6-C   marketplace
   - 6-D   agriculture

7. Justin wrote an <u>itinerary</u> for his trip through Mexico.
   - 7-A   poem
   - 7-B   schedule
   - 7-C   library
   - 7-D   introduction

8. Worried she had a fever, Alex got the <u>thermometer</u>.
   - 8-A   family doctor
   - 8-B   hot soothing soup
   - 8-C   tool for measuring heat
   - 8-D   medicine for colds

9. <u>Nomadic</u> people in the desert often moved to find new food sources.
   - 9-A   native
   - 9-B   suffering
   - 9-C   hidden
   - 9-D   wandering

10. The business began to <u>prosper</u> after some early setbacks.
   - 10-A   succeed
   - 10-B   confine
   - 10-C   explain
   - 10-D   appear

11. <u>Apathy</u> most nearly means
    11-A without direction.
    11-B without feelings.
    11-C underhanded.
    11-D overreacting.

12. Luis got right to the point and avoided <u>superfluous</u> explanation.
    12-A unclear
    12-B unfair
    12-C extra
    12-D exciting

13. The scout leader read the <u>roster</u> of the campers on the trip.
    13-A stories
    13-B rules
    13-C goals
    13-D list

14. <u>Pitfall</u> most nearly means
    14-A disadvantage.
    14-B distance.
    14-C application.
    14-D uncertainty.

15. The <u>congenial</u> teacher met her new class with a smile.
    15-A replacement
    15-B pleasant
    15-C unprepared
    15-D beginner

16. <u>Infinite</u> most nearly means
    16-A cloudy.
    16-B discrete.
    16-C endless.
    16-D negative.

17. The scientist carefully transported the <u>volatile</u> dynamite.
    17-A explosive
    17-B refined
    17-C standard
    17-D coarse

18. <u>Brawl</u> most nearly means
    18-A speak.
    18-B fight.
    18-C cooperate.
    18-D investigate.

19. To complete his geography paper, Brian consulted an <u>atlas</u>.
    19-A journal
    19-B news articles
    19-C book of maps
    19-D biography

20. Bringing only food and water was a <u>pragmatic</u> choice.
    20-A rowdy
    20-B curious
    20-C debated
    20-D practical

21. <u>Ultimatum</u> most nearly means
    21-A unfair decision.
    21-B final demand.
    21-C total surrender.
    21-D moving speech.

22. Lisa was <u>ambivalent</u> about the candidates and did not vote.
    22-A undecided
    22-B protective
    22-C furious
    22-D worried

23. Stan used a quick <u>maneuver</u> to avoid an auto accident.
    23-A helpful lesson
    23-B unclear motive
    23-C call for assistance
    23-D skillful movement

24. The cunning spy used <u>guile</u> to trick her captors.
    24-A speed
    24-B quests
    24-C force
    24-D deceit

25. The <u>valiant</u> firefighter saved the man from the blaze.
    - 25-A unlikely
    - 25-B unusual
    - 25-C brave
    - 25-D courteous

26. Mayor Smith met <u>reproach</u> for her dishonest actions.
    - 26-A speed
    - 26-B discovery
    - 26-C joy
    - 26-D blame

27. The lost children sought <u>refuge</u> from the winter cold.
    - 27-A a new friend
    - 27-B a place of shelter
    - 27-C enjoyment
    - 27-D employment

28. Many blamed plain <u>avarice</u> for the country's economic troubles.
    - 28-A greed
    - 28-B abundance
    - 28-C concepts
    - 28-D interest

29. Thomas was <u>baffled</u> by the difficult math problems.
    - 29-A cornered
    - 29-B amused
    - 29-C angered
    - 29-D confused

30. <u>Ravage</u> most nearly means
    - 30-A ruin.
    - 30-B explore.
    - 30-C hide.
    - 30-D demand.

31. We wanted to <u>gauge</u> the costs before we accepted the project.
    - 31-A earn
    - 31-B estimate
    - 31-C allow
    - 31-D invent

32. While the man lived a life suited for a prince, his sister lived like a <u>pauper</u>.
    - 32-A poor person
    - 32-B kind person
    - 32-C religion
    - 32-D business

33. We eagerly read the <u>brochure</u> about the zoo tour.
    - 33-A visitors
    - 33-B journey
    - 33-C animals
    - 33-D pamphlet

34. As the river rose, locals built a high <u>levee</u>.
    - 34-A foundation for buildings
    - 34-B collection of money
    - 34-C protection from floods
    - 34-D assortment of laws

35. The truck became stuck in a <u>quagmire</u> in the jungle.
    - 35-A destination
    - 35-B swamp
    - 35-C highway
    - 35-D plant

practice test

PARAGRAPH COMPREHENSION

TIME: 13 Minute • 15 Questions

Directions: This test contains 15 items measuring your ability to obtain information from written passages. You will find one or more paragraphs of reading material followed by incomplete statements or questions. You are to read the paragraph(s) and then mark the lettered choice that best completes the statement or answers the question on your answer form.

Your score on this test will be based on the number of questions you answer correctly. You should try to answer every question. Do not spend too much time on any one item.

1. One of the novice surfer's biggest challenges is keeping the board on the surface of the water. If the front of the board dips into the water or the back of the board angles down under the surface when you lie on it, you will not be able to catch a wave. If this occurs, move closer to the middle of the board. This is the position you will start in when heading for your first wave. When paddling into the ocean, move one arm at a time to keep a steady, even pace. To stand on your board, use slow movements, looking in front of you and pushing your upper body upward. Rise to a high crouch and keep looking up. With a lot of practice, you'll be ready to catch your first wave.

   As used above, the word <u>novice</u> means
   - 1-A   distant.
   - 1-B   dangerous.
   - 1-C   older.
   - 1-D   beginner.

2. The Sydney Opera House is one of the most unique and famous pieces of architecture in Australia and in the world. In 1956, the government of New South Wales, Australia, asked architects to develop and submit plans for an opera house in Sydney. Of the more than 200 entries, architect Jørn Utzon's design was chosen by the government panel. The development and construction of the building lasted from 1957 to 1973. Finally, in 1973, the building was opened by Queen Elizabeth II. Today, the Sydney Opera House's distinct white structure has become an icon of the city and of all of Australia.

   From this passage, you can infer that the Sydney Opera House
   - 2-A   is Queen Elizabeth's favorite building.
   - 2-B   was not built by an Australian citizen.
   - 2-C   does not look like other opera houses.
   - 2-D   is the world's most successful opera house.

3. Millions of drivers watch as their windshield wipers push aside rain, sleet, or snow to create a clear view of the road. Few probably consider who invented these small wonders, however. While riding on a streetcar in New York City, Mary Anderson noticed that drivers opened their windows during bad weather, just so they could see the road. Upon returning to her home in Birmingham, Alabama, Anderson invented the first windshield wiper. Patented in 1903, her simple device included a manually controlled lever, a moveable arm, and a rubber blade. Drivers could move the lever to make the blade wipe precipitation from the car windshield. Before long,

windshield wipers were a standard feature on most automobiles.

This paragraph is mainly about

3-A   a handy invention.

3-B   the patent system.

3-C   life in Birmingham, Alabama.

3-D   the life of Mary Anderson.

4. The Champagne-Ardennes region of France, world-famous for its sparkling wine, has a rich history filled with great prosperity and great strife. The region's location made it an important trading route with Eastern Europe. The wealth brought to the region through trade led to the construction of a massive cathedral in the city of Reims during the twelfth century. This became the traditional site for the crowning of French kings. The region was later devastated during the French Wars of Religion. Unrest continued for several generations, until the reign of Louis XIV brought peace to the region. Today, Champagne-Ardennes is home to more than one million people and has recently become a popular tourist destination for travelers from all over the world.

Wealth first came to Champagne-Ardennes through

4-A   wine.

4-B   trade.

4-C   wars.

4-D   tourism.

5. Jane Addams, a Nobel Peace Prize winner, is famous for her efforts to help underprivileged people. During a trip to Europe, Addams and her friend Ellen G. Starr visited a home for the poor and got the idea to start a similar program in the United States. As a result, Addams and Starr began their organization, Hull House. Hull House offered Chicago residents a place where they could sleep, eat, learn, and socialize. Addams raised money for Hull House and made speeches advocating the rights of people living in poverty. Although her health was poor and she could not travel to the ceremony, Addams was awarded the Nobel Peace Prize in 1931.

What does the word advocating mean as used above?

5-A   supporting

5-B   wondering

5-C   approaching

5-D   weakening

QUESTIONS 6 TO 8 ARE BASED ON THE FOLLOWING PASSAGE.

With so much emphasis on hand washing as an integral step in preventing the spread of colds and flu, it is important to know the proper hand-washing procedure. First, wet hands with clean running water and apply soap. Rub hands together to create lather and scrub all areas of the hands, including nails. Continue rubbing your hands for fifteen to twenty seconds, out of the water stream. A good rule of thumb for washing your hands is to imagine singing "Happy Birthday" twice. Rinse hands well and dry using a paper towel or air dryer. If soap and water are not available, clean hands with an alcohol-based hand sanitizer. Keeping the hands clean significantly reduces the amount of germs and bacteria that enter the body.

6. From this passage, you can infer that

6-A   few people wash their hands properly.

6-B   towels are better than air dryers are.

6-C   germs and bacteria can cause illness.

6-D   only hot water works for hand washing.

7. As used above, the word <u>integral</u> means
   7-A difficult to do.
   7-B done rarely.
   7-C easy to forget.
   7-D very important.

8. This paragraph is mainly about
   8-A why germs affect people.
   8-B how sicknesses spread.
   8-C how to cleanse the hands.
   8-D how to use hand sanitizer.

9. Rockets are by no means a new invention. The first rockets were probably used in or before the 1200s, likely in China. After scientists accidentally invented explosive black powder, it did not take long for them to find many ways to use it. By igniting black powder inside a hollow piece of bamboo, these scientists could make primitive rockets. These rockets were used on the battlefield or to carry beautiful fireworks into the night sky. Today, rockets are used as weapons, for learning and entertainment, and most famously to deliver astronauts into space. This ancient technology still has much to offer people today and in the future.

   This paragraph is mainly about
   9-A life in ancient China.
   9-B the history of rockets.
   9-C modern space travel.
   9-D battles of ancient times.

10. Foster care is the temporary placement of a child under the age of 18 with a guardian or guardians who will care for him or her after a family court or a child welfare agency, such as a state's Department of Social Services, deems the child's parents unable to care for the child. Foster care is usually a short-term situation until a permanent home is found for the child. Foster care can be provided in someone's home or at a care facility. Permanent placement consists of reunification with the biological parents, adoption, or transfer of guardianship.

Which of the following is a TRUE statement according to this passage?
   10-A A care facility is not a permanent placement.
   10-B People over 18 are commonly put in foster care.
   10-C Foster children are never returned to their parents.
   10-D Children in the foster care system are rarely adopted.

QUESTIONS 11 AND 12 ARE BASED ON THE FOLLOWING PASSAGE.

Language differences can cause great confusion. Dr. L.L. Zamenhof noticed this when he lived in a crowded Russian city where the inhabitants spoke Russian, Polish, German, and Jewish languages. The different languages seemed to create divisions between people and sometimes led to prejudices. Zamenhof decided to invent a new language called Esperanto. Esperanto was meant to become a worldwide second language that all people could learn. Zamenhof hoped that the new language would create communication between nations and usher in world peace. Esperanto was a combination of European languages, but people in Italy used it most. Today, few people speak the language, but it does come in handy for students studying how languages develop.

11. Esperanto became most popular in
    11-A Italy.
    11-B Germany.
    11-C Israel.
    11-D Russia.

12. As used above, the word <u>usher</u> means
   12-A slow.
   12-B fight.
   12-C stop.
   12-D bring.

13. On Halloween night in 1938, Orson Welles directed and narrated a radio broadcast adapted from H.G. Wells' novel *The War of the Worlds*. The broadcast, which was aired over the Columbia Broadcasting System radio network, claimed that space aliens had invaded Grover's Mills, New Jersey. The news-style broadcast caused some listeners to believe that the events were actually happening! Some listeners panicked because of the broadcast, and many people were furious when they learned the truth. The incident made national newspaper headlines, and it helped to make Orson Welles famous.

   From this passage, you can infer that
   13-A people were scared by the broadcast.
   13-B nobody believed in space aliens.
   13-C Welles and Wells were related.
   13-D Welles's career suffered after 1938.

14. Each October, the skies near Albuquerque, New Mexico, fill with a rainbow of colors as more than 700 hot-air balloons take part in the Albuquerque International Balloon Fiesta. The nine-day event is the largest hot-air balloon festival in the world and is also one of the most photographed because of its uniqueness and beauty. The first festival was in 1972 and included only thirteen participants. The festival continued to grow over the years and today is considered the premier event for hot-air balloon pilots. More than 100,000 spectators gather at the launch site each day of the festival to catch a rare glimpse of the inflation and liftoff of hundreds of vibrantly colored hot-air balloons.

   Which of the following is the best title for this passage?
   14-A "How Hot Air Balloons Work"
   14-B "Things to Do in Albuquerque"
   14-C "America's Favorite Sky Sports"
   14-D "The Albuquerque Balloon Fiesta"

15. The Seven Mile Bridge in Key West, Florida, is one of the longest bridges in the world. It connects the Middle Keys to the Lower Keys by creating a passageway between the Gulf of Mexico and the Florida Straight. The total length of the bridge is 35,862 feet or 6.79 miles. Constructed between 1978 and 1982, the bridge incorporates some elements of an older bridge built between 1909 and 1912. The older bridge was destroyed by a hurricane in 1935. Because of the vastness and beauty of the Seven Mile Bridge, it has appeared in many Hollywood movies and television programs.

   Construction of the Seven Mile Bridge was completed in
   15-A 1909.
   15-B 1935.
   15-C 1978.
   15-D 1982.

ANSWER KEY AND EXPLANATIONS

Arithmetic Reasoning

1. C	7. A	13. C	19. D	25. C
2. B	8. A	14. B	20. B	26. B
3. B	9. C	15. D	21. A	27. D
4. B	10. C	16. C	22. B	28. C
5. C	11. B	17. A	23. C	29. B
6. D	12. C	18. B	24. B	30. C

1-C   1 gallon = 4 quarts = 16 cups

        4 gallons = 16 × 4 = 64 cups

2-B   0.55 + 0.12 = 0.67

        260 × 0.67 = 174.2

        The entire shipment weighs 174.2 lbs.

3-B   3 hrs. 32 min.

       − 2 hrs. 54 min.

       Borrow from 3 hours so that you can subtract the number of minutes:

        2 hrs. 92 min.

      − 2 hrs. 54 min.

                38 min.

4-B   The profit for the entire 62 rolls of wrapping paper is 62 × $2.10 = $130.20.

5-C $330 \text{ yds.} \times \dfrac{3 \text{ ft.}}{1 \text{ yd.}} = 990 \text{ ft.}$

6-D   Using the book, admission costs $4.00 per person, a savings of 0.50 per person.

        4.50 − 4.00 = 0.50

        Fraction of the regular cost = $\dfrac{0.50}{4.50} = \dfrac{50}{450} = \dfrac{1}{9}$

        Percentage of the regular cost = $100 \times \dfrac{1}{9} = 11\dfrac{1}{9}$

7-A   Add the costs:

        $8.50

        $5.20

       +$3.20

        $16.90

If Tina already gave the clerk $10, she needs $6.90.

8-A Add the minutes and divide by 5.

$32 + 23 + 35 + 30 + 25 = 145$

$145 \div 5 = 29$

The average time Latisha spent playing the piano per day over the 5 days was 29 minutes.

9-C $\dfrac{3^3}{3^2} = \dfrac{3 \times 3 \times 3}{3 \times 3} = \dfrac{27}{9} = 3$

10-C $420 is 70% of the original price of the sofa: $100\% - 30\% = 70\%$.

Original price $= 420 \div 0.70 = \$600$

11-B 9:40 to 10:00 $=$ 20 min.

10:00 to noon $=$ 2 hrs.

Noon to 2:30 $=$ 2 hrs. 30 min.

4 hrs. 50 min.

12-C Add the individual prices to get:

Cost of food: $4.95 + $4.50 + $2.50 + $2.25 = $14.20

Tip: $14.20 \times 0.15 = $2.13

Total: $14.20 + $2.13 = $16.33

13-C Vehicles involved $=$ 6 blue cars

$=$ 4 black cars

$=$ 2 red cars

Total $=$ 12 cars

Total NOT blue $=$ 6 cars

Percentage NOT blue $= \dfrac{6 \text{ not blue}}{12 \text{ cars total}} = \dfrac{1}{2} = 50\%$

14-B Time already performed + Time left to perform = Total length of scene.

Time already performed = Total length of scene − Time left to perform.

$= 16\dfrac{1}{4} - 2\dfrac{1}{2}$

$= 16\dfrac{1}{4} - 2\dfrac{2}{4}$

$= 15\dfrac{5}{4} - 2\dfrac{2}{4}$

$= 13\dfrac{3}{4}$ minutes already performed

15-D Adults: $10.00

Children: $5.50

3 Adults + 2 Children = $(3 \times \$10.00) + (2 \times \$5.50) = \$30.00 + \$11.00 = \$41.00$

16-C $4 \times (2 \text{ hrs.} + 15 \text{ min.}) = 9 \text{ hrs.}$

17-A   The highest peak in the number of burglaries occurred in 2003.

18-B   In 2005, the number of burglaries was about 400 and the number of thefts was about 200, so the difference is about 200.

19-D   The highest peak in the number of motor vehicle thefts occurred in 2009.

20-B $\frac{1}{4}$ inch = 10 miles

Let x = the number of miles it takes to get from one town to another.

$$\frac{\frac{1}{4}}{10} = \frac{\frac{19}{8}}{x}$$

$$\frac{190}{8} \times \frac{4}{1} = \frac{190}{2} = 95 \text{ miles}$$

21-A   Add each item individually. Then find the total cost.

Sleeping bag:	$56.00
Water bottles:	10($1.25) = $12.50
Boots:	$32.50
Shirts:	2($21.99) = $43.98
Socks:	3($3.50) = $10.50
Total spent:	$155.48

$200.00 − $155.48 = $44.52

22-B   85 dimes = 8.5 × $0.10 = $8.50

$15.50 − $8.50 = $7.00

There is $7.00 worth of nickels in the bag.

7.00 ÷ 0.05 = 140 nickels.

23-C   The cost of $4\frac{1}{2}$ dozen is $4\frac{1}{2} \times \$2.10 = 4.5 \times 2.10 = \$9.45$.

The stickers sell for 2 for $0.50. A dozen sell for 6 × $0.50, or $3.00.

The selling price of $4\frac{1}{2}$ dozen is $4\frac{1}{2} \times \$3.00 = 4.5 \times \$3.00 = \$13.50$.

Profit = $13.50 − $9.45 = $4.05

24-B   Move the (intended) decimal two places to the left: 15% = 0.15.

30 subscriptions at $12.50/subscription = 375 × 0.15 = $56.25

25-C

New York to London	$525 each way
New York to San Francisco	− $379 each way
Difference	$146 one way

Multiply by 2 to find the difference for a round-trip ticket.
$146 × 2 = $292

26-B 1 foot = 12 inches
8 feet = 8 × 12 = 96 inches

27-D Divide the total number of passengers by the number of passengers per bus load:
678 ÷ 48 = 14.13

Because after 14 round trips there is a remainder, the bus will have to make one more trip, for a total of 15 round trips.

28-C $$\text{average} = \frac{\text{total of all terms}}{\text{number of terms}}$$

$$= \frac{57.4 + 58.9 + 64.3 + 69.3 + 74.7 + 79.4}{6} = \frac{404}{6} = 67.3$$

The average daily mean temperature is approximately 67.3°.

29-B Set up a proportion of their actual heights to the lengths of their shadows. All measurements should be in the same units, inches.

$$\frac{\text{height}}{\text{length of shadow}} =$$

$$\frac{68}{40} = \frac{N}{30}$$

$$\frac{17}{10} = \frac{N}{30} \quad \text{(Cross-multiply)}$$

$$10N = 510 \quad \text{(Divide by 10 to find } N\text{)}$$

$$N = 51 \text{ inches}$$

30-C $2\frac{1}{2}$ cups × 4 = 10 cups of flour needed

2 cups of flour = 1 pound

$$\frac{10 \text{ cups}}{2 \text{ cups/pound}} = 5 \text{ pounds}$$

Mathematics Knowledge

1. C	6. C	11. C	16. C	21. B
2. D	7. D	12. B	17. B	22. D
3. A	8. A	13. C	18. B	23. D
4. A	9. B	14. B	19. B	24. B
5. B	10. A	15. C	20. A	25. C

1-C From the diagram you can see that there are two right triangles (*BAD* and *BCD*), each having legs of 8 feet and 15 feet, with a supporting wire as the hypotenuse of each triangle. Using the Pythagorean theorem:

$$BD^2 = AD^2 + AB^2$$
$$8^2 + 15^2 = 64 + 225 = 289$$

$$BD = \sqrt{289} = 17$$
$$BD = AC$$

Therefore, the door requires $17 + 17 = 34$ feet of wire.

2-D Solve for C: $C + 3 = Y$ and $Y = 6$.

$$C + 3 = 6$$
$$C = 6 - 3$$
$$C = 3$$

3-A Look at the differences between the consecutive terms:
$-2, +3, -4, +5, -6$

The next term will be $43 - 6 = 37$.

4-A Change the signs of the second term and add.

$$\begin{aligned} 2x^2 + 2x + 4 \\ \underline{-3x^2 - 3x - 5} \\ -x^2 - x - 1 \end{aligned}$$

or $-(x^2 + x + 1)$

5-B $D = R \times T$

$$T = \frac{D}{R}$$

$$= \frac{385 \text{ miles}}{55 \text{ mph}} = 7 \text{ hours}$$

6-C $\left(2\sqrt{3}\right)^2 = \left(2\sqrt{3}\right)\left(2\sqrt{3}\right) = 4 \times 3 = 12$

7-D Multiply by 6:

$$3p + 2p = 5$$
$$5p = 6$$
$$p = \frac{6}{5}$$

8-A Represent the angles as:

$$3x + 6x + 9x = 180$$
$$18x = 180$$
$$x = 10$$

The angles are 30°, 60°, and 90°. The triangle is a right triangle.

9-B $\dfrac{24}{6} = 4$

Area of a square = $s^2 = 4$

$s = \sqrt{4} = 2$

Volume of a cube = $s^3 = 2^3 = 8$

10-A Let x = games lost

$x + 12$ = games won

$$x + x + 12 = 32$$
$$2x + 12 = 32$$
$$x = 10$$

11-C $\sqrt{8} = \sqrt{4 + 2} = \sqrt{4} \times \sqrt{2} = 2\sqrt{2}$

$\sqrt{32} = \sqrt{16 \times 2} = \sqrt{16} \times \sqrt{2} = 4\sqrt{2}$

$2\sqrt{2} + 4\sqrt{2} = 6\sqrt{2}$

12-B Let x = width of rectangle

Length of rectangle = $3x + 2$
Perimeter = $2l + 2w = 60$

$$2(x) + 2(3x + 2) = 60$$
$$2x + 6x + 4 = 60$$
$$8x + 4 = 60$$
$$8x = 56$$
$$x = 7$$

13-C Multiply by 100 to make the coefficient an integer.

$$14m = 0.28$$
$$m = 0.02$$

14-B   Original area $= \pi r^2$

Reduced area $= \pi \left(\dfrac{1}{5}r\right)^2 = \dfrac{1}{25}\pi r^2$

Therefore, 4% of the original remains.

15-C   Multiply the coefficients and add the exponents of the same base.

$2 \times 3 = 6$

$x^2 \times x^3 = x^{(2+3)} = x^5$

$y \times y^2 = y^{(1+2)} = y^3$

$6x^5y^3$

16-C   Short Trip: Longer Trip:

$$\dfrac{D}{T} \qquad\qquad\qquad \dfrac{D}{T}$$

$$\dfrac{120}{1\frac{3}{4}} = \dfrac{360}{x}$$

$$120x = 630$$

$$x = \dfrac{630}{120} = 5\dfrac{1}{4} \text{ hours}$$

17-B $\dfrac{a}{b} = \dfrac{1}{2}$

$2a = b$

Multiply both sides by 10:

$20a = 10b$

18-B   Pair numbers starting at the decimal point. Add a zero if necessary to complete a pair.

19/44/81

Each pair of numbers represents 1 digit in the square root.

19-B $6\sqrt{3}^2 = 6 \times \sqrt{3} \times \sqrt{3} = 6 \times 3 = 18$

20-A

$$\begin{array}{r} x + 5 \\ \times\; x - 5 \\ \hline x^2 + 5x \\ -\,5x - 25 \\ \hline x^2 - 25 \end{array}$$

21-B Area of 1 indentation: 2 ft. × 1 ft. = 2 ft.²
Area of 6 indentations: 6 × 2 ft.² = 12 ft.²
Area of door: 7 × 3 = 21 ft.²
Area of door − area of indentations: 21 ft.² − 12 ft.² = 9 ft.²

22-D Let x = the number

$9 = 0.09x$
$900 = 9x$ (Multiply by 100.)
$100 = x$

23-D Area of circle = $36\pi = \pi r^2$

Radius of circle = 6

Side of square = 12

Perimeter of square = 48

24-B $x^2 + 4x - 2 =$

$(-2)^2 + 4(-2) - 2 =$

$+4 - 8 - 2 =$

-6

25-C Simple interest = principal × rate × time

$\$4,000 \times 0.055 \times 1 = \$220$
$\$220 + \$4,000 = \$4,220$

Word Knowledge

1. A	8. C	15. B	22. A	29. D
2. A	9. D	16. C	23. D	30. A
3. D	10. A	17. A	24. D	31. B
4. B	11. B	18. B	25. C	32. A
5. C	12. C	19. C	26. D	33. D
6. A	13. D	20. D	27. B	34. C
7. B	14. A	21. B	28. A	35. B

1-A A *pseudonym* is an *assumed name*. Many authors, such as Samuel Clemens, use different names when they write. This word comes from the Greek word parts *pseud* (false) and *onym* (name).

2-A *Substandard* means *below a standard*. The prefix *sub-* means under or below. Other words using this prefix include submarine (under the water) and subhuman (below human). The other answer choices do not fit the meaning of this prefix.

3-D A *depot* is a *warehouse* for storing things. Armies and other large groups often keep their equipment at depots. The other answer choices may deal with certain aspects of military life, but they do not match the vocabulary word.

4-B *Unkempt* means *messy*, sloppy, and not taken care of. A child's room may be unkempt if he or she does not pick up clothes, books, or toys. In this sentence, you can determine Mom is mad because of a messy bedroom.

5-C A *tycoon* is a person who has made a great deal of money in a particular business. There are steel tycoons, hotel tycoons, Internet tycoons, and even amusement park tycoons. The sentence uses the word *ironic* to suggest that a tycoon is very different from a poor man.

6-A A *drought* is a *lack of rain* or a period of unusually dry weather. During droughts, farms often suffer. Crops do not get the water they need, and they often die. Droughts can present serious problems to farms both large and small.

7-B An *itinerary* is a *schedule* or a listing of times, places, and events for a trip. In this sentence, Justin creates a list of things he wants to do when he is in Mexico.

8-C A *thermometer* is a *tool for measuring heat*. Alex thinks she might have a fever. As you know, fevers make the body warmer, and a thermometer will measure that warmth. If she does have a fever, the doctor, soup, and medicine might come in handy, but none of them can measure her temperature like a thermometer can.

9-D *Nomadic* means *wandering*, traveling, and having no permanent place to live. In the past, many groups of people were nomads. They traveled from place to place in search of food, water, and other important resources. Some people are still nomadic today.

10-A *Prosper* means to *succeed*, be fortunate, and flourish. The sentence tells you that the business prospered after early setbacks, or troubles. That means the business overcame its problems and became successful.

11-B *Apathy* means *without feelings*. An apathetic person does not feel interest, emotion, or excitement. You can get clues to the word's meaning by examining its parts. The prefix *a-* means *without*. The word part *-pathy* comes from the Greek *pathos*, which means compassion or feeling.

12-C *Superfluous* means *extra*, additional, and unnecessary. In this sentence, Luis "got right to the point," which means he expressed what he wanted to say. Then he did not give any *superfluous*—extra—information.

13-D A *roster* is a *list*, usually containing names and other information about people. The scout leader had a list of the campers he would be leading. This *roster* would allow him to make sure everyone was present.

14-A A *pitfall* is a *disadvantage*, trap, or other source of danger. People use this word in many contexts, but the original pitfall is a hidden hole dug in the ground that is used to capture people or animals.

15-B *Congenial* means *pleasant*, agreeable, and suitable. The sentence contains some context clues. First, you learn that *congenial* refers to a way people may act. Then you learn that a *congenial* person is likely to smile at others.

16-C *Infinite* means *endless*, boundless, and too large to ever be measured. The word part *finite* refers to something that can be measured. Adding the prefix *in-* (not) makes the word *infinite* mean *not measureable*.

17-A *Volatile* means *explosive* or potentially violent. You can get a clue from the sentence, which says that dynamite is *volatile*—likely to explode. The word can also be used figuratively to refer to tense situations or disagreements between people.

18-B A *brawl* is a noisy quarrel or squabble. Therefore, the best synonym for *brawl* is *fight*.

19-C An *atlas* is a book of maps. The sentence contains an important clue: Brian is working on a *geography* paper. Geography is the study of different lands on the planet. An atlas would be very helpful in learning about geography.

20-D *Pragmatic* means dealing with what is necessary, useful, and ordinary. Therefore, *practical* is a good synonym for *pragmatic*. A pragmatic person would likely value basic things, such as food and water, over anything that is fancy or unnecessary.

21-B An *ultimatum* is a last proposal or condition—in other words, a *final demand*. For example, a businessperson who is tired of bargaining may make a final demand, or an *ultimatum*, about a business deal.

22-A *Ambivalent* refers to having mixed feelings or an *undecided* perspective. The sentence suggests that people may be *ambivalent* about difficult choices, such as elections, and this feeling may not be resolved.

23-D A *maneuver* is a *skillful movement*. In this sentence, Stan may have used a quick spin of the steering wheel to move his car away from a dangerous driving situation.

24-D *Guile* is craftiness, cunning, or deception. Therefore, a good synonym for *guile* is *deceit*. Spies are known for being skillful at deceit, and this spy used a trick to get herself out of trouble.

25-C *Valiant* means courageous, excellent, or stout-hearted. *Brave* is the best answer choice to define the word. A firefighter would have to be *valiant* to accomplish such a feat.

26-D To *reproach* someone is to find fault and show disapproval. Therefore, the best synonym for *reproach* is *blame*. In this sentence, Mayor Smith acted dishonestly. People blamed her for her misdeeds.

27-B *Refuge* is a place of shelter. People can seek shelter from danger or discomfort. Children outside on a cold winter day would likely seek *refuge* in a warm, dry house.

28-A *Avarice* is a deep state of *greed*. Economic troubles do not typically arise from abundance, concepts, or interest. Greed, however, has caused many problems with economies throughout history.

29-D To be *baffled* is to be puzzled, perplexed, or generally *confused*. In this sentence, difficult math problems left Thomas confused or *baffled*.

30-A To *ravage* something is to bring havoc or terrible damage—in other words, to bring *ruin*. For example, Vikings were known to *ravage* their enemies by burning towns, defeating armies, and kidnapping civilians.

31-B To *gauge* means to *estimate*. In this sentence, the speaker wanted to *gauge* or estimate the costs of a project. People can gauge many things, from emotions to measurements. *Gauge* can also be used as a noun. A gas gauge, for instance, is a tool that estimates the amount of gasoline in a vehicle.

32-A A *pauper* is a person who is penniless or impoverished. In other words, a *pauper* is a *poor person*. The sentence gives a hint by telling you that the lifestyle of a prince is very different from the lifestyle of a *pauper*. Princes are usually quite wealthy.

33-D A *brochure* is a *pamphlet*, a small booklet that lists important facts about a person, place, or thing. A zoo brochure might include a map, a list of tours, pictures of animals, and a schedule of events.

34-C A *levee* is a bank or hill that is usually made by humans to keep bodies of water from flooding. In the sentence, people work to build a levee while a river rises.

35-B A *quagmire* is a *swamp*. Other synonyms for *quagmire* include marsh, bog, or mire. These are all places where a truck may become stuck. The word *quagmire* may also be used figuratively to refer to a difficult or complicated problem.

Paragraph Comprehension

1. D	4. B	7. D	10. A	13. A
2. C	5. A	8. C	11. A	14. D
3. A	6. C	9. B	12. D	15. D

1-D You may not be familiar with the word *novice*, but you can determine its meaning using clues from the passage. One clue is that the passage contains information about basic surfing skills and safety. Another clue is that the author says, "You'll be ready to catch your first wave" after "a lot of practice." You can now safely determine that *novice* means *beginner*.

2-C To make an inference, use what you've read to figure out more about the topic. You read that the Sydney Opera House is a "unique and famous" building with a "distinct" structure. Its design resulted from a competition between top architects. Using these details, you can safely infer that the Sydney Opera House does not look like the average opera house.

3-A This passage mentions several topics, including patents, Birmingham, and Mary Anderson. However, each of these topics serves primarily to explain the main idea, which is the windshield wiper. The paragraph is mostly about the windshield wiper, a handy invention.

4-B The passage explains that wine, trade, wars, and tourism all impacted Champagne-Ardennes. However, the region's wealth first developed thanks to a trading relationship with Eastern Europe. This is a detail contained in the passage.

5-A The word *advocating* means *supporting*. Jane Addams made speeches that supported the rights of people living in poverty. This was part of her overall campaign to help underprivileged people.

6-C The author states that washing your hands is a good way to prevent colds and flu. In addition, hand washing helps keep germs and bacteria from entering the body. Readers can connect these ideas and use what they already know to infer that germs and bacteria can cause illnesses.

7-D Something that is *integral* is *very important*. The author explains why washing your hands is an integral—very important—step in staying healthy.

8-C This passage does mention germs, sicknesses, and hand sanitizer, but these are just details that support the main idea. The main idea in the passage, or what it's all about, is how to properly cleanse one's hands.

9-B To answer this main idea question, consider what the passage is mostly about. The passage does mention ancient China, battles, and space travel. All of these details, however, join to form the real main idea—the rocket. The main idea is the rocket, so the second answer choice is best.

10-A A care facility for foster children is only a short-term solution. Permanent placement for these children would involve them returning to their biological parents, being adopted, or having their guardianship transferred permanently to other adults.

11-A Esperanto combined several languages, but it was not popular in many countries. The author writes that Esperanto became most popular in Italy. That detail provides the answer to this question.

12-D The author writes that Zamenhof wanted his language to usher in world peace. He believed that his language would allow all people to communicate more efficiently. Zamenhof wanted to help bring peace to the world. The word *usher* means *bring*.

13-A When Orson Welles made his broadcast, many people thought it was true. According to the passage, the people panicked over the news that space aliens were invading Earth. From this information, you can safely infer that people were scared by the broadcast.

14-D A good title usually refers to the main idea of a passage. To determine the best title among these choices, ask yourself what the passage is mostly about. The passage does not explain how hot-air balloons work. The passage is not really about things to do in Albuquerque or American sky sports—the passage only discusses one thing to do and one sky sport. You can now tell that the passage is mostly about the Albuquerque Balloon Fiesta, which would be a good title.

15-D This passage gives several dates and other numbers. To find the correct date of the completion of the Seven Mile Bridge, you may look back to the passage. The year 1909 refers to the time when construction on the previous bridge started; 1935 was when that bridge was destroyed. Construction of the Seven Mile Bridge began in 1978. It was not completed until 1982, which is the correct answer.

ARITHMETIC REASONING

1. Ⓐ Ⓑ Ⓒ Ⓓ   7. Ⓐ Ⓑ Ⓒ Ⓓ   13. Ⓐ Ⓑ Ⓒ Ⓓ   19. Ⓐ Ⓑ Ⓒ Ⓓ   25. Ⓐ Ⓑ Ⓒ Ⓓ
2. Ⓐ Ⓑ Ⓒ Ⓓ   8. Ⓐ Ⓑ Ⓒ Ⓓ   14. Ⓐ Ⓑ Ⓒ Ⓓ   20. Ⓐ Ⓑ Ⓒ Ⓓ   26. Ⓐ Ⓑ Ⓒ Ⓓ
3. Ⓐ Ⓑ Ⓒ Ⓓ   9. Ⓐ Ⓑ Ⓒ Ⓓ   15. Ⓐ Ⓑ Ⓒ Ⓓ   21. Ⓐ Ⓑ Ⓒ Ⓓ   27. Ⓐ Ⓑ Ⓒ Ⓓ
4. Ⓐ Ⓑ Ⓒ Ⓓ   10. Ⓐ Ⓑ Ⓒ Ⓓ   16. Ⓐ Ⓑ Ⓒ Ⓓ   22. Ⓐ Ⓑ Ⓒ Ⓓ   28. Ⓐ Ⓑ Ⓒ Ⓓ
5. Ⓐ Ⓑ Ⓒ Ⓓ   11. Ⓐ Ⓑ Ⓒ Ⓓ   17. Ⓐ Ⓑ Ⓒ Ⓓ   23. Ⓐ Ⓑ Ⓒ Ⓓ   29. Ⓐ Ⓑ Ⓒ Ⓓ
6. Ⓐ Ⓑ Ⓒ Ⓓ   12. Ⓐ Ⓑ Ⓒ Ⓓ   18. Ⓐ Ⓑ Ⓒ Ⓓ   24. Ⓐ Ⓑ Ⓒ Ⓓ   30. Ⓐ Ⓑ Ⓒ Ⓓ

MATHEMATICS KNOWLEDGE

1. Ⓐ Ⓑ Ⓒ Ⓓ   6. Ⓐ Ⓑ Ⓒ Ⓓ   11. Ⓐ Ⓑ Ⓒ Ⓓ   16. Ⓐ Ⓑ Ⓒ Ⓓ   21. Ⓐ Ⓑ Ⓒ Ⓓ
2. Ⓐ Ⓑ Ⓒ Ⓓ   7. Ⓐ Ⓑ Ⓒ Ⓓ   12. Ⓐ Ⓑ Ⓒ Ⓓ   17. Ⓐ Ⓑ Ⓒ Ⓓ   22. Ⓐ Ⓑ Ⓒ Ⓓ
3. Ⓐ Ⓑ Ⓒ Ⓓ   8. Ⓐ Ⓑ Ⓒ Ⓓ   13. Ⓐ Ⓑ Ⓒ Ⓓ   18. Ⓐ Ⓑ Ⓒ Ⓓ   23. Ⓐ Ⓑ Ⓒ Ⓓ
4. Ⓐ Ⓑ Ⓒ Ⓓ   9. Ⓐ Ⓑ Ⓒ Ⓓ   14. Ⓐ Ⓑ Ⓒ Ⓓ   19. Ⓐ Ⓑ Ⓒ Ⓓ   24. Ⓐ Ⓑ Ⓒ Ⓓ
5. Ⓐ Ⓑ Ⓒ Ⓓ   10. Ⓐ Ⓑ Ⓒ Ⓓ   15. Ⓐ Ⓑ Ⓒ Ⓓ   20. Ⓐ Ⓑ Ⓒ Ⓓ   25. Ⓐ Ⓑ Ⓒ Ⓓ

WORD KNOWLEDGE

1. Ⓐ Ⓑ Ⓒ Ⓓ   8. Ⓐ Ⓑ Ⓒ Ⓓ   15. Ⓐ Ⓑ Ⓒ Ⓓ   22. Ⓐ Ⓑ Ⓒ Ⓓ   29. Ⓐ Ⓑ Ⓒ Ⓓ
2. Ⓐ Ⓑ Ⓒ Ⓓ   9. Ⓐ Ⓑ Ⓒ Ⓓ   16. Ⓐ Ⓑ Ⓒ Ⓓ   23. Ⓐ Ⓑ Ⓒ Ⓓ   30. Ⓐ Ⓑ Ⓒ Ⓓ
3. Ⓐ Ⓑ Ⓒ Ⓓ   10. Ⓐ Ⓑ Ⓒ Ⓓ   17. Ⓐ Ⓑ Ⓒ Ⓓ   24. Ⓐ Ⓑ Ⓒ Ⓓ   31. Ⓐ Ⓑ Ⓒ Ⓓ
4. Ⓐ Ⓑ Ⓒ Ⓓ   11. Ⓐ Ⓑ Ⓒ Ⓓ   18. Ⓐ Ⓑ Ⓒ Ⓓ   25. Ⓐ Ⓑ Ⓒ Ⓓ   32. Ⓐ Ⓑ Ⓒ Ⓓ
5. Ⓐ Ⓑ Ⓒ Ⓓ   12. Ⓐ Ⓑ Ⓒ Ⓓ   19. Ⓐ Ⓑ Ⓒ Ⓓ   26. Ⓐ Ⓑ Ⓒ Ⓓ   33. Ⓐ Ⓑ Ⓒ Ⓓ
6. Ⓐ Ⓑ Ⓒ Ⓓ   13. Ⓐ Ⓑ Ⓒ Ⓓ   20. Ⓐ Ⓑ Ⓒ Ⓓ   27. Ⓐ Ⓑ Ⓒ Ⓓ   34. Ⓐ Ⓑ Ⓒ Ⓓ
7. Ⓐ Ⓑ Ⓒ Ⓓ   14. Ⓐ Ⓑ Ⓒ Ⓓ   21. Ⓐ Ⓑ Ⓒ Ⓓ   28. Ⓐ Ⓑ Ⓒ Ⓓ   35. Ⓐ Ⓑ Ⓒ Ⓓ

PARAGRAPH COMPREHENSION

1. Ⓐ Ⓑ Ⓒ Ⓓ   4. Ⓐ Ⓑ Ⓒ Ⓓ   7. Ⓐ Ⓑ Ⓒ Ⓓ   10. Ⓐ Ⓑ Ⓒ Ⓓ   13. Ⓐ Ⓑ Ⓒ Ⓓ
2. Ⓐ Ⓑ Ⓒ Ⓓ   5. Ⓐ Ⓑ Ⓒ Ⓓ   8. Ⓐ Ⓑ Ⓒ Ⓓ   11. Ⓐ Ⓑ Ⓒ Ⓓ   14. Ⓐ Ⓑ Ⓒ Ⓓ
3. Ⓐ Ⓑ Ⓒ Ⓓ   6. Ⓐ Ⓑ Ⓒ Ⓓ   9. Ⓐ Ⓑ Ⓒ Ⓓ   12. Ⓐ Ⓑ Ⓒ Ⓓ   15. Ⓐ Ⓑ Ⓒ Ⓓ

answer sheet

Practice Test 3

ARITHMETIC REASONING

TIME: 36 Minute • 30 Questions

Directions: This test has 30 arithmetic questions followed by four possible answers. Decide which answer is correct and then mark the space on your answer form with the same number and letter as your choice. Don't forget to use scrap paper to work out problems and organize your thoughts.

Your score on this test will be based on the number of questions you answer correctly. You should try to answer every question. Do not spend too much time on any one question.

1. During a five-day workweek, Jan's flower shop sold 1,275 bouquets of roses. There were 245 bouquets sold on Monday, 117 sold on Tuesday, 383 sold on Wednesday, 323 sold on Thursday, and the rest were sold on Friday. How many bouquets of roses were sold on Friday?

   1-A   155
   1-B   192
   1-C   201
   1-D   233

2. In a day, Kevin's bakery uses 51 pounds of sugar. If 1 pound equals 454 grams, how many kilograms does the bakery use in a day? (Round to the nearest tenth.)

   2-A   23.2 kg.
   2-B   29.4 kg.
   2-C   33.6 kg.
   2-D   35.1 kg.

3. Olivia is reviewing her grocery bill. She purchased 1 box of cereal for $3.29, 2 pounds of strawberries for $1.99 per pound, 3 bottles of soda for $0.89 per bottle, and 2 salad mixes for $3.59 each. How much change should she receive from $20?

   3-A $1.79
   3-B $2.88
   3-C $3.17
   3-D $0.25

4. What is $\frac{1}{4}$ of 572?

   4-A   307
   4-B   234
   4-C   211
   4-D   143

5. It takes Selena 8 minutes to peel 1 pound of potatoes. How many pounds can she peel in 1 hour?

   5-A   6 lbs.

   5-B $7\frac{1}{2}$ lbs.

   5-C $8\frac{1}{3}$ lbs.

   5-D   9 lbs.

6. Weather forecasters predict that the tri-state area will have a record snowfall of 96 inches this winter. Last year, the area received 66 inches of snow. According to the forecasters, how many more feet of snow will the area receive this year?

   6-A   2.5 ft.

   6-B   3 ft.

   6-C   4.5 ft.

   6-D   5 ft.

7. Janice discovered that her test scores represent 5 points for every quarter of an hour she studies. At this rate, if she spends 4 hours studying for her history test, what grade should she expect to receive?

   7-A   60

   7-B   75

   7-C   80

   7-D   95

QUESTIONS 8 AND 9 REFER TO THE FOLLOWING CIRCLE GRAPH.

Post-High School Plans (1,250 students surveyed)

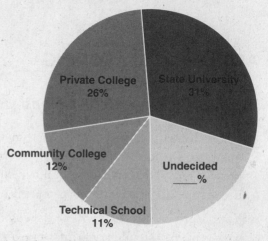

8. According to the graph, how many students are undecided about their post–high school plans?

   8-A   100

   8-B   150

   8-C   200

   8-D   250

9. According to the graph, how many more students plan to attend a private college than a community college?

   9-A   105

   9-B   175

   9-C   210

   9-D   225

10. If the average household uses 96 gallons of water per day, how many quarts are used per hour? (1 gallon = 4 quarts)

    10-A   4

    10-B   8

    10-C   12

    10-D   16

11. Ryan attended a conference in Michigan. He spent $475 on airfare, $119 per night for three nights at a hotel, and $320 on food and expenses. How much did Ryan's trip cost?

11-A $914

11-B $1,089

11-C $1,152

11-D $1,245

12. The ages of five employees at the local movie theater are as follows:

Megan: 18

Suzanne: 20

William: 34

Travis: 27

Nicolas: 31

What is the average age of these employees?

12-A 24

12-B 26

12-C 29

12-D 31

13. The bookstore is having a sale. Buy two books at regular price and receive 50% off a third book. The 50% is taken off the least expensive book. The books Bill wants to purchase cost $12.35, $14.56, and $11.80. How much should Bill expect to spend?

13-A $32.81

13-B $33.79

13-C $34.17

13-D $35.22

14. At the gym, Todd puts one 45-pound weight on each end of a barbell. If the barbell weighs 20 pounds, how much will Todd be lifting?

14-A 90 lbs.

14-B 110 lbs.

14-C 125 lbs.

14-D 130 lbs.

15. A store sells tires for $56 each. During a promotion, the store gives customers 10% off their total when they purchase 4 tires. How much money will Kenny save if he purchases 4 tires during this promotion?

15-A $12.50

15-B $20.74

15-C $22.40

15-D $28.13

16. To check the quality of a shipment of 600 cell phones, a sampling of 50 phones was carefully inspected. Of this sample, 3 were defective. Based on these findings, what is the probable percentage of defective phones in the original shipment?

16-A 2%

16-B 3%

16-C 5%

16-D 6%

17. If one quart of floor wax covers 500 square feet, how many gallons of wax are needed to cover a 6,000-square foot home?

17-A 1 gal.

17-B 2 gal.

17-C 3 gal.

17-D 4 gal.

18. In 2008, a high school basketball team won 54 of 90 games. What percentage of games did the team lose last year?

18-A 40%

18-B 43%

18-C 51%

18-D 55%

19. How many seasons (1 season per year) did Roberto Clemente play baseball if he played from 1955–1972?

19-A 17

19-B 18

19-C 19

19-D 20

20. At a long jump competition, an athlete jumped 20 feet, 19 feet, 21 feet, and 24 feet. What was the average distance the athlete jumped?

20-A 20 ft.

20-B 21 ft.

20-C 22 ft.

20-D 23 ft.

21. For her birthday, Lily received a $25 gift card to a department store. If she used the gift card to purchase a purse that cost $37.50, how much money did she have to add?

21-A $10.50

21-B $11.50

21-C $12.50

21-D $13.50

22. Mandy is preparing a budget for her New Year's party. She has a total of $180 to spend. If she spends 52% of her money on food and drinks, how much money is left for decorations?

22-A $68.60

22-B $74.80

22-C $79.20

22-D $86.40

23. A book of 10 garbage stickers costs $16.00. Each individual sticker costs $1.75. Helen needs 15 garbage stickers. What is the minimum amount she must pay?

23-A $24.75

23-B $25.25

23-C $26.50

23-D $27.25

24. A teacher has 30 feet of ribbon. If she gives each of her 18 students an equal share of the ribbon, how many inches of ribbon should each student receive?

24-A 12 in.

24-B 15 in.

24-C 20 in.

24-D 23 in.

25. A science teacher divides $\frac{3}{4}$ of a gram of a soil specimen among her 25 students. If equal portions are prepared for each student, how many grams of soil should each student receive?

25-A 0.01 g.

25-B 0.03 g.

25-C 0.40 g.

25-D 0.25 g.

26. The value of 42 nickels, 12 quarters, and 170 dimes is

26-A $19.35.

26-B $20.25.

26-C $21.45.

26-D $22.10.

27. Garrison earns $10.50 an hour for a 40-hour week and $1\frac{1}{2}$ times the base pay for overtime. How much will he make if he works 52 hours in a week?

27-A $420

27-B $489

27-C $609

27-D $655

28. The population of Middletown has increased from 40,000 to 60,000 in the last twenty years. What is the percentage of increase in the population?

28-A 50%

28-B 65%

28-C 70%

28-D 85%

29. Thirty men and 20 women started a 5-kilometer race. During the race, 6 men and 3 women dropped out. What percentage of people dropped out of the race?

29-A 9%

29-B 11%

29-C 15%

29-D 18%

30. Wendy won the 100-meter freestyle with a time of 40 seconds. How many meters/second did she swim?

30-A 2 m/s

30-B 2.5 m/s

30-C 2.9 m/s

30-D 3 m/s

practice test

MATHEMATICS KNOWLEDGE

TIME: 24 Minutes • 25 Questions

> **Directions:** This is a test of your ability to solve 25 general mathematical problems. Select the correct response from the choices given and then mark the space on your answer form that has the same number and letter as your choice. Don't forget to use scrap paper to work out problems and organize your thoughts.
>
> Your score on this test will be based on the number of questions you answer correctly. You should try to answer every question. Do not spend too much time on any one question.

1. Solve for Y: $Y - 3 = 3 - Y$
   - **1-A**   0
   - **1-B**   1
   - **1-C**   2
   - **1-D**   3

2. When 4 is added to 4 times a number, the result is 4. What is the number?
   - **2-A** -4
   - **2-B**   0
   - **2-C**   8
   - **2-D**   12

3. A child sailed a toy boat across a small pond at a rate of 10 feet per minute. If it took $3\frac{1}{2}$ minutes for the boat to sail across the pond, how many feet did it sail?
   - **3-A**   25 ft.
   - **3-B**   35 ft.
   - **3-C**   3.5 ft.
   - **3-D**   30.5 ft.

4. Five is approximately what percent of 75?
   - **4-A**   6.7%
   - **4-B**   10%
   - **4-C**   15%
   - **4-D**   66.7%

5. What is the next term in the following sequence? 6, 10.5, 15, 19.5,____
   - **5-A**   24
   - **5-B**   24.5
   - **5-C**   25
   - **5-D**   34.5

6. What is the sum of $(4x^2 + 8x + 9) + (3x^2 - 2x - 8)$?
   - **6-A** $7x^2 + 6x + 1$
   - **6-B** $12x^2 - 16x + 72$
   - **6-C** $x^2 + 6x + 1$
   - **6-D** $7x^2 + 6x - 1$

7. By how many inches will the perimeter of a rectangle increase if the length increases by 4 inches and the width by 5 inches?
   - **7-A**   9 in.
   - **7-B**   10 in.
   - **7-C**   18 in.
   - **7-D**   28 in.

8. One-sixth of the audience of parents and children at a play consisted of girls, and $\frac{1}{12}$ of the audience consisted of boys. What percent of the audience consisted of children?
   - **8-A**   16%
   - **8-B**   25%
   - **8-C**   50%
   - **8-D**   75%

9. $(3x + 2)(4x + 5) =$

   9-A $7x + 7$

   9-B $12x^2 + 7x - 3$

   9-C $12x^2 + 7x + 3$

   9-D $12x^2 + 23x + 10$

10. Deshawn and Kelly left the beach at the same time. Deshawn drove west at 50 miles per hour, and Kelly drove east at 55 miles per hour. How many miles apart will they be in 3 hours?

   10-A   15 miles

   10-B   105 miles

   10-C   150 miles

   10-D   315 miles

11. Divide: $\dfrac{28x^4}{7x^2}$

   11-A $4x$

   11-B $4x^2$

   11-C $4x^6$

   11-D $4x^8$

12. A circle is inscribed in a square with a side of 4. Express the area of the circle in terms of π.

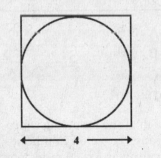

   12-A 2π

   12-B 4π

   12-C 8π

   12-D 16π

13. A classified ad in the *Daily News* costs $50 for the first 2 lines, $40 for the next 3 lines, and $20 for each additional line. Find the cost of a 9-line classified ad.

   13-A $190

   13-B $180

   13-C $170

   13-D $90

14. Ten percent of 10% of 10 is what number?

   14-A   0.01

   14-B   0.1

   14-C   1

   14-D   10

15. If $2 - x = x - 2$, then find $\dfrac{4}{x}$.

   15-A   0

   15-B   1

   15-C   2

   15-D   4

16. Find the first term in the following series: ____, 8, 32, 128.

   16-A   1

   16-B   2

   16-C   4

   16-D -4

17. If $(3x + 3)$ is multiplied by 3, the result is 36. What is the value of x?

   17-A   12

   17-B   9

   17-C   6

   17-D   3

18. A pulley with a 6-inch diameter is belted to a pulley with a 3-inch diameter, as shown in the figure. If the larger pulley runs at 180 rotations per minute, how fast does the smaller pulley run in rotations per minute?

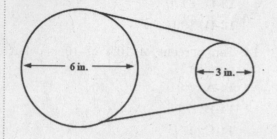

18-A   90 rpm

18-B   180 rpm

18-C   360 rpm

18-D   1,080 rpm

19. If an item costs $6.30 after a 30% discount, what was its original price?

19-A $63.00

19-B $21.00

19-C $9.00

19-D $1.89

20. The base of a rectangular tank is 5 feet by 5 feet and its height is 48 inches. Find the number of cubic feet of water in the tank when it is $\frac{1}{2}$ full?

20-A   4 cu. ft.

20-B   48 cu. ft.

20-C   50 cu. ft.

20-D   100 cu. ft.

21. $2\sqrt{5} + \sqrt{45} =$

21-A $2\sqrt{50}$

21-B $5\sqrt{5}$

21-C $2\sqrt{3}$

21-D $3\sqrt{5}$

22. A rectangular yard has a perimeter of 280 feet. If the ratio of length to width is 3:4, find the diagonal of the yard in feet.

22-A   280 ft.

22-B   140 ft.

22-C   100 ft.

22-D   40 ft.

23. If a car uses $2\frac{1}{2}$ gallons of gas for 50 miles, how many miles can be driven with 10 gallons of gas?

23-A   200 miles

23-B   250 miles

23-C   500 miles

23-D   1,250 miles

24. In triangle ABC, $AC = BC$. If angle $A = (4x + 10)°$, and angle $B = (2x +30)°$, find the number of degrees in angle C.

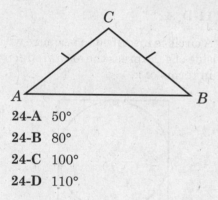

24-A   50°

24-B   80°

24-C   100°

24-D   110°

25. Which of the following represents the distance traveled in 4 hours by a car traveling at $4x - 9$ miles per hour?

25-A $16x - 9$

25-B $16x - 36$

25-C $4x - 36$

25-D $4x^2 - 9$

WORD KNOWLEDGE

TIME: 11 Minute • 35 Questions

Directions: This test has 35 questions about the meanings of words. Each question has an underlined word. Select the answer choice that is closest in meaning to the underlined word and then mark the space on your answer form with the same number and letter as your choice.

Your score on this test will be based on the number of questions you answer correctly. You should try to answer every question. Do not spend too much time on any one item.

1. Chronic most nearly means
   1-A afflicted.
   1-B persuaded.
   1-C defenseless.
   1-D unrelenting.

2. The judge denied bail for the millionaire, fearing he would use his vast resources to flee the country.
   2-A wealthy
   2-B suitable
   2-C gigantic
   2-D miserly

3. The rancher needed a durable pair of boots to wear to work.
   3-A fancy
   3-B light
   3-C tough
   3-D muddy

4. Unilateral most nearly means
   4-A self-moving.
   4-B one-sided.
   4-C harassed.
   4-D recharged.

5. Imponderable most nearly means
   5-A unknown.
   5-B external.
   5-C appropriate
   5-D undecided.

6. On Monday morning, the employees discussed the agenda for the week.
   6-A work
   6-B party
   6-C vacations
   6-D schedule

7. The Internet makes it easy to correspond with friends and family around the world.
   7-A visit
   7-B feast
   7-C talk
   7-D play

8. Spontaneous most nearly means
   8-A cheerful.
   8-B impulsive.
   8-C loving.
   8-D satisfied.

9. Hypertension most nearly means
   9-A to have a cold.
   9-B low blood sugar.
   9-C high blood pressure.
   9-D to be in good health.

10. The store prepared for the semiannual sale.
    10-A substantial
    10-B half-off
    10-C fabulous
    10-D half-year

11. His friend agreed to <u>reimburse</u> him for the loan.
11-A repay
11-B thank
11-C charge
11-D include

12. <u>Unruly</u> most nearly means
12-A nosey.
12-B rowdy.
12-C jaded.
12-D simple.

13. <u>Inadequate</u> most nearly means
13-A brisk.
13-B probable.
13-C insufficient.
13-D commanding.

14. The hurricane forced the couple to <u>postpone</u> their travel plans until the following week.
14-A rethink
14-B control
14-C expire
14-D delay

15. The hero thwarted the mad scientist's <u>devious</u> plan.
15-A usual
15-B lively
15-C cunning
15-D humorous

16. <u>Unscathed</u> most nearly means
16-A unharmed.
16-B uninterested.
16-C misunderstood.
16-D misrepresented.

17. <u>Cohesion</u> most nearly means
17-A calm.
17-B unity.
17-C present.
17-D forward.

18. The child <u>wavered</u> about whether to choose chocolate or vanilla ice cream.
18-A repeated
18-B hesitated
18-C proceeded
18-D considered

19. The students disliked the new girl because she seemed <u>aloof</u>.
19-A kind
19-B funny
19-C beautiful
19-D standoffish

20. The lush watering hole in the middle of the desert was only a <u>hallucination</u>.
20-A hope
20-B feeling
20-C vision
20-D mystery

21. <u>Affluence</u> most nearly means
21-A wealth.
21-B courage.
21-C intellect.
21-D fitness.

22. <u>Ecology</u> most nearly means
22-A the study of landforms.
22-B loving to be outside.
22-C study of the environment.
22-D overly polluted.

23. The couple cited <u>irreconcilable</u> differences on their divorce petition.
23-A destructive
23-B frustrated
23-C uncommon
23-D irresoluble

24. The <u>barren</u> soil threatened to ruin the family farm.
24-A soaked
24-B infertile
24-C complex
24-D auburn

25. <u>Wretched</u> most nearly means
    25-A tired.
    25-B strict.
    25-C miserable.
    25-D moveable.

26. <u>Degenerate</u> most nearly means
    26-A immerse.
    26-B worsen.
    26-C perch.
    26-D repose.

27. The collector put the antique car up for <u>auction</u>.
    27-A public sale
    27-B free of charge
    27-C inspection
    27-D rotation

28. The tabloid accused the senator of having a <u>torrid</u> affair with his lawyer.
    28-A serene
    28-B lengthy
    28-C perceptive
    28-D passionate

29. The police charged the driver with a moving <u>violation</u>.
    29-A ticket
    29-B permit
    29-C misdeed
    29-D security

30. <u>Unassuming</u> most nearly means
    30-A airy
    30-B modest
    30-C chic
    30-D dreary

31. <u>Protrude</u> most nearly means
    31-A fulfill.
    31-B bank.
    31-C project.
    31-D weep.

32. <u>Biosphere</u> most nearly means
    32-A to live forever.
    32-B too energetic.
    32-C to take shape.
    32-D globe of life.

33. The formula <u>facilitated</u> the kitten's growth, allowing her to gain weight.
    33-A assisted
    33-B prolonged
    33-C calmed
    33-D plagued

34. The principal <u>expelled</u> the student from school for fighting in the halls.
    34-A consented
    34-B barred
    34-C conjoined
    34-D opened

35. The guests thanked their <u>gracious</u> host for treating them so well.
    35-A exhausted
    35-B unwilling
    35-C friendly
    35-D talented

PARAGRAPH COMPREHENSION

TIME: 13 Minute • 15 Questions

Directions: This test contains 15 items measuring your ability to obtain information from written passages. You will find one or more paragraphs of reading material followed by incomplete statements or questions. You are to read the paragraph(s) and then mark the lettered choice that best completes the statement or answers the question on your answer form.

Your score on this test will be based on the number of questions you answer correctly. You should try to answer every question. Do not spend too much time on any one item.

1. Duane Hanson, born in 1925, was an artist like none other. Using fiberglass, resin, and even automotive putty, Hanson built life-sized statues of people. Each statue had a theme. At first, Hanson made statues of people in tension, distress, or even violence. Later, the artist used his work to examine common people in everyday situations. Hanson made highly realistic statues of regular people such as tourists, custodians, athletes, construction workers, and supermarket shoppers. Each statue was clothed and given accessories; some viewers actually thought the statues were humans! Before Hanson's death in 1996, he made a lasting contribution to the artistic field of hyperrealism, or making art that looks like real life.

From this passage, you can infer that

1-A athletes are the best models for statues.

1-B Hanson's statues almost looked alive.

1-C resin is the best material for statues.

1-D Hanson did not like hyperrealist art.

2. Icing a cake takes patience and practice. After a cake has completely cooled, transfer it to a plate or cake dish. Top the cake with about a cup of icing. Using either a spatula or a butter knife, spread a thin layer of icing all over the top and down the sides of the cake. This layer, called a crumb coat, should be thin enough that the cake is still visible through the icing. After the cake is completely covered, it is ready for the final icing layer. Top the cake with more icing and follow the same instructions that you used for the crumb coat. This layer of icing should completely cover the cake; the cake should no longer be visible through the icing. Smooth the sides and top with a spatula.

A crumb coat is

2-A the first layer of frosting.

2-B a spatula or butter knife.

2-C the final layer of frosting.

2-D a plate or cake dish.

3. Writers can use words to create beautiful stories and poems, but calligraphers can make the words themselves look beautiful. Calligraphy is the visual art of writing. A calligraphy artist works to draw each letter and word with grace and elegance. The word "calligraphy" comes from the Greek term for "beauty writing." Some works of word art are displayed in frames. Others are so fancy that they are actually difficult to read; they are more like paintings than writings. Most calligraphy created today, however, is functional. Oftentimes calligraphic

writing is used for cards, diplomas, and certificates. Most of the world's written language systems can be written in calligraphy, so this art form can be found throughout history and around the globe.

Calligraphy would probably be used to write

3-A shopping lists.

3-B class notes.

3-C a party invitation.

3-D a phone number.

4. The Painted Desert in northern Arizona is a magnificent sight to behold. The desert stretches more than 160 miles from the Grand Canyon to the Petrified Forest. The desert gets its name for the multitude of colors—ranging from lavenders to shades of gray with vibrant tints of red, orange, and pink—that color the sand and rock that make up the many buttes and badland hills in the area. Created from layers of eroded siltstones, mudstones, and shale, the layers contain a large amount of iron and manganese compounds that color the rock and sand to give the desert its "painted" appearance.

This paragraph is mainly about

4-A materials in the soil.

4-B the Grand Canyon.

4-C Western landscapes.

4-D the Painted Desert.

5. Henry David Thoreau (1817–1862) was an American poet, an author, and a philosopher. Most of his poems reflect upon nature, philosophy, environmentalism, and simple living. His book of reflections, *Walden*, is considered an American classic. It is about his two-year journey of simple living in a cabin owned by fellow poet and essayist Ralph Waldo Emerson in Concord, Massachusetts. In addition to writing, Thoreau was heavily involved in the anti-slavery movement.

His essay *Civil Disobedience* is about his resistance to the government and was said to have much influence on Martin Luther King Jr. and Mahatma Gandhi. Thoreau wrote more than twenty volumes of stories, articles, essays, journals, and poetry.

From this passage, you can infer that

5-A Thoreau dealt with politics and societal issues.

5-B Thoreau and Emerson had little in common.

5-C Thoreau and Gandhi were very close friends.

5-D Thoreau did not like being around other people.

6. Tailgating is more than fans gathering in a parking lot before a sporting event, concert, or other attraction. It has become a social event—some even consider it a sport in itself! A tailgate party is a gathering held before a major attraction or event. In the past years, tailgating has gained popularity at college football games. Participants bring tents, chairs, food, and drinks to celebrate prior to the event. Documents say the practice may date as far back as the Civil War era, when those who supported the soldiers gathered near battlefields with baskets of food.

Which of the following is the best title for this passage?

6-A "How to Throw a Great Party"

6-B "America in the Civil War Era"

6-C "Parties in the Parking Lot"

6-D "The World's Favorite Sports"

QUESTIONS 7 AND 8 ARE BASED ON THE FOLLOWING PASSAGE.

Though often unseen, skunks live quietly among people in neighborhoods across the United States. They often live close to homes that provide easy access to garbage or warm, dark places for skunks to sleep. In the wild, skunks live in underground burrows not far from the surface, and they dig for insects and trap small rodents for food. Though they are best known for their foul-smelling spray, skunks only spray when threatened—and only then as a last resort. Skunks first make their fur stand on end as they stomp on the ground, rise onto their hind legs, and growl. If you are sprayed by a skunk, thoroughly wash your skin with tomato juice or vinegar, and flush your eyes with cold water.

7. What does the word <u>burrows</u> mean as used above?

    7-A tunnels

    7-B rocks

    7-C houses

    7-D neighborhoods

8. From this passage, you can infer that

    8-A skunks often use their spray.

    8-B skunks' legs are not very strong.

    8-C skunks like sunny, bright places.

    8-D skunk spray is hard to clean off.

9. The term "baby talk" refers to silly, nonsensical words and sounds. Researchers on child development have discovered that this sort of talk does not benefit infants very much. Infants are experiencing the most dramatic growth and learning process of their lives. They need to learn not only what words mean, but also how language works. How can adults help? Some adults speak to infants as they would speak to other adults, with long sentences and flat tones. Researchers believe that this does not help infants much, either. The infant cannot focus on and absorb information that way. Instead, researchers believe that the best communication with infants in-volves short, simple sentences spoken in a lively, exaggerated tone. This allows the infant to pick up new words and learn about communication.

From this passage, you can infer that

    9-A "baby talk" comes naturally to adults.

    9-B infants and adults think differently.

    9-C "baby talk" is helpful for infants.

    9-D adults cannot communicate with infants.

10. Treasure hunting is not just for kids. Geocaching is a new activity that is similar to treasure hunting, but participants use global positioning system (GPS) units instead of maps. Geocaching participants hide small containers filled with trinkets and other small souvenirs in different places around the globe. After hiding the containers, which are called geo-caches, participants list the location of their cache on the Internet. Then, other geocachers use GPS units to locate various geocaches. All people need to begin geocaching is an Internet connection, a GPS unit, and a spirit of adventure.

As used above, the word <u>souvenirs</u> means

    10-A maps.

    10-B small items.

    10-C GPS units.

    10-D adventures.

11. At 2,178 miles, the Appalachian National Scenic Trail is the longest foot-path in the United States. The idea for the trail came from Benton MacKaye, a forester who wanted others to enjoy nature, during the 1920s. The trail was completed in 1937 and has been open to the public since that time. The path, which runs from Maine to Georgia, passes through fourteen states. The Appalachian Trail Conservancy

manages the trail, and thousands of volunteers care for it. Every year, many Americans hike at least part of the Appalachian Trail.

Which of the following is an UNTRUE statement?

11-A Benton MacKaye was a forester.

11-B Many volunteer workers care for the trail.

11-C The trail was completed in 1937.

11-D The trail is not open to the public.

12. Chopsticks are eating utensils traditionally used in China, Japan, Korea, Vietnam, Tibet, and Nepal. Used to pick up pieces of food, chopsticks consist of a pair of sticks held between the thumb and fingers of one hand. They can be made of a variety of materials including bamboo, plastic, ivory, wood, bone, and metal. Different cultures use different varieties and lengths of chopsticks. These eating utensils are originally from China and were used as early as the Shang Dynasty. Etiquette dictates that chopsticks must be used in one hand, usually the right hand.

Chopsticks were first made in

12-A Korea.

12-B China.

12-C Nepal.

12-D Japan.

QUESTIONS 13 TO 15 ARE BASED ON THE FOLLOWING PASSAGE.

Iceland's frosty features not only provide a breathtaking backdrop, but also provide some of the most challenging hiking, biking, climbing, and exploration activities in the world. Iceland is home to Vatnajokull, which, at 3,300 square miles, is the largest glacier in Europe. Vatnajokull provides an exciting destination for tourists daring enough to head for the top. These adventurers rely on skilled guides to help them avoid the dangerous cracks below the surface. Iceland's mountains, including the capital city's Mount Esja, provide hikers and bikers with many steep, winding trails to traverse. After a vigorous trip, tourists can relax in one of Iceland's many geothermal pools, where they can enjoy Icelandic culture among the country's residents.

13. As used above, the word <u>traverse</u> means

13-A melt.

13-B travel

13-C relax.

13-D guide.

14. This paragraph is mainly about

14-A countries to tour in Europe.

14-B places to visit in Iceland.

14-C the history of a large glacier.

14-D how geothermal pools work.

15. As used above, the word vigorous means

15-A secret.

15-B disappointing.

15-C interesting.

15-D active.

ANSWER KEY AND EXPLANATIONS

Arithmetic Reasoning

1. C	7. C	13. A	19. B	25. B
2. A	8. D	14. B	20. B	26. D
3. B	9. B	15. C	21. C	27. C
4. D	10. D	16. D	22. D	28. A
5. B	11. C	17. C	23. A	29. D
6. A	12. B	18. A	24. C	30. B

1-C   Add the number of bouquets sold on Monday, Tuesday, Wednesday, and Thursday.

$$
\begin{array}{r}
245 \\
117 \\
383 \\
+\ 329 \\
\hline
1{,}074
\end{array}
$$

Subtract this amount from the total amount of bouquets sold.

$$
\begin{array}{r}
1{,}275 \\
-\ 1{,}074 \\
\hline
201
\end{array}
$$

This means that 201 bouquets were sold on Friday.

2-A   Multiply 51 pounds by 454 grams:

$51 \times 454 = 23{,}154$

1 kilogram = 1,000 grams

Divide 23,154 by 1,000:

$$
1{,}000\overline{)23{,}154}^{\ 23.154}
$$

Rounded to the nearest tenth, the bakery uses 23.2 kilograms of sugar per day.

3-B   Calculate the cost for each item group first. Then find the sum of these purchases.

cereal =	1 box =	$3.29
strawberries =	2 lbs. =	$3.98
soda =	3 bottles =	$2.67
salad mixes =	2 mixes =	$7.18

$3.29
$3.98
$2.67
+ $7.18
―――――
$17.12

Subtract this amount from $20:

$20.00
−$17.12
―――――
$2.88

4-D   Multiply $\frac{1}{4}$ by 572:

$$\frac{1}{4} \times \frac{572}{1} = \frac{572}{4}$$

$$4\overline{)572} \quad 143$$

$\frac{1}{4}$ of $572 = 143$

5-B   There are 60 minutes in 1 hour.

Divide 60 by 8:

$$\begin{array}{r} 7.5 \\ 8\overline{)60} \\ -56 \\ \hline 4\,0 \end{array}$$

Selena can peel $7\frac{1}{2}$ pounds of potatoes in 1 hour.

6-A   There are 12 inches in 1 foot.

$$12\overline{)96} \quad 8$$

8 feet = amount of snow predicted

$$12\overline{)66} \quad 5.5$$

5.5 feet = last year's snowfall

$8 - 5.5 = 2.5$

Forecasters are predicting an additional 2.5 feet of snow this winter.

7-C   There are 4 quarters in every hour. Janice receives 5 points for every quarter of an hour she studies.

$4 \times 5 = 20$

She spends 4 hours studying.

$4 \times 20 = 80$

Janice will receive a grade of 80 if she studies for 4 hours.

8-D   The circle graph must total 100%.

Add the known sectors:

$$
\begin{array}{r}
31 \\
26 \\
12 \\
+\,11 \\
\hline
80
\end{array}
$$

$100 - 80 = 20$

This means that 20% of students are undecided about their post–high school plans. Multiply 20% by the number of students surveyed.

$1{,}250 \times 0.20 = 250$

Of the 1,250 students surveyed, 250 students are undecided about their post–high school plans.

9-B   According to the circle graph, 26% of students plan to attend a private college and 12% plan to attend a community college. Multiply these amounts by the number of students surveyed.

$0.26 \times 1{,}250 = 325$
$0.12 \times 1{,}250 = 150$

Subtract to find how many more students plan to attend a private college than a community college.

$325 - 150 = 175$

This means that 175 more students are planning to attend a private college than a community college.

10-D   Find out how many gallons are used per hour. Remember, there are 24 hours in a day.

$$24\overline{)96}\;\;^{4}$$

This means that the average household uses 4 gallons of water per hour. There are 4 quarts in every gallon.

$4 \times 4 = 16$

The average household uses 16 quarts of water every hour.

11-C Add up all of Ryan's expenses.

Airfare = $475
Hotel = $119 × 3 = $357
Food and Expenses = $320

$$
\begin{array}{r}
\$475 \\
\$357 \\
+\ \$320 \\
\hline
\$1,152
\end{array}
$$

Ryan's trip cost $1,152.

12-B Add up the ages of the 5 employees:
18 + 20 + 34 + 27 + 31 = 130

Divide by the number of employees:

$$\frac{130}{5} = 26$$

The average age of the employees is 26.

13-A Take 50% off the least expensive book:
$11.80 × 0.50 = $5.90

Add this amount to the price of the other two books:

$$
\begin{array}{r}
\$5.90 \\
\$12.35 \\
+\ \$14.56 \\
\hline
\$32.81
\end{array}
$$

Bill should expect to pay $32.81.

14-B The barbell has two ends.

45 + 45 = 90
90 + 20 = 110

Todd will be lifting 110 pounds.

15-C Figure out the total cost of 4 tires:
4 × $56 = $224

Multiply by 10%:
$224 × 0.10 = $22.40

Kenny will save $22.40 if he purchases 4 tires during this promotion.

16-D Fraction of defective cell phones:

$$\frac{3}{50} = \frac{6}{100}$$

Percentage of defective cell phones = 6%

17-C   1 quart waxes 500 sq. ft. Since 4 quarts = 1 gallon, 1 gallon waxes $500 \times 4 = 2,000$ sq. ft.

$$\frac{6,000}{2,000} = 3\, \text{gallons}$$

18-A   Subtract the number of games won from the total number of games played.

$$90 - 54 = 36$$

$$\text{percentage lost} = \frac{\text{number lost}}{\text{number of games played}}$$

$$\frac{36}{90} = 0.40$$

The team lost 40% of the games it played.

19-B   Break the problem into two steps. Remember there is one season per year. Be sure to count the first year.

1955–1965	10 seasons
1965–1972	+ 8 seasons
Total =	18 seasons

20-B   Add the distances and divide by 4:

$$\frac{20 + 19 + 21 + 24}{4} = \frac{84}{4} = 21\, \text{feet}$$

21-C   Subtract the amount of the gift card from the cost of the purse:
$37.50 − $25.00 = $12.50

22-D   100% − 52% = 48% left over for expenses

$$0.48 \times 180 = \$86.40$$

23-A   1 book of 10 stickers = $16.00

5 stickers at $1.75 = $8.75

$16.00 + $8.75 = $24.75

24-C   There are 12 inches in every foot.

$$30 \times 12 = 360$$

Divide by the number of students.

$$18\overline{)360}^{\,20}$$

Each student should receive 20 inches of ribbon.

25-B Divide the sample of $\frac{3}{4}$ gram of soil among 25 students.

$\frac{3}{4}$ gram ÷ 25 (students)

$\frac{3}{4}$ gram × $\frac{1}{25}$ students = $\frac{3}{100}$ = 0.03

Each student received 0.03 gram of soil.

26-D Find the amount of each group first. Then add the products together.

nickels = 42 × 0.05 = $2.10
quarters = 12 × 0.25 = $3.00
dimes = 170 × 0.10 = $17.00

$2.10
$3.00
+ $17.00
———
$22.10

27-C 52 − 40 = 12 hours overtime

Salary for 12 hours overtime:

$1\frac{1}{2} \times \$10.50 \times 12 = \frac{3}{2_1} \times \$10.50 \times 12_6 = \$189$

Salary for 40 hours regular time:
$10.50 × 40 − $420

Total salary = $420 + $189 = $609

28-A Amount of increase = 60,000 − 40,000 = 20,000

Fraction of increase = $\frac{20,000}{40,000} = \frac{1}{2}$

Percentage of increase = 50%

29-D The percentage is found from the fraction of dropouts.

$\frac{dropouts}{total} = \frac{6+3}{30+20} = \frac{9}{50} = 0.18$

When the decimal is moved two places to the right, 0.18 becomes 18. Therefore, 18% of the runners dropped out of the race.

30-B The problem wants meters per second.

$\frac{100 \text{ meters}}{40 \text{ seconds}} = 2.5 \text{ meters/second}$

Mathematics Knowledge

1. D	6. A	11. B	16. B	21. B
2. B	7. C	12. B	17. D	22. C
3. B	8. B	13. C	18. C	23. A
4. A	9. D	14. B	19. C	24. B
5. A	10. D	15. C	20. C	25. B

1-D

$$Y - 3 = 3 - Y$$
$$\underline{+Y = +Y} \qquad \text{Add } Y \text{ to both sides.}$$
$$2Y - 3 = 3$$
$$\underline{+3 = +3} \qquad \text{Add 3 to both sides.}$$
$$2Y = 6$$
$$\frac{2Y}{2} = \frac{6}{2} \qquad \text{Divide both sides by 2.}$$
$$Y = 3$$

2-B   Let $x =$ the number

$$4 + 4x = 4$$
$$\underline{-4 = -4} \qquad \text{Subtract 4 from both sides.}$$
$$4x = 0$$
$$\frac{4x}{4} = \frac{0}{4} \qquad \text{Divide both sides by 4.}$$
$$x = 0$$

3-B   Distance = Rate × Time

$$\text{Distance} = \frac{10\,\text{ft.}}{\text{min.}} \times 3\frac{1}{2}\,\text{min.} = 10\,\text{ft.} \times 3\frac{1}{2} = 35\,\text{ft.}$$

4-A

$$\frac{5}{75} = \frac{x}{100}$$
$$75x = 500 \qquad \text{(Cross multiply.)}$$
$$x = \frac{500}{75} = 6.7 \qquad \text{(Divide by 75.)}$$

5-A   Add 4.5 to each term to get the next term:
$19.5 + 4.5 = 24$

6-A $(4x^2 + 8x + 9) + (3x^2 - 2x - 8)$

$$4x^2 + 8x + 9$$
$$\underline{+3x^2 - 2x - 8}$$
$$7x^2 + 6x + 1$$

7-C Original Perimeter $= 2l + 2w$

New perimeter $= 2(l + 4) + 2(w + 5)$

$= 2l + 8 + 2w + 10$

$= 2l + 2w + 18$

Difference is $(2l + 2w + 18) - (2l + 2w) = 18$

8-B Let $x =$ number of people in the audience.

$\frac{1}{6}x + \frac{1}{12}x = \frac{2}{12}x + \frac{1}{12}x = \frac{3}{12}x$ or $\frac{1}{4}x = 25\%$

9-D $(3x + 2)(4x + 5) =$
$12x^2 + 15x + 8x + 10 =$
$12x^2 + 23x + 10$

10-D Since they are going in opposite directions, their distances are added.

Deshawn: $50 \times 3 = 150$ miles
Kelly: $55 \times 3 = 165$ miles

$150 + 165 = 315$ miles

11-B Divide the coefficients and subtract the exponents:

$\frac{28x^4}{7x^2} = 4x^{(4-2)} = 4x^2$

12-B Area of a circle $= \pi r^2 = \pi 2^2 = \pi 4 = 4\pi$

13-C 2 lines at \$50 = \$50
3 lines at \$40 = \$40
4 lines at \$20 per line = \$80

\$50 + \$40 + \$80 = \$170

14-B $0.10 \times 0.10 \times 10 = 0.1$

15-C $2 - x = x - 2$
$\quad 2 = 2x - 2$
$\quad 4 = 2x$
$\quad 2 = x$

$\frac{4}{x} = \frac{4}{2} = 2$

16-B Each term is the previous term times 4. The first term is $\frac{8}{4} = 2$.

17-D $3(3x + 3) = 36$
$\quad 9x + 9 = 36$
$\quad 9x = 27$
$\quad x = 3$

18-C   One revolution of the larger wheel causes more than one revolution of the smaller. This problem can be solved using a proportion:

$$\frac{6}{3} = \frac{x}{180}$$

$$3x = 1,080$$

$$x = 360$$

19-C $0.70x = \$6.30$

           $7x = \$63.00$

             $x = \$9.00$

20-C   Convert 48 inches to feet:

$$\frac{48}{12} = 4 \text{ feet}$$

Volume $= l \times w \times h$

$5 \times 5 \times 4 = 100$

$= 100$ cubic feet when the tank is full

$\frac{1}{2} \times 100 = 50$ cubic feet when half full

21-B $\sqrt{45} = \sqrt{5 \cdot 9} = \sqrt{5} \cdot \sqrt{9} = 3\sqrt{5}$

           $2\sqrt{5} + 3\sqrt{5} = 5\sqrt{5}$

22-C   Perimeter: $2l + 2w = 280$ feet

$$2(3x) + 2(4x) = 280$$

$$6x + 8x = 280$$

$$14x = 280$$

$$x = 20$$

$3x = 60$

$4x = 80$

The rectangle is 60 feet by 80 feet. This is a 3-4-5 right triangle, so the diagonal is 100 feet.

23-A $\dfrac{2\frac{1}{2}}{50} = \dfrac{10}{x}$

$$2\frac{1}{2} \cdot x = 500$$

$$x = 200$$

24-B Triangle *ABC* is an isosceles triangle; therefore, angle *A* = angle *B*.

$$4x + 10 = 2x + 30$$
$$x = 10$$
$$4(10) + 10 = 50$$
$$2(10) + 30 = 50$$

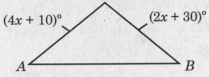

$$\text{Angle } A + \text{Angle } B + \text{Angle } C = 180°$$
$$50° + 50° + \text{Angle } C = 180°$$
$$\text{Angle } C = 180° - 100° = 80°$$

25-B Distance = Rate x Time
$$= (4x - 9) \times 4$$
$$= 16x - 36$$

Word Knowledge

1. D	8. B	15. C	22. C	29. C
2. C	9. C	16. A	23. D	30. B
3. C	10. D	17. B	24. B	31. C
4. B	11. A	18. B	25. C	32. D
5. A	12. B	19. D	26. B	33. A
6. D	13. C	20. C	27. A	34. B
7. C	14. D	21. A	28. D	35. C

1-D The root *chron* refers to time. *Chronic* means marked by a long duration or frequent recurrence. *Unrelenting* is an acceptable synonym for *chronic*. The other words do not fit the definition of the underlined word.

2-C The context clue in this sentence is *flee the country*. This implies that the millionaire has many resources at his disposal. *Vast* means very great in amount or size. An acceptable synonym for *vast* is *gigantic*.

3-C The context clue in this sentence is *wear to work*. Ranchers trek across rough terrain as they work. Therefore, a rancher would need a *tough* pair of boots. The other choices do not fit the context of the sentence.

4-B The prefix *uni-* means *one*. *Unilateral* means *one-sided* or independent. For example, a *unilateral* decision is one that is made without considering opposing viewpoints. The other choices are not synonyms for *unilateral*.

5-A The prefix *im-* means *not* and the suffix *-able* means *capable*. *Imponderable* means not capable of being pondered. An acceptable synonym for *imponderable* is un-

known. The other choices are not synonyms for *imponderable*.

6-D From the context of the sentence, you can tell that *agenda* means *schedule*. The employees discuss the *schedule* on Monday morning so they know what they need to do during the workweek.

7-C By using the Internet, people can communicate with others through e-mail or online videos. From the context of the sentence, you can tell that *correspond* means *talk*. The other choices are not acceptable substitutes for *correspond*.

8-B The suffix *-ous* means *full of*. *Spontaneous* means full of spontaneity. An acceptable synonym for *spontaneous* is *impulsive*. The other choices are not synonyms for *spontaneous*.

9-C The prefix *hyper-* means *too much*. This helps you figure out that *hypertension* means *high blood pressure*. The other words don't fit the definition of *hypertension*.

10-D The prefix *semi-* means *half* and *annual* means *year*. *Semiannual* means *half-year*. Though the other choices could apply to a sale, these words aren't synonyms for *semiannual*.

11-A The context clue in this sentence is *loan*. This tells you that *reimburse* means *repay*. The other choices do not fit the context of the sentence.

12-B The prefix *un-* means *not*. *Unruly* means out of control. *Rowdy* is an acceptable synonym for *unruly*. *Nosey*, *jaded*, and *simple* aren't synonyms for *unruly*.

13-C The prefix *in-* means *not* and *adequate* means *enough*. *Inadequate* means not enough. *Insufficient* has the same meaning. The other choices don't fit the definition of *inadequate*.

14-D The context clue in this sentence is *until the following week*. From this, you can tell that *postpone* means *delay*. *Rethink*, *control*, and *expire* aren't synonyms for *postpone*.

15-C The context clue is this sentence is *mad scientist*. Scientists are generally intelligent, so you can assume that his plan would be *cunning*. The other choices don't fit the context of the sentence.

16-A The prefix *un-* means *not* and *scathe* means *to do harm*. *Unscathed* means *unharmed*. The other choices don't fit the definition of *unscathed*.

17-B The prefix *co-* means *together*. *Cohesion* means the state or act of sticking together. An acceptable synonym for *cohesion* is *unity*.

18-B The context of the sentence tells you that the child is trying to decide between chocolate or vanilla ice cream. The word *wavered* means *hesitated*. The other choices don't fit the context of the sentence.

19-D The context of the sentence tells you that the students perceive something negative about the new girl. The only negative choice is *standoffish*. The other choices are qualities that most people would admire.

20-C From the sentence, you can tell that a *hallucination* is something that is not real. An acceptable synonym for *hallucination* would be *vision*. The other choices don't fit the context of the sentence.

21-A The word *affluence* means abundant flow or supply. The best synonym for *affluence* is *wealth*. The other words are desirable traits, but they aren't synonyms for *affluence*.

22-C The suffix *-logy* means *study of* and *eco-* refers to the environment. *Ecology* means *study of the environment*. Though the other choices are related to the environment, they don't fit the definition of *ecology*.

23-D The prefix *irr-* means *not* and the suffix *-able* means *capable of*. *Irreconcilable* means not able to be reconciled. An acceptable synonym for *irreconcilable* is *irresoluble*.

24-B From the context of the sentence, you can tell that there is something wrong with the soil. *Barren* means *infertile*, meaning that the soil cannot produce crops. This would ruin the farm because there would be no crops to sell.

25-C *Wretched* means deeply afflicted. An acceptable synonym would be *miserable*. For example, "The employee felt *wretched*" means that the employee felt *miserable*.

26-B   *Degenerate* means *worsen*. For example, "The conversation quickly *degenerated* when the father brought up his old grudge." The other choices are not synonyms for *degenerate*.

27-A   *Auction* refers to a *public sale*. During an *auction*, items are sold to the highest bidder. The other choices do not fit the definition of *auction*.

28-D   From the context of the sentence, you can tell that *torrid* means *passionate*. Substituting the other choices would not retain the integrity of the sentence.

29-C   From the context of the sentence, you can tell that the driver did something wrong. Therefore, you can assume that *violation* means *misdeed*. The driver had committed a wrongdoing. The other choices do not fit the context of the sentence.

30-B   The prefix *un-* means *not* and *assuming* means presumptuous. Unassuming means not presumptuous. An appropriate synonym is *modest*. The other words don't fit the definition of *unassuming*.

31-C   The prefix *pro-* means *forward*. *Protrude* means to thrust forward or *project*. For example, "The ledge *protruded* from the hilltop."

32-D   The root *bio* means *life* and *sphere* refers to a globular body, like the earth. *Biosphere* refers to a globe of life.

33-A   The context clue in this sentence is *gain weight*. This tells you that *facilitated* means *assisted*. The other choices don't fit the context of the sentence.

34-B   After fighting in the halls, the student was *expelled*, or *barred* from school. Expulsion is very serious because the student can never return. These situations often involve repeated bad behavior.

35-C   *Gracious* means marked by kindness or courtesy. An acceptable synonym for this is *friendly*. *Exhausted* and *unwilling* don't fit the context of the sentence. The host may be *talented*, but this is not a synonym for *gracious*.

Paragraph Comprehension

1. B	4. D	7. A	10. B	13. B
2. A	5. A	8. D	11. D	14. B
3. C	6. C	9. B	12. B	15. D

1-B Duane Hanson made life-sized statues that showed people in everyday situations. He clothed them and gave them accessories. Some people who saw the statues thought they were real people. Using information such as this, you can infer that Hanson's statues almost looked alive.

2-A This passage mentions layers of frosting, spatulas and butter knives, and plates and cake dishes. Only one of these, however, is identified as the crumb coat. Look back to the passage if you don't remember. The correct answer is that the first layer of frosting is called the crumb coat.

3-C *Calligraphy* means *beauty writing* and is usually reserved for fancy occasions. Shopping lists, class notes, and phone numbers are typically functional writings and are not meant to be fancy. Party invitations, however, may be fancy. Calligraphy would most likely be used to write a party invitation.

4-D This passage mentions many topics, including materials in soil, the Grand Canyon, and the appearance of the landscape in the West. All of these details support the "bigger picture," which is the passage's main idea. This passage is mostly about the Painted Desert of northern Arizona.

5-A To make an inference, readers use what they've read and what they already know to learn something else about the topic. In this passage, you can make an inference about Thoreau. The passage says that he was involved with the anti-slavery movement. He also wrote about resisting the government. From this information, you can infer that he dealt with politics and society.

6-C The title of a passage should reflect the main idea of the passage. The passage does not really tell how to throw a party. It only briefly mentions the Civil War era, and it says little about sports. The real main idea is tailgate parties, which are parties in parking lots. "Parties in the Parking Lot" would be the best title to reflect the main idea.

7-A The author explains that skunks live in burrows. You can use clues in the passage to determine what the word *burrows* means. These burrows are likely "warm, dark places." They are underground and allow skunks to dig for insects. From the answer choices, you can tell that *tunnels* is the closest match.

8-D You can use what you've read to make inferences, or determine new information about the topic. The material in the passage suggests that skunks *do not* use their spray often, skunks *can* stand on their hind legs, and skunks like their homes dark. These inferences are not correct. Choice D is correct. The author explains that people need to use tomato juice or vinegar to thoroughly wash their skin if they are sprayed, which demonstrates that the spray is hard to clean.

9-B   Adults often have difficulty communicating with infants. "Baby talk" is thought to be ineffective. Regular adult-type speech does not work well, either. Adults have to use a particular kind of speech to help infants understand, because infants and adults think differently. You can make this inference using the information in the passage.

10-B   People often create geocaches that contain trinkets and other *souvenirs*. A souvenir is a small item. Like trinkets, souvenirs are small—and they have to be small to fit in geocache containers. The other answer choices may relate to the geocaching experience, but the correct definition of *souvenirs* is *small items*.

11-D   Three of these answer choices contain true information, and only one makes a false claim. The last one, choice D, contains an untrue statement. The Appalachian National Scenic Trail *is* open to the public, as explained in the passage.

12-B   The passage tells you that chopsticks were first made in China. Chopsticks were later used in places such as Korea, Nepal, and Japan.

13-B   The passage says that hikers, bikers, and other visitors to Iceland will find winding trails to *traverse*. You can tell from the sentence that these people are moving around. Hikers and bikers are often on the move. Trails are great places to do this. The word *traverse* does not match with *melt*, *relax*, or *guide*. *Traverse* means *travel*.

14-B   The author mentions tour destinations in Europe, glaciers, and geothermal pools. The majority of the information in this passage, however, is about visiting Iceland. This paragraph is mainly about places to visit in Iceland.

15-D   The author says that visitors may have *vigorous* trips. These trips may include hiking, biking, climbing, and exploring frozen mountains. This sounds like a lot of activity, and the author suggests that visitors should relax when they finish. You can use these context clues to determine that *vigorous* means *active*.

NOTES

NOTES

NOTES

NOTES

Peterson's
Book Satisfaction Survey

Give Us Your Feedback

Thank you for choosing Peterson's as your source for personalized solutions for your education and career achievement. Please take a few minutes to answer the following questions. Your answers will go a long way in helping us to produce the most user-friendly and comprehensive resources to meet your individual needs.

When completed, please tear out this page and mail it to us at:

Publishing Department
Peterson's, a Nelnet company
2000 Lenox Drive
Lawrenceville, NJ 08648

You can also complete this survey online at **www.petersons.com/booksurvey.**

1. **What is the ISBN of the book you have purchased? (The ISBN can be found on the book's back cover in the lower right-hand corner.)** _____

2. **Where did you purchase this book?**
   ❑ Retailer, such as Barnes & Noble
   ❑ Online reseller, such as Amazon.com
   ❑ Petersons.com
   ❑ Other (please specify) _____

3. **If you purchased this book on Petersono.com, please rate the following aspects of your online purchasing experience on a scale of 4 to 1 (4 = Excellent and 1 = Poor).**

	4	3	2	1
Comprehensiveness of Peterson's Online Bookstore page	❑	❑	❑	❑
Overall online customer experience	❑	❑	❑	❑

4. **Which category best describes you?**
   ❑ High school student
   ❑ Parent of high school student
   ❑ College student
   ❑ Graduate/professional student
   ❑ Returning adult student

   ❑ Teacher
   ❑ Counselor
   ❑ Working professional/military
   ❑ Other (please specify) _____

5. **Rate your overall satisfaction with this book.**

Extremely Satisfied	Satisfied	Not Satisfied
❑	❑	❑

6. Rate each of the following aspects of this book on a scale of 4 to 1 (4 = Excellent and 1 = Poor).

	4	3	2	1
Comprehensiveness of the information	❑	❑	❑	❑
Accuracy of the information	❑	❑	❑	❑
Usability	❑	❑	❑	❑
Cover design	❑	❑	❑	❑
Book layout	❑	❑	❑	❑
Special features (e.g., CD, flashcards, charts, etc.)	❑	❑	❑	❑
Value for the money	❑	❑	❑	❑

7. This book was recommended by:
- ❑ Guidance counselor
- ❑ Parent/guardian
- ❑ Family member/relative
- ❑ Friend
- ❑ Teacher
- ❑ Not recommended by anyone—I found the book on my own
- ❑ Other (please specify) _____

8. Would you recommend this book to others?

Yes	Not Sure	No
❑	❑	❑

9. Please provide any additional comments.

_____

_____

_____

_____

_____

Remember, you can tear out this page and mail it to us at:

> Publishing Department
> Peterson's, a Nelnet company
> 2000 Lenox Drive
> Lawrenceville, NJ 08648

or you can complete the survey online at **www.petersons.com/booksurvey.**

Your feedback is important to us at Peterson's, and we thank you for your time!

If you would like us to keep in touch with you about new products and services, please include your e-mail address here: _____